AF653470

THE POETRY OF SWAMI VIVEKANANDA AND SRI AUROBINDO

A Study in Indian Philosophy

THE POETRY OF SWAMI VIVEKANANDA AND SRI AUROBINDO

A Study in Indian Philosophy

ARUNA LOLLA

Prestige

an international publishing house

Published by
Prestige Books
New Delhi 110 058
Ph. 011-25507139
email: prestigebooks@gmail.com
website: asiabookclub.com

Associate Office
60/29-45 Parramatta Road,
Concord, NSW 2137
Australia

ISBN: 81-85218-079-0
© Author 2011

All rights reserved. No part of this book may be reproduced or utilized in any form or by any means, electronic or mechanical, including photocopy, microfilm, microfiche, recording, e-mail, web publication, or any information storage and retrieval system, without the written permission of the copyright owner.

Printed at Chaman Offset Press, New Delhi 110 002

Contents

Foreword

Swami Vivekananda and Sri Aurobindo were poet-philosophers of modern India and pioneers of Sublime poetry in English.

As the author recounts in the book, Swami Vivekananda began writing poetry and composing songs from an early age, all of which reveal the imprint of his initial spiritual inspirations. Carebanu Cooper who did an illustrious research on the literary aspect of the Swami puts it, "the Soul became his persona, the 'Reflector true—Thy pulse so timed to mine" ("To My Own Soul"). It was Swami Vivekananda's mission to bring out 'the most wonderful truths' from our Upanishads and *Puranas*, from the monasteries and the possession of selected bodies of people and broadcast them to the world so that 'the truths may run like fire all over the country.' To quote the Swami himself,

> The abstract *Advaita* must become living—poetic—in everyday life; out of hopelessly intricate mythology must come concrete moral forms; and out of bewildering *Yogi*-ism must come the most scientific and practical psychology—and all this must be put in a form so that a child may grasp it. That is my life's work.(*C.W* 5: 104-5).

"Swami Vivekananda was a soul of puissance if ever there was one, a very lion among men—we say Behold, Vivekananda still lives in the soul of his Mother and in the souls of her children," writes Sri Aurobindo and recalls an esoteric experience he underwent during his imprisonment thus: "I was hearing constantly the voice of Vivekananda speaking to me for a fortnight, in my solitary meditation and felt his presence." The fundamental difference of Swami Vivekananda's philosophy and of Sri Aurobindo, i.e. Sri Aurobindo's Yoga is for the "sake of divine," not for the sake of mankind alone. Both of them expressed their viewpoint in their short poems and sonnets.

Sri Aurobindo regards poetry of the future 'a voice of eternal things.' Poetry shall restore to humanity, the sense of the eternal and the presence of the Divine.' Sri Aurobindo emphasizes, poetry shall be 'a voice of intuitive experience and rhythm and chant of the revelation of an eternal presence.' The objective of Sri Aurobindo is creation of an 'altered perfected art of poetry' and his theory is an attempt to 'put the poetic spirit once more in the shining front of the powers and guides of the ever-progressing soul of humanity."

The mankind would invent 'novel and unprecedented forms' for the subtler vaster spirit of the new poetry. To satisfy the new poetic vision, subtler inner changes are of primary importance in all the existing forms of poetry. To develop this new kind of poetry, it is imperative that the old habits of speech and rhythmic movement have to be substituted by new movements and new connotations and usage of poetic word if the future poetry has to be the soul's self-expression . Sri Aurobindo says, "The poetic word is a vehicle of the spirit, the chosen medium of the soul's self-expression." 'It's way of seeing, it's type of feeling' are completely different to the old method.

An intuitive poetic speech can alone be the fit medium of the poetry of the future. The poetic speech can express itself from 'the boundless finite's last expanse, the cosmic empire of the overmind." Then poetry becomes a true '*Mantra* of the Real.' Sri Aurobindo's aim is to manifest the secret god in the life or to unveil the divine and establish that divinity in earthly life.

> The Truth-Light Capture Nature by surprise .
> A stealth of God compel the heart to bliss.
> And earn grow unexpectedly divine. (*Savitri*, 55)

To unmask this true meaning of creation is the work Sri Aurobindo assigns to new poetry. This great vision of the seer is reflected in his short poems too. He made poetry a vehicle for the expression of the soul.

Through the comparison of the short poems and sonnets of two poets, a vast and clear picture of the evolution of spirituality and Sublime poetry has emerged. Scholars working in this area can draw unique insight from this book and can take the research forward. Aruna has made a pioneering effort in this field of great potential and I express my best wishes in her future endeavours.

T.V. Nagaranjani

Dr. T.V. Nagaranjani hails from a family of Aurobindonians and is a regular speaker at Sri Aurobindo Bhavan, Hyderabad. She did her Masters, M.Phil. and Ph.D. from the University of Hyderabad in the discipline of Telugu literature and is presently working at Rajabahadur V.R.R. Women's College, Hyderabad.

To

The Divine

&

My Parents

Preface

Spiritual experience is acknowledged as the highest human experience and poetry as its most apt vehicle of expression. The prevailing climate of rampant materialism and predominance of a sensate culture heightens our need for such enlightening poetry. India has always been hailed as the land of spirituality, which has mothered countless sages and seers from the days of yore. The vast philosophic-religious literature that has come down to us from ancient times is but the fruit of this spiritual search.

The present publication, which is based on the author's research work for Ph.D degree deals with the philosophical poetry of the two most important philosopher-poets of modern India, Swami Vivekananda and Sri Aurobindo. The schools of philosophy they had established and the two modes of devotion they had followed are still very relevant in India and the rest of the world. These two saints were also very effective poets who could write poetry of a high order celebrating their spiritual experiences and elucidating their philosophies. The short poems and sonnets of these poets form a microcosm within the macrocosm of their philosophical teachings. In the present study, an attempt has been made to analyze and compare those short poems and sonnets, which encapsulate the essential teachings and religious ideas of the two seers.

While studying their contribution to the present age and making a comparative assessment in the explicit medium of poetry, the critique illumines the fact that the Sublime poetry is the ultimate poetry of all times. The future poetry, as Sri Aurobindo envisions, would be the poetry of the Soul. The study also explores the relationship between poetry and religious thought.

I express my deep sense of gratitude to the Divine for His showers of blessings and His presence with me in times of need and joy, during this research, as always. In fact, most of the ideas and chapter plans have emerged in the silence and serenity of the worship room at home. Throughout the course, it has been a sublime feeling that Goddess Saraswati Herself is behind the book-racks of the libraries I consulted and Her unseen hand is passing on the exact book or journal that was required for my work of the day.

I am very much indebted to a visible form of Saraswati, my guide and beacon, Prof. C. Vijayasree, Department of English, Osmania University who has been my favourite teacher right from my college days. Her patience, scholarly suggestions and directions have contributed greatly in shaping the thesis into its present form. Her paper on the poetry of Swami Vivekananda was particularly helpful.

I owe special thanks to Dr. T.V. Nagaranjani whose learned expositions on the teachings of Sri Aurobindo and the Mother have enhanced the spiritual light and vision in me. Her Sunday lectures on *Savitri* and *The Life Divine* at Sri Aurobindo Bhavan, Hyderabad, have given me the required insight and motivation to delve deep into the subject. Again, I am thankful to her for kindly writing a foreword to this book.

While working on my thesis I had wide interactions on the subject with some of the distinguished scholars and devotees of Sri Aurobindo and the Mother including Prof. Mangesh Nadkarni (Retired from EFL University) whose workshop on *Savitri* at Nainital bestowed a special experience on me, Dr. Ananda Reddy, Director of SACAR, Pondicherry, Dr. Prema Nandkumar and others. I am extremely thankful to them for enriching my knowledge and understanding of the subject.

I have been very fortunate to have listened to great scholars including Swami Prakashananda Saraswati (over Television) of Barsana *Dham* Austin, U.S.A and *Brahmasri* SamaVedam Shanmukha Sarma, a widely acclaimed orator who spoke on various scriptures at Hyderabad. My knowledge of philosophy has been substantiated through their insightful talks and lectures.

My heartfelt thanks to all my teacher figures and benefactors like Prof. V.V. Ramana Rao (Principal, Annamacharya Institute of Technology and Sciences), Prof. Varadacharya (a senior colleague, Dept. of English, TKR Engg. College), Professors of English, Osmania University, Dr. Sumita Roy and Dr. A. Subba Rao for their guidance and good wishes. I also thank the Dean, School of Humanities, Prof. Mohan G. Ramanan and Prof. Sachidanand Mohanty of University of Hyderabad for encouraging me to publish this work.

I owe warm gratitude to my friends and colleagues, Ms. Prabha, Mr. M. Umesh, Ms. K. Kavitha, Mr. Mattaiah Yadav, Mr. Die Ter Schemmer (Akhilesh Chidanand), and others for their assistance and moral support in this endeavor.

My thanks are also due to the people associated with Sri Aurobindo *Ashram*, Pondicherry, including Mr. P.R. Srinivasa Murty (*Promisse*' Auroville Foundation) and Mr. Ravikanti Mihir (In charge of Pharmaceutical wing at the *Ashram*) who facilitated my work of data collection and stay at the Ashram guest house for two weeks.

This publication would not have been possible within a short time of three months without the prompt and kind attention given by Prof. R.K. Dhavan and Ms. Renu and other staff of Prestige Books, Delhi. I am thankful to all of them.

I would be failing in my duty if I do not acknowledge the moral, physical and academic support and inspiration provided by my parents Prof. P. Rajeswari and Prof. L.S.N. Murty, my brother, Dr. L. Ramesh and sister, Dr. L. Padmavathi in carrying out this research and publication work. I am deeply indebted to them for their affection and encouragement in my education and career development. The gladdening presence of my little nieces Ananya and Garima and playing with them sometimes relieved me from monotony and weariness.

I am thankful to all others who helped or inspired me in completing this work.

Aruna Lolla

Abbreviations

C.W.: *The Complete Works of Swami Vivekananda.*
LSVEWD: *The Life of Swami Vivekananda by his Eastern and Western Disciples.*
Selections from C.W.: *Selections from the Complete Works of Swami Vivekananda.*
SABCL: *Sri Aurobindo Birth Centenary Library.*
SABDA: *Sri Aurobindo Book Distributing Agency*

Chapter 1

Introduction

Spiritual experience is acknowledged as the highest human experience and poetry as its most apt vehicle of expression. The prevailing climate of rampant materialism and predominance of a sensate culture heightens our need for such enlightening poetry. India has always been hailed as the land of spirituality, which has mothered countless sages and seers from the days of yore. Swami Vivekananda aptly points out that "No people have spent so much energy as the early Indians in defining the nature of Reality" (*C.W.* 2: 372). Their quest was earnest, intense and persevering. It is expressed beautifully by the three verses of *Brihadaranyaka Upanishad*:

> From the unreal (*asat*) lead me to the real (*sat*)!
> From darkness lead me to light!
> From death lead me to immortality! (1.3.28. qtd. Mannumel 7)

The vast philosophic-religious literature that has come down to us from ancient times is but the fruit of this spiritual search. Though its intensity was to a large extent on the decline during the succeeding centuries, the concern for the 'beyond' has remained. It could not be lost. When it reached on occasions a very low ebb owing to political upheavals and social and economic vicissitudes, some great leader or other appeared on the scene who by his "inspired" life and teaching kept the ancient torch of wisdom burning in the land. In this long cultural history, several invasions by foreign forces mounted strong attack on the old faith. But it somehow survived the shock with the adaptation and assimilation, which are the characteristic features of Brahminism as well as its progeny, Hinduism. The philosophy of spirituality and devotion renewed itself from time to time assuming different names and forms. During the middle ages, the *Bhakti* movement ushered in a rich tradition of poetry. As Nirmalya Ghatak points out, the higher aspects of mystic aspiration are to be found in Swami Ramananda Tirtha and Tulsi Das in the north, in Tukaram and the Maratha saints in the west and especially in Manikka-Vasagar and the Saiva saints of the south. Meerabai, Andal and Thyagaraju sang ecstatically of their spiritual experiences (20). With the establishment, however, of the British rule, yet another phase of religious reawakening occurred in the Indian context. Contact with the West and English education ushered in a new era for Hinduism. In fact, the past hundred and fifty years have been marked by new religious forces silently working towards a great reawakening of the old faith.

The spiritual heritage of the nation has been given a new dimension by modern philosopher-patriots like Swami Vivekananda and Sri Aurobindo. The schools of philosophy they had established and two modes of devotion they followed are still very relevant in India and the rest of the world. The West has deep roots in their metaphysics, who are, at the same time, well posted in the ancient Indian thoughts embodied in the Vedas, Upanishads, *Bhagavad Gita*, Sankhya, *Yoga*, Vedanta, Tantra, Kashmir Shaivism and Shakta systems. They developed their theories of *Advaita* and Integral *Yoga* on such a background and their own personal spiritual experience, explains Rama Shanker Srivastava (Foreword iii). These two saints were also very effective poets who could produce poetry of a high order celebrating their spiritual experiences and elucidating their philosophies.

The short poems and sonnets of these poets form a microcosm within the macrocosm of their philosophical teachings. In the present study an attempt has been made to analyze and compare those short poems and sonnets, which encapsulate the essential teachings and religious ideas of the two seers. In Swami Vivekananda's poetry, every verse is under girded with the concepts of *Brahman*, man's freedom, strength and fearlessness beautifully wrought in various poetic styles. Although his poetic output is not voluminous, the combination of intellect and emotion, with their appropriate styles, arrests the attention of the reader. The main bulk of

Sri Aurobindo's lyrical poetry is "suffused with a philosophical or mystical glow," writes K.R. Srinivasa Iyengar and asserts that "At no period of his life was he blind to the spiritual reality behind the material façade; never did he countenance either of the classic negations—the total denial of phenomenal life or the total denial of spiritual life" (1995: 160). His poetry is no doubt dominated by the experiences of his adventures in the realms of the supramental and the superconscious, yet his poetry reveals a unique blend of western and eastern attitudes, modes and techniques in the literary tradition.

As we read the poetry of these two sages, we read apart from metaphysics all aspects of Indian Religion like its scriptures, mythology and common religious symbols for these are essential props of their poetry. By comparing the traditional *Advaita* theory of Swami Vivekananda with Sri Aurobindo's synthetic *yoga*, as expressed in the explicit medium of poetry, we get a comprehensive picture of India's philosophical thought and its suitable techniques of prosody. The following is a statement of the objectives of the study, the methodology adopted, the scope of the work and the chapterization of the thesis. The main objectives of the study are:

i) to study the poetry of Swami Vivekananda and Sri Aurobindo from the view point of its scriptural basis, thus highlighting the need for a new critical approach for analyzing the philosophic-spiritual poetry;
ii) to study the aesthetic aspect and the poetic tools of sublime poetry;
iii) to understand the Indian philosophy in its contempoprised and comprehensive form and to highlight the primacy and eternal significance of the scriptural texts, viz., the Vedas, the Upanishads, the *Gita*, the *Shaddarshanas*, etc., and show how they form the source and substratum of all modern and synthetic philosophies as well as their poetic expression; and

iv) to study the contribution of Swami Vivekananda and Sri Aurobindo to Indian philosophy and Indian English poetry.

Swami Vivekananda and Sri Aurobindo have been chosen for the present study as they are contemporary Indian philosophers of worldwide reputation. It may be asserted that no philosopher ever invents a system of thought, if by 'invention' we mean something absolutely new and not known before. "Whenever a philosopher produces a 'new' system of thought, he does so by renewing and enlarging previous knowledge" that has been laid down by the scriptures explains N. Jaya Shanmukham (3). Referring to the creative work of the philosopher, Sri Aurobindo observes:

> What he does is to take up the material available to him in the past history of thought, to choose, select, reject, to present new light on old ideas, to develop latent suggestions, to bring into prominence what was before or not so trenchant and definite, to give a fresh, striking and illuminating sense to old terms, to combine what was before not at all or else ill-combined; in doing so he creates; his philosophy, though not new in its materials, is new in the whole effect it produces and the more powerful light that in certain directions it conveys to the thinking mind (*Mother India*. July 1966: 13).

This statement about the creative philosopher holds right in the case of Swami Vivekananda and Sri Aurobindo also as they have drawn their basic philosophies from the scriptures and have gone beyond them following the lead of their own inner light. Sri Aurobindo has emphasized this point more than once:

- Even the *Upanishads*, and the *Gita* were not final, though everything may be there in seed.
- The traditions of the past are very great in their own place, in the past, but I do not see why we should merely repeat them and not go farther.
- Why should the past be the limit of spiritual experience?

(Sri Aurobindo, *On Himself*: 125)

This 'going farther' and recording one's own spiritual experience is best accomplished in the poetic-medium owing to its metaphysical potential. The seer glimpses the contours of ultimate possibility, the mystic poet hymns his "gloried fields of trance" (Iyengar 1972: 153).

Keeping the above stated objectives in view the work has been done by following the three steps mentioned below:

All the poems of Swami Vivekananda (both in English and translated works) and the selected short poems and sonnets of Sri Aurobindo constitute the sample of this study. A close textual reading of these poems is complemented by historicization of these texts within the socio-spiritual matrix of the poets' times. These poems are discussed and analyzed in the dissertation from literary (paraphrase and poetic devices) and philosophical (central theme/concept) angles. The poems are broadly classified into two categories, namely, devotional and philosophical poems based upon their central theme and essence. The underlying philosophic concepts are explained first and then their poetic presentation by the two sages is elucidated in the subsequent sections in the concerned chapters.

Swami Vivekananda's poems are collected from fourth, fifth, sixth and eighth volumes of *Complete Works of Swami Vivekananda* (Abbreviated as *C.W.*) and those of Sri Aurobindo from the anthology *Collected Poems*. The poems of Swami Vivekananda have been collected and published by the Advaita Ashrama as an anthology bearing the title, *In Search of God and Other Poems*. Some of the poems have been taken from this anthology also.

Conceptual explanation is drawn primarily from the *Bhagavad Gita* and some Vedic and Upanishadic texts. For example, the concepts of *Advaita, Brahma,* creation and meditation are studied form *Mandukya*, *Svetasvatara*, *Aitareya* and *Taittiriya* Upanishads respectively. The concepts of Involution, Evolution and Transformation are traced from sources like the *Bhagavad Gita*, the *Rig Veda*, etc. Apart from them, certain selected essays and critical writings in prose by and about Swami Vivekananda and Sri Aurobindo are consulted from a wide range of books, journals and research papers.

A comparative assessment of the philosophical ideas and style of versification of the two masters has been made and presented in the concluding chapter. The major part of the thesis demonstrates the influence of Indian philosophy upon the poetry of Swami Vivekananda and Sri Aurobindo.

The previous research on the works of the two poet-philosophers is extensive. The explorative works of Carebanu Cooper, Ananda Coomaraswamy, Sanat Kumar Rai Chaudhuri, R.K. Dasgupta, Swami Harshananda, Swami Jitatmananda, Jacob Kattackal, C.L. Khatri, Swami Nikhilananda, Akhouri Rajendra Prasad, S.J. Thomas Mannumel, C. Vijayasree, etc., are particularly helpful in gaining an insight into the poetic works and ideas of Swami Vivekananda. The scholarly articles and books on the philosophy and poetry of Sri Aurobindo by Jagdish Saran Agarwal, Sisir Kumar Ghose, Vinayak Krishna Gokak, K.R. Srinivasa Iyengar, Syamala Kallury, Mangesh Nadkarni, Prema Nandakumar, S.K. Prasad, M.P. Pandit, Rishabhchand, S. Krishna Sarma, Satprem, K.D. Sethna, Rama Shanker Srivastava, Aniruddha Sircar, etc., are very enlightening on the subject.

As regards the scope of this work, incomplete short poems, longer poems and prose writings of the two authors are not covered by the present study. All the poems of Swami Vivekananda are studied although six of them couldn't be discussed in this work (These six poems are: "An Interesting Correspondence," "To My Own Soul" "A Blessing," "Many Happy Returns," "One More Circle" and "Whom to Fear"—which is a translated work). Careful scrutiny has been made in choosing the short poems and sonnets of Sri Aurobindo in order to do justice to them in terms of analysis and interpretation. No theory of Philosophy can be taken as the ultimate limit that would seal the spiritual research of mankind. The spiritual aspirant keeps discovering new permutations and combinations of the eternal laws to cater to his needs and temperament as well as to those of his age. A collection of such 'discoveries' has taken the form of scriptures in India from the days of yore. The scriptures, then, are inexhaustible and infinite like the Eternity itself. For this reason, the scriptural study for the purpose of this work is delimited to selective sources only.

The dissertation is divided into six chapters. The first chapter is introduction, while the second elucidates philosophical concepts and their presentation in poetic form. The third and fourth chapters are devoted to philosophical poetry of Swami Vivekananda and Sri Aurobindo respectively. The fifth chapter discusses devotional poetry of both the poets. And the sixth one presents a comparative assessment of the two philosophical standpoints and the two poets. A brief overview of the dissertation is presented below.

Chapter I, the introductory chapter, briefly states the area of research, the main objectives of the study, the methodology adopted, the scope of the work and the chapterization of the thesis.

Chapter II briefly reviews some principal concepts of Indian philosophy with a view to understanding how they are synthesized in the Neo-Vedantism of Swami Vivekananda and the integral spirituality of Sri Aurobindo. The philosophy of Hinduism is traced from the six scriptures: *Shrutis* (constituted by the Veda), *Smiritis*, *Itihasas*, *Puranas*, *Aagamas* and *Shad-darshanas* (six systems of philosophy). Then the philosophy of the Veda, the Upanishads, the *Gita* and the six systems or schools of thought are presented in some detail. After a comprehensive and brief elucidation of the chief scriptural sources an attempt is made to explore the age-old method of broadcasting the philosophical thought, that is through poetry. The interdependence of poetry and philosophy is established, based on the use of poetic form by sages of all ages.

Chapter III is devoted to a study of the philosophical poems of Swami Vivekananda. The first section gives a brief sketch of Swami Vivekananda. The succeeding three sections of the chapter discuss his poems under three broad themes of:

i) Descent to the Relative;
ii) Ascent to the Absolute; and
iii) Synthetic estimate of the concept of *Advaita*.

An effort is made to trace the scriptural sources of the concepts contained in these poems and is presented at the end of the respective section. Apart from this conceptual study the literary aspects are also studied. Here, the progression of thought, the symbols and images used along with the method of expression are analyzed.

Likewise, Chapter IV discusses philosophical poetry of Sri Aurobindo. As in the third chapter, the first section presents in brief—the life, literature and the general principles of philosophy of Sri Aurobindo. The next three sections of the chapter analyze his poems under the following three categories:

i) Descent or Involution
ii) Ascent or Evolution
iii) Transformation—which are the three chief components of Integral *Yoga*

Sri Aurobindo's style of versification and poetic devices are studied here. The scriptural background of each concept is presented at the end of the respective section.

Chapter V discusses those poems, which are addressed to a personal deity and effuse devotional fervor, of both the poets. There are three groups of devotional poems viz., those devoted to Shiva, to Kali and to Krishna, which are discussed in three sections respectively. The two poets see the omnipotent power operating in the creation, preservation and dissolution of the universe sometimes as Kali and sometimes as Shiva or as Krishna. Even when they identify this power by name of a personal god, they only refer to the Absolute, the Formless and the Nameless *Brahma*. Besides this, the influence of respective streams of devotion, namely, Shaivism (esp. Kashmir Shaivism), Shaktism and Vaishnavism is also evident. For this reason a brief explanation of the stream of devotion concerned, namely Shaivism, Shaktism and Vaishnavism, is presented at the beginning of the respective section. Poems on Kali and Krishna of both the poets overflow with ardent adoration and devout self-surrender. The fervent longing of the devotee to reach the Divine or the yearning of the self to discover the Self set the tone of these poems. Swami Vivekananda's "My Play is Done," "Kali The Mother," etc., and Sri Aurobindo's poems like "Krishna," "The Cosmic Dance—Dance of Krishna, Dance of Kali" are some of the fine examples of this genre.

In Chapter VI, the final chapter of the thesis, the philosophical ideas and styles of versification of Swami Vivekananda and Sri Aurobindo are compared and contrasted. Swami Vivekananda and Sri Aurobindo have presented the spiritual philosophy behind Hinduism in such a way that they seem to have touched upon the cardinal truth behind all religions. Also both have deftly nativized English to explain Indian philosophy in its most comprehensive and contemporary form to the entire world, whose essence is the divinity of man in a universe that is one. Both the prophets and their disciples have emphasized the ideal of living in the world as a free soul for the uplift of humanity. As R.K. Dasgupta points out, neither *Advaita Vedanta* nor Integral *Yoga* pronounces a moratorium on the material universe, they only put on it the imprint of the Absolute (293). While a lightening-like energy characterizes Swami Vivekananda's verse, Sri Aurobindo's poetry is suffused with Supramental Light. Total self-surrender and an advocating of equal vision is the common method of Divinization promulgated by both the sages. This chapter compares and contrasts the basic ideologies, the method of *sadhana*, the style of versification and the literary devices used by both the masters. In this comparative assessment, their intellectual background, their response to the colonial encounter, their message to the world and the like have also been discussed. The chapter also takes a note of the contribution and influence of the two sage-poets.

While studying their contribution to the present age and making a comparative assessment in the explicit medium of poetry, the dissertation attempts to demonstrate that the ancient scriptural texts, like the *Gita*, the Upanishads, etc., are the source and substratum of these modern or synthetic philosophies. The study also attempts to explore the relationship between poetry and religious thought. P.T. Raju's enlightening statement in this context, closely describes the present endeavour:

> Comparative philosophy must have a philosophical aim. Only when the aim is clarified, can the work be given a definite shape. The aim has to illuminate the perspective; then the traditions thrown into perspective take on a definite meaning and significance (Preface v).

Thus the aim of comparative philosophy is the elucidation of the nature of Man, God, Creation and varying pathways to Liberation in order that a comprehensive philosophy of life and a plan for thought and action may be found. In choosing the poetry of these two philosophers for a critical study, the present work attempts to theorize on the nature of spiritual poetry, relationship between poetry and philosophy and the philosophical substratum of the poetry of the two sages, Swami Vivekananda and Sri Aurobindo, and the metaphysical undercurrent of Indian poetry in English in general. It is with this end in view that the present study has been undertaken.

Chapter 2

Fusion of Philosophy and Poetry: Context of the Study

One finds innumerable tributes of reverence to the Indian scriptures in poetic language throughout the works of Swami Vivekananda and Sri Aurobindo. For example, in his 'Three Lectures on the Vedanta Philosophy' (1894), Swami Vivekananda speaks of those who disparage Vedanta philosophy as something misty and says: "True mystic philosophy . . . is as clear as a summer sky, it is full of brightness and full of warmth" (qtd. Dasgupta 8). He makes this point more picturesquely in his lecture 'The Freedom of the Soul' delivered in London on 5th November 1896, in which he very appropriately calls the *Bhagavad Gita* 'the last of the Upanishads': "The *Gita* is like a bouquet composed of the beautiful flowers of spiritual truths collected from the Upanishads" (*C.W.* 2: 189). And Sri Aurobindo hails the scripture in metaphorical language thus:

> The *Gita* is an unfathomable ocean of inexhaustible treasure of gems. We may go on diving into that ocean for taking out those gems throughout our lives, but there is no end of them, one never reaches the bottom of the ocean . . . Just by having a gem or two from it the poor becomes rich, a serious thinker becomes a wise man of Knowledge, the hostile turns into a lover of God. (qtd. Maheshwari 1)

The *Bhagavad Gita*, besides other scriptural texts, has been a constant source of inspiration for the two poet-philosophers. The poetic style as well as the thought-content of the Indian scriptures are greatly adored by them both. A brief review of some principal concepts of Indian philosophy, are presented in this chapter, with a view to understand how they are synthesized in the integral spirituality of Swami Vivekananda and Sri Aurobindo. A study on interdependence of philosophy and poetry is presented after the review.

2.1 The Philosophy of India

The word 'Philosophy' is derived from the Greek word '*philos*' (love) and '*Sophia*' (wisdom), which etymologically means the love of wisdom. The term wisdom is too rich in connotation and is not the sum total of empirical and intellectual knowledge but the appreciation and appraisal of the higher values of life. According to S. Radhakrishnan, "while the Salvation of the soul is the end of religion, the discovery of truth is the object of Philosophy." Cicero described Philosophy as "the director of our lives, friend of virtue and enemy to vice." Windelhand says "Philosophy is the critical science of universal value." According to Herbert Spencer 'Philosophy' is concerned with everything as a universal science." To Aristotle Philosophy is the science which considers truth; Plato states that "Philosophy is a way of living and dying." Ludwig Wittgenstein says "Philosophy is a battle against the bewitchment of our intelligence by means of language" (qtd. Mohapatra 3, 4). The idea of philosophy in the West has not been parallel to that in India. The Sanskrit word equivalent to philosophy is *Darshanam,* which literally means 'seeing' and the Indian systems start neither from a *priori* principle nor from the observed facts, as is usually understood, but from some transcendental experience in which the truth about the nature of the universe is directly perceived. The philosophy of India has not been the result of accumulation of thought and ideas, promulgated by different philosophers at different periods of history. It is like the organic growth of a full grown tree into its branches and fruits from the power of a seed which merely unfolds itself by inner growth and differentiation, and not by external accretion. 'Indian Philosophy,' being a confluence of several faiths and schools of thought, is extremely comprehensive.

Let us begin with the study of principal scriptures and religious systems of India or 'Hinduism' as it is presently known.

From the philosophical standpoint, Hinduism is non-dualistic, and from the religious standpoint monotheistic. The Hindu philosophy asserts the essential non-duality of God, individual soul and universe, the apparent distinctions being created by mere names and forms. It believes that the ultimate reality is one, so all these apparent distinctions are due to our ignorance. Although Hinduism accepts large numbers of gods, in reality it regards them as diverse manifestations of the one God. The Hindu Trinity of Brahma, Vishnu and Shiva represents the three aspects of Godhead each controlling the process of creation, preservation and destruction, respectively. However, Hindu monotheism does not discard the various deities of different faiths and cults but includes them as the manifestations of the One.

God in the Hindu faith has been described as omnipresent, omnipotent, omniscient, infinite, all merciful and impersonally personal. His spirit pervades the whole universe. He is beyond all forms and names. He is the soul of our souls, it is in Him that we live, through Him that we exist, and without Him there cannot be anything. Worship of different deities and idols is aimed at achieving mental concentration while catering to the personal faith and orientation of the devotees. The different idols are the symbols of the Divine energy or of the attributes of God, which are difficult to grasp without some outward form. The Vedanta philosophy does not teach the worship of many gods, but of the one God who is called by many names and appears in any form in accordance with the beliefs of the worshippers. Thousands of names are given to that Supreme Being who is in fact nameless and formless. He is extra-cosmic, as well as intra-cosmic, and is immanent as well as transcendent. He appears as if with a form to a dualist and without a form to a non-dualist. He is one, yet His aspects are many. He is personal, impersonal, and beyond both.

Hinduism is considered as the *Sanatana* (eternal) *Dharma*. It is eternal because God only is real and He is Eternal. This Ultimate Reality which is all pervading is the efficient and material cause of the universe. The human soul is divine and the entire universe is a manifestation of the Supreme soul. From this perspective the *Sanatana Dharma* or Hinduism does not subscribe to a certain set of dogmas or creeds, but enjoins or recommends in the attainment of God consciousness through spiritual unfoldment which is being and becoming God. It is being and becoming the Absolute *Brahman*. Hinduism is *Sanatana* because, the God being the central pivot of religion, is eternal.

Hinduism does not shut out inquiry; on the other hand, it stimulates inquiry absolutely free from prejudice and prepossessions. Religion of Vedanta may be called the science of the soul. Just as modern science does not deal with dogmas and does not insist upon belief in the authority of any person or book, but depends entirely upon correct observation and experience of the facts of nature to discover the laws which govern the phenomena of the universe, Hinduism or Vedanta also does not deal with dogmas or creeds but explains, through logic and reason, the true nature of the soul. It is stated in the Upanishads that "This *Atman* should be heard about, reflected upon and understood."

This science of soul discusses such questions as whether or not the soul can exist independently of the body, whether or not it existed before the present birth. whether it is free or bound? Thus it is concerned about the immortality of soul, freedom of will and bondage, law of *karma*, etc. Vedanta philosophy admits the existence of a multitude of individual souls, called *Jivatmas,* and distinguishes these from the Supreme Soul i.e. *parabrahma*. The Upanishads speak of two souls, namely the real soul and the apparent soul. The real soul is not attached to the world. It is without body or form, beyond pain and pleasure, whereas the apparent soul is attached to the world. It is with a body and form. It experiences pain and pleasure as a result of its own actions, good or bad. When the apparent soul realizes the oneness of the two souls, its grief or bondage vanishes. This oneness of the two souls has been stated by such Vedic statements as 'That thou art'; 'This self is *Brahman*'; 'I am He.'

Hinduism admits the reality of the *jiva* or the individual soul embodied in a relative state. It holds that after death the individual soul assumes a new body and that his rebirth is governed by the law of *karma*. The doctrine of rebirth, based upon the law of cause and effect, is the most plausible of all the speculations regarding the nature of the soul and its existence after death. The human soul undergoes many a cycle of birth and death according to its deeds. According to Vedas, man in his life has to suffer the consequences of the actions of his previous life. Hinduism divides the *karma* into (a) those which have not yet begun to bear fruit (*ararabdha karma*) and which have already begun to bear fruit (*prarabdha karma*). *Ararabdha karma* is again sub-divided into two classes: (a) *sanchita karma* i.e. *karma* accumulated from past lives, and (b) *kriyamana* or *sanchayamana karma* i.e. *karmas* that are being gathered in this life. A soul is born again and again, high or low, depending upon the merit or demerit of its action. Only a liberated soul does not take any physical form.

The embodiment of self is apparent and not real. Therefore its birth and death are also apparent only. After the attainment of the self-knowledge, the *jivatma* realizes itself to be *Brahman*, infinite and all pervading. A knower of *atman* is called *jivanmukta*. He is free from bondage of joy and sorrow. Death has no terror for a free soul, because a change of body is like a change of garments. A free soul, while living in the body, may experience disease, old age, or decay; may feel hunger, thirst and grief, but having realized that these are the characteristics of the body, the mind or the senses, he does not take them seriously and so is not overwhelmed by them. A free soul lives, thinks and works with a sense of immortality.

Of all the living religions, the Hindu faith is the most ancient. It was not founded by any individual prophet and is not composed of the teachings of any particular group of saints or teachers. The scriptures are the fountainheads of Hinduism. Hindu scriptures can be classified under six heads: (1) *Shrutis*, (2) *Smritis*, (3) *Itihasas*, (4) *Puranas*, (5) *Aagamas*, and (6) *Darshanas*. '*Shrutis*' literally mean that which is heard. The great sages heard and experienced the eternal truths and recorded their experiences for the benefit of people. These constitute the four Vedas. The Vedas contains such divine revelations thus forming the most authoritative source of the religion.

The '*Smritis*' literally mean that which is remembered. They stand next in importance to *Shrutis*. *Smritis* are founded on the teachings of the Vedas. They explain and elucidate religious obligations. They form parts of the code of laws which guide the individuals, families and communities in their daily conduct, their manners and customs.

The '*Itihasas*' (i.e. the epics of the historic period) are the two well known epics, the *Ramayana* (written by sage Valmiki) and the *Mahabharata* (written by sage Veda Vyasa). They contain living stories of absorbing interest through which the fundamental teachings of Hinduism are illustrated dramatically and impressed upon the minds of the people. The philosophical essence in these epics is presented through analogies and parables.

The *Puranas* are of the same class as the *Itihasas*. They popularize the philosophy of the Vedas. The aim of *Puranas* is to give a concrete form to the teachings of the Vedas by means of myths, stories, legends and the lives of saints and kings and sometimes through allegories. They present religion in a concrete form. There are eighteen *Puranas* of which the *Bhagavata* and the *Vishnu Purana* are the most popular. It is believed that sage Veda Vyasa was the author of the eighteen *Puranas* besides the epic *Mahabharata*.

Another class of popular scriptures is *Agamas*. Though they do not derive their authority from the Vedas, but they are not antagonistic to their teachings. They are theological treatises and manuals of worship. The three chief sects, Shaivism, Shaktism and Vaishnavism derive their doctrines and dogmas from the *Aagmas*.

There are six *Darshanas*. '*Darshana*' literally means light or vision. These six or '*Shad*'-*darshanas* are (i) *Nyaya*, (ii) *Vaisheshika*, (iii) *Sankhya*, (iv) *Yoga*, (v) *Mimamsa*, (vi) Vedanta. Each *Darshana* prescribes a way of looking at truth. They are treated as the way of life and form of life. Mainly the Vedas, the Upanishads, the *Bhagavad Gita* and *Shaddarshansas* are the fundamental scriptures of Hindu philosophy and considered a great storehouse of knowledge and wisdom. Let us start the scriptural study with the philosophy of the Vedas, considering their monistic and spiritual aspects.

2.2 The Philosophy of the Vedas

Hindu thought and philosophy from the period of the *Rig Veda* till our own times has adhered to the view that "*ananta vau vedah*" i.e. 'endless are the Vedas.' In the words of Wilson, an eminent western orientalist, "The Vedas give us abundant information of antiquity." There are four Vedas viz. *Rig*, *Yajur*, *Sama* and *Atharva*. According to Max Muller, the *Rig Veda* is the most ancient book in the world. Again each Veda consists of three parts known as (1) the Mantras, (2) the *Brahmanas*, and (3) the Upanishads. Out of four Vedas, the *Rig Veda* is the chief Veda. The following are some of the aspects of the Vedas which elucidate its philosophical interpretations:

Various theories have been put forward in modern times by scholars regarding the problem of gods in the Vedas. It is held that in the Veda, there is a progression from a multitude of gods to a single God and then to a unity of the world (polytheism to monotheism and then to monism). Max Mueller who made an attempt to study the nature of gods in Vedas, could not find any appropriate term that would fit into the nature of God. In the Vedas there are many gods and practically every one of them is described as the 'One God' and the 'Supreme God' when that god is worshipped. Max Muller invented a Greek term to designate this doctrine of 'one God' what has now become well known as 'Herotheism.' Raja Ram Mohan Roy holds the view that the Vedic gods allegorically represent the characteristics of the ultimate God. The different gods and goddesses of the Vedic hymns are the different facets of the one and the same God. The Vedic philosophy does not stop even at monotheism. This tendency towards the one God culminates in monism. There are hymns in the Vedas which allude to monism e.g.: "*Ekam sat vipra bahudha vadanti*" (Truth is one; the scholars say it in different ways).

Faith in the Vedas must not be misconstrued as dogmatism. Religions are serviceable only so far as they are spiritual. In Vedas there are intuitive experiences of the great seers of Divinity. The study of the *Rig Veda* is indispensable for any adequate understanding of Indian thought. Sri Aurobindo is of the opinion that the Vedas are replete with suggestions of secret doctrines and mystic philosophies. To him the Vedic gods and goddesses are the symbols of psychological processes. The Sun god, for example, symbolizes intellect, while Fire and Soma represent determination or will and feeling respectively. Generally the *Jnana Kanda* deals with the spiritual aspects of the Vedas.

In *Rig Veda* the conception of *Rita* is of great significance. This universal moral system is termed '*Rita*' in the Vedas, '*Apurva*' in the *Mimamsa* and *Adrishta* in the *Nyayavaisheshika*. Gods like Mitra (the Sun god) and Varuna (the rain god) not only bring about 'nature's ordered course, but also maintain the moral order in the universe. The *Rita* of the Vedas establishes a standard of morality. It is the *satya* or the truth of things. Virtue is conformity to the law of God, which includes the love of man. The Vedas assume a very close and intimate relationship between man and gods. The life of man has to be led under the very eye of God. Consistency is the central feature of good life. The 'good man' of Vedas does not alter his ways. Kindness and hospitality are considered as great virtues. In short, the ultimate aim of the Vedas is the general good of the entire mankind.

The concept of *Rita-Chit* or Truth-consciousness is developed magnificently in the Aurobindonean concept of Supermind. This in turn leads to his aspiration for transformation of nature into Supernature. These concepts have been studied in poetic form in the fourth chapter and scriptural sources have been traced and explained. Let us now turn our attention to a brief study of the Upanishadic philosophy.

2.3 The Philosophy of Upanishads

The central theme of the Upanishads is the search for what is true. Radhakrishnan says that Upanishad means knowledge which destroys error and enables one to approach the truth. Shankara points out "True knowledge of *Brahman* is called Upanishad." The thought current of the Upanishads is, in a way, a continuation of that in the *Brahmanas* and the *Aranyakas*. However, the trend in the Upanishads, unlike in the latter, is definitely against ritualism and strongly favours *upasana* (meditation) and *jnana* (knowledge). In the more philosophical portions of the Upanishads, the discussions generally center round the fundamental cause of the world, if there is one, and its nature as also its evolution into this world. This cause is usually called '*Brahman*.' As against this, there is a parallel mode of enquiry, into the existence or otherwise, of a permanent subjective entity behind the body-mind complex. This is called '*atman*' (the Self or the soul).

Destiny of the living beings here and hereafter, including some eschatological questions, form another topic of the Upanishads. Ignorance of one's real nature as the cause of bondage and its eradication through the practice of certain virtues like self-control and speaking the truth are also touched upon. The seers of Upanishadic Philosophy inquired into the ultimate Reality from different standpoints and persisted in their inquiry till the Reality was fully known. According to R.D. Ranade, the metaphysical problem of the Upanishads was "Cosmo-theo-psychological problem" (qtd. Mohapatra 6).

According to the Upanishads, the ultimate reality is *Brahman*. *Brahman* is infinite, eternal, omnipotent, omniscient and self-consciousness. It is the self of all. *Brahman* is the subtle essence pervading the whole living and non-living world. According to *Maitri* Upanishad, "That from which all these living things have been born, in which they live and lastly into which they will be merged, that is *Brahman*." In the *Brihadaranyaka* Upanishad it is stated that the sun, the moon, heaven, earth, days, nights, months and years, seas and rivers, etc., follow their own course due to the order of *Brahma*. So also in the discussion between Yajnavalkya and Vidagdha Sakalyamit was concluded after much reasoning that *Brahman* alone is the God of universe. The *Brahman* is infinite. It is transcendent as well as immanent. In the *Shvetashvatara* Upanishad God has been described as immanent and transcendent in the same verse: "God is standing silently in heaven like a tree and yet the whole universe is filled by Him." In the *Kenopanishad* (1-2-8) the Self has been called" the ear of ears, the mind of minds, the speech of speeches and the life of lives." The *Taittiriya* Upanishad (11-3) says: "That from which the mind returns along with speech and cannot attain it, that is the ultimate reality. The highest *Brahman* which is *ananda*, is just *atman* as realized in the *turiya* state."

The following are some of the important aspects of the Upanishads like epistemological, philosophical, synthetic, spiritual, moral, cultural, and optimistic aspects which elaborate these concepts:

The epistemological method observes the philosophical aspect of knowledge in the Upanishads. It is mainly concerned with the self-knowledge (*Atma-Jnana*). By this self-knowledge, one can realize *Brahman* which is supreme and which is indefinable. In *Brihadaranyka* Upanishad *Brahman* is mentioned as "Unseen but seeing, unheard but hearing, unperceived but perceiving, unknown but knowing." Our intellectual capacities are not adequate for comprehension of *Brahman*. The *Kena* Upanishad (11-3) says "It is unknown to those who know and known to those who do not know." However, seers have realized *Brahman* and obtained self-knowledge through intuition (qtd. Mohapatra 130-34). The Ultimate Reality in the subjective aspect is known as intellectual self (*prajna*) and the intuitive self (*turiya*). One can realize *Bràhman* only in the intuitive stage.

Coming to the philosophical aspect, Bloomfield, in his work *The Religion of the Vedas* writes that, "There is no important form of Hindu thought, heterodox Buddhism included, which is not rooted in the Upanishads. *Sankhya-Yoga*, *Nyayavaisheshika*, Vedanta etc., all derive their basic tenets from the Upanishads." As Ranade points out "Upanishads contain no one system of philosophizing one over another like Alps over Alps" (qtd. Baird and Bloom 76). Most of the *Yoga* philosophy is found in the *Shvetashvatara* Upanishad. In this Upanishad one finds the description of *asana*, *pratyahar*, *pranayam* and *dhyana*. The God of *Yoga* has been described in the *Kathopanishad*. The categories, five elements and time, mind, soul and liberation are mentioned in the *Shvetashvatara* Upanishad. So also the quality of "*Akasha*" and "*Puritat*" are mentioned in the *Chandogya* and *Brihadaranyaka* Upanishads, respectively. Shankara developed his monistic philosophy on the basis of the Upanishads. The *Brahman* in *Advaita* Vedanta is similar to the Upanishadic *Brahman*. Shankara's doctrine of *Maya* also has its roots in the Upanishads.

As regards the synthetic aspect, the Upanishads have different views regarding *Brahman*, *atman* and *moksha*. Sometimes the views are contrary and contradictory to one another. It may be considered in the terms of Hegel as thesis, antithesis and synthesis. As for instance, it is stated that *Brahman* is *saguna* and *nirguna*, *para* and *apara*, transcendent and immanent. The various aspects of the dialectical process are replaced by the synthetic method. In the fourth chapter of the *Brihadaranyaka* Upanishad, Yajnavalkya synthesizes the several standpoints explained by King Janak. Such kind of synthesis is found also in *Chandogya*, and *Prashna* Upanishads.

The Upanishads are profoundly concerned with the spiritual aspect of life. Only after self-realization can one achieve the spiritual knowledge. In order to realize the self, the concentration of mind by restraining the senses from the external objects is to be cultivated. Soul is the inner dweller, it cannot be realized by running after worldly desires and objects. The self cannot be realized either by speech or by intellect or by hearing many things (*Kathopanishad*, 1-2-20), but it can be realized by truth, austerity, real knowledge and the life of celibacy (*Mundaka* Upanishad-III-1.5). Besides devotion, initiation from the teacher and meditation are necessary for self-realization. When the inquirer realizes the self as identical with *Brahman*, the Absolute, that is the last stage of self-realization. In the *Brihadaranyaka* Upanishad and in the Chandogyopanishad it has been said that one must identify the 'I' with the Absolute. It is clear that the spiritual aspect of Upanishads insists on a transformation of the whole nature of man.

The Upanishads work as a practical guide to our moral and cultural life. The *Taittiriya* Upanishad deals with the five sheaths (*kosha*) viz.: physical sheath, vital sheath, mental sheath, consciousness sheath and bliss sheath, which are considered as scientific approaches to the transformation (*rupantara*) of self. The moral purpose appears to be more explicit in the Upanishads than in the Vedas. The ultimate end according to the Upanishads is the realization of the Soul. The law of *karma* and the highest freedom of life in Upanishads are the counterparts of the moral world. God consciousness is bound to be transmuted into good. Morality, according to the Upanishads, expresses the true nature of things.

About the optimistic aspect, the Upanishads aim at an integral life. In the *Ishopanishad* it is mentioned that "full is that, and full is this. Out of the full comes the full. When from the full the full is taken, the full itself remains." The *Brihadaranyaka* says, "Lead me from the unreal to the Real. Lead me from darkness to light! Lead me from death to immortality." Such an integralist and optimistic approach forms the foundation of Sri Aurobindo's Integral *Yoga* (Harshananda 9-49).

2.4 The Philosophy of the *Bhagavad Gita*

The *Bhagavad Gita* presents a synthesis of *Karma*, *Jnana* and *Bhakti*. This sacred book is very popular among the Hindus and forms a part of Bhishma-parva of the *Mahabharata*. The message of the *Bhagavad Gita* (*Gita* hereafter) is universal in its scope. It presents the quintessence of Hinduism. According to William Von Humboldt, *Gita* is "the most beautiful, perhaps the only philosophical song existing in any known tongue." According to Radhakrishnan "the *Gita* appeals to us not only by its force of thought and majesty of vision, but also by its fervour of devotion and sweetness of spiritual emotion" (1968: 47). While investigating upon the originality of *Gita*, Swami Vivekananda says that *yoga*, *Bhakti* etc. had each strong adherents even before its advent but they all quarreled among themselves, each claiming superiority for his own chosen path without ever trying for a reconciliation among these different paths. "It was the author of the *Gita* who for the first time tried to harmonize these. He took the best from what all the sects then existing had to offer, and threaded them in the

Gita (*Selections from C.W.* 370). The central teaching of the *Gita* has been beautifully summarized in this sentence of Annie Besant: "It is meant to lift the aspirant from the lower levels of renunciation where objects are renounced, to the loftier heights where desires are dead, and where the yogi dwells in calm and ceaseless contemplation, while the body and mind are actively employed in discharging the duties that fall on his lot in life" (qtd. Mohapatra 130).

It is verily a blend of the mystical and the activistic. Such a blend is a characteristic excellence of the heritage of Hinduism. The essence of mysticism is some kind of absorption. Absorption in action is possible through selfless dedication. Dedicated action is more than mere disinterested action. Disinterested action as such may not be sustained long; it runs the risk of death by inaction. The mystic touch of dedication transforms it into divine action, revitalizing it on a superior plane and infusing into it a superhuman potency. Dedicated action thus gets charged with a sublime efficiency. The mystic opens himself to the Infinite in his moments of absorption. He renders himself receptive to the divine impact and gets actually divinised himself (qtd. Mohapatra 106). The following is the threefold pathway of the *Gita*, comprising of *Bhakt*, *Karma* and *Jnana*.

The *Gita* has been variously described as a gospel of work, a gospel of pure knowledge and a gospel of devotion. The emphasis which the *Gita* lays on devotion (*Bhakti*) is no doubt superior to any other. It insists in clear terms on the supremacy of the Divine as the Supreme *purusha* or *purushottama*. Devotion to the supreme is its dominant note, and the path of work as well as the path of knowledge is perfectly attuned to it. *Bhakti-yoga* (i.e. the path of devotion to God) is the quest of union through sanctified sentiment. It is the *yoga* of love, the greatest of mystic schools. True love of God originates from knowledge of the Lord's glory and greatness. It is fostered and converted into a flaming energy by *nishkama karma, Abhyasa Yoga* and *Jnana-yoga.* When love deepens and ends in absolute surrender, the grace of God descends on the devotee. It destroys the distinction between *bhakti* and *jnana* by bringing both to their common end of experience of God, in which to know Him is to love Him, and vice-versa. When this experience is attained, it destroys the cloud of ignorance, and one realizes God.

Jnana yoga, the path of knowledge, advocates the method of discrimination between the real and the unreal, refusing to accept anything other than the one Reality. *Jnana* according to the *Gita* does not stop with a mere intellectual understanding of philosophical concepts; it is illumination accompanying the attainment of God. In the path of knowledge, the aspirant has to realize that the world is illusory and *Brahman* alone is real. He has to develop a firm conviction through reasoning that *Brahman* is not this universe, nor the mind, nor the intellect, nor the senses, neither happiness nor misery and so on, till by this process of elimination he finally comes to the core of things and realizes the Absolute. In order to realize the Absolute one has to rise above 'I' and 'mine,' which cause the bondage of the soul. The *Gita* says:

> Even the most sinful man can cross over the ocean of *samsara* by means of the boat of knowledge alone. As fire well-kindled reduces fuel to ashes, so the fire of knowledge reduces all actions to ashes. The culmination of action is in knowledge. Having obtained knowledge, one soon embraces peace or bliss (*Bhagavad Gita*, IV 38).

Although the *Gita* is primarily a gospel of action or of work, a closer scrutiny would reveal that it culminates on a note of spiritual realization, because the action which the *Gita* holds forth as an ideal is not selfish or self-centered action but illuminated action, inspired by deep devotion and sustained by conscious surrender and consecration. Sri Krishna says in the *Gita* that men and women are destined to work i.e., *Svadharma*. *Karma-yoga* is mainly based on *nishkama-karma* (desire less action) and not the mere renunciation of *karma* or action. Without action a man cannot attain the state of non-action. One has to renounce all attachment and the fruit deriving from the action. Action is man's *svadharma*, the fruit or result thereof is not his concern. Without *jnana* and *bhakti*, renunciation of desire and attachment is not possible in *karma*.

A synthesis of action, knowledge and devotion, the *Gita* accepts God as the ultimate cause and ground of sustenance of this universe. *Ishvara*, and '*Brahman*' are some of the epithets used to describe Him. However, it is to be noted that Sri Krishna often identifies himself with the God and freely uses the words 'I' or 'Me' to denote Him. He has two *prakriti*s or natures—the *para prakriti* and the *apara prakriti.* The former comprises the *jivas* or living beings and the latter consists of the three gunas: *sattva, rajas* and *tamas*. The *jivas* are described as of His part or *amsha*—birth less, deathless and eternal. They wear and discard the bodies as a man wears new clothes discarding the old and worn out. The body is called *kshetra* or the field since the fruits of actions are reaped through. The *jiva*, who is essentially the *atman*, identifies itself with the *kshetra* due to ignorance and hence suffers the agonies of birth, disease, old age and death.

The three paths of *Gita* can be described as follows: the first is the path of knowledge. *Gita* helps man to know himself, to know his real nature i.e. to know his soul, the *atman*. The second is the path of action; the *Gita* teaches *nishkama karma*, which means to work for the well being and the peace of his society, without a desire for the results. The third is the path of devotion, through which one develops intense love and longing for God. One can lead a spiritual life in which all the three, *jnana*, *karma* and *bhakti*, have their rightful place. The *Gita* treats *yoga* or spiritual life as organic whole involving the discipline of our will, i.e. the *Karma Yoga*; the discipline of our emotions, i.e. the *Bhakti yoga*; the discipline of our intellect i.e. the *Jnana yoga*. These three disciplines cannot be compartmentalized or isolated from one another as they are required integrally for man's spiritual realization. It can be seen that there is an element of *bhakti* in *Karma-yoga*. A *karmayogi* always feels that he is a servant of God. Without *bhakti*, it is impossible to perform any action in a perfect manner. A *karmayogi* considers God as the Doer and himself as only an instrument in the hands of God. He surrenders all actions, their agency and their results to God. For him work is worship. *Bhakti* is the essence of *Karma-yoga*. *Bhakti* is an unconditional devotion towards God. The *Gita* says that true devotion is always balanced by *karma-yoga* on one side and *jnana-yoga* on the other. That is, true *Bhakti* is always accompanied by moral awareness on one side and detachment and discrimination on the other. *Bhakti* is never blind. It is enlightened love for God. Just as there is an element of *bhakti* in *Karma-yoga*, there is an element of *jnana* in *Bhakti-yoga*. According to the *Gita*, *jnana* also includes the cultivating and practice of various virtues of head and heart, which lead an aspirant to *jnana*. In the path of knowledge i.e. *jnana-yoga*, the aspirant has to realize that the world is illusory and *Brahman* alone is real. *Brahman* is the real knowledge which is called *atman* and therefore the *jnana* is *atma-jnana* (i.e. knowledge of oneself). By this *atma-jnana* one gets devoted to God. This *Jnana-yoga* is the reasoned exposition of philosophical knowledge and spiritual realization or *moksha*. This synthetic approach for God-realization finds an explicit place in Swami Vivekananda's gospel of spiritual-humanism. Apart from a zealous scientific interpretation of the scripture he has added a more practical and human dimension to it when he declared "The new religion demanded by the age must be a harmonious fusion of *yoga*, devotion, knowledge and work" (*C.W.* 2: 484).

2.5 *Puranic* Aspect of Hinduism

The *Ramayana*, the *Mahabharata* and the other *Puranas* constitute the epics of Hindu religion. For over two thousand years, the *Ramayana* and the *Mahabharata* have been influencing deeply the religious, moral and literary thoughts of India. In fact Swami Vivekananda has declared that the *Ramayana* and the *Mahabharata* are the two encyclopedias of the ancient Aryan life. Vedas are treated as the original source of all epics. The two great epics are neither the outcome of poetical imagination, nor pure myth or allegory. But, in fact, mythology function and allegory are undoubtedly closely interwoven in these two epics.

The *Ramayana* of Valmiki is essentially an epitome of virtue. Its hero, Sri Rama, the model of virtue, the man of perfection, is made the incarnation of Vishnu, who took form on earth for repression of wrong and rehabilitation of virtue. Sri Rama is called *Purushottama*, having all the noble and virtuous qualities. Sri Rama stands for duty, self-sacrifice, compassion, protection, heroism, and justice. It is a *dharmashashtra*, a sacred text teaching righteousness. It propounds the principles of eternal law or *Sanatana Dharma* and presents the ideals of good conduct, which every human being should emulate. The *Ramayana* brings out the strengths and weaknesses of the Aryan culture. The superiority of the Aryans lay in the sternness of their character, their spirit of sacrifice, supreme regard for truth, love and adventure and perseverance. Sri Rama is the embodiment of the high ideals of Hindu life. In him is presented the strange combination of a faithful and dutiful son, an affectionate brother, a loving husband, a stern, relentless warrior, and an ideal king. Sri Rama's younger brothers, Lakshmana Bharata and Shatrughna represent ideal brothers while Sita is a dutiful wife.

The *Mahabharata* of Vyasa is so comprehensive in its scope that there is a popular saying that what is not in the *Mahabharata* is not to be found on the land of the Bharatas. It is an epic par excellence. The *Mahabharata* refers to the six systems of the Hindu philosophy and their conflict. It is an authoritative book on law, morality, and social and political philosophy, laying down rules for the attainment of *dharma*, *artha*, and *kama*, called *trivarga*. It also shows the way to liberation (i.e. *moksha*) expounding the highest religious philosophy of India, and inculcating reverence for Narayana, the Supreme Spirit.

2.6 Six Systems of Hindu Philosophy

As already mentioned earlier the Hindu philosophers developed six principal systems of philosophy, viz. *Vaisheshika*, *Nyaya*, *Sankhya*, *Yoga*, *Mimamsa* and Vedanta.

The *Vaisheshika* philosophy of Kannad traces the origin of the universe to the combination of atoms and molecules. It maintains that these atoms and molecules were not created by God, but were co-eternal with Him. The power, which combines two atoms and makes aggregates of atoms, comes from God, who is personal. He possesses knowledge, desires and will, and God is the lord of all phenomena. According to this system of philosophy, ether, time, space, self and mind are eternal substances of nature. The *summum bonum* is *moksha* or release from rebirth and thus from bondage or suffering. Next is the *Nyaya* philosophy of Gautama. Its object is the true knowledge of nature, soul and God, and the attainment of ultimate freedom.

The *Sankhya* system of Kapila considers the rational consideration of self and non-self, *purusha* and *prakriti* or eternal energy. Kapila denied the existence of God as Creator, but admitted the existence of the individual soul as an eternal, infinite and immortal entity. His philosophy narrates the qualities e.g., *sattva*, *rajas* and *tamas*, in case of evolution. Its *summum bonum* is release from bondage, suffering and rebirth. *Moksha* is gained ultimately only through knowledge.

The *Yoga* philosophy of Patanjali devotes itself to the higher psychology of the human mind and explains the science of concentration and meditation, the science of breath, clairvoyance, telepathy, and various other psychic powers, and shows the way by which one can attain God-consciousness (*samadhi*). Patanjali's yogic system of philosophy is very complete in itself. Devotion to God and practical discipline of *Chittavritti nirodha* (i.e. control of one's mind) are emphasized as essential aids to obtaining *moksha*.

The *purva-Mimamsa* is an orthodox school of philosophy propounded by Jaimini, which examines the various injunctions of the ritualistic portions of the Vedas (karma-kanda). It points out that the highest duty of man is to follow these injunctions as strictly as possible. This system may be called the philosophy of *karma* or ritualistic work. It explains the authoritative sources of knowledge, the relation between word and thought.

Lastly the system of Vedanta, which is commonly known as *Advaita* Vedanta of Shankaracharya, is confined to the study of the Vedas and the Upanishads. Vedanta implies literally 'end of knowledge' or the end of the Vedas. This is the most popular philosophy of India today. The monistic *Advaita*-vedanta philosophy guides man above all knowable objects of perception, and directs his soul towards the eternal and absolute Being, through which man finds solution to all problems. According to *Advaita*-vedanta, *Brahman* only is real and the world is unreal. *Brahman* must be one and not many. From one, many have come into existence, and the individual souls are the manifestations of absolute *Brahman*. From this absolute *Brahman* the phenomenal universe emerges and in the end it returns into *Brahman*, and this view is maintained by the monistic religion of Vedanta.

Developing a dualistic phase of Vedanta, Ramanuja said that the world, God (*Brahman*) and souls are real. Our ignorance is the cause of bondage and suffering; it can be avoided by true knowledge, which is known as *Brahma-jnana*. *Moksha* is a state of bliss, where the individual self identifies itself with *Brahman*.

The traditional *Advaita* which forms the central axis of the teachings of Swami Vivekananda is also given a humanistic perspective as attested in his writings. For example, he writes "True religion teaches man that 'every being is only your own self multiplied' (*C.W.* 5: 14) and that we have to worship the living God, the Man-God who wears a human form and yet is universal" (*C.W.* 6: 265).

2.7 Religious Systems

The Indian philosophical tradition is exceedingly complex and varied. Some of the systems exist today while others exerted their main influence in past ages. Here is an elaboration of three of the above mentioned systems while studying the attempts of their religious systematization. The three religio-philosophical systems, which form the essential background of the philosophical ideas of Swami Vivekananda and Sri Aurobindo, namely *Advaita*, *Vishishtadvaita* and *Yoga* are discussed in some detail hereunder. The information on the three systems has been taken from the treatise, *Indian and Far Eastern Religious Traditions* written by Robert D. Baird and Alfred Bloom in addition to the notes taken from the television lectures of Swami Prakashanand Saraswati, which were broadcasted on the *Sanskar* channel during the years, 2003-4.

To start with *Advaita* Vedanta, this position is called Vedanta because it is based on the Upanishads which come at the end of the Veda, and *Advaita* because it is a nondual (a + *dvaita*) system. Shankara (788-820 A.D.), with whom this system is commonly associated, was the son of a Shivaguru and was born in the Malabar country of the Deccan. Since Shankara believed himself to be interpreting *Shruti*, most of his position is found in his commentaries, which include digressions in which he attempts a refutation of all opposing positions. His main commentary is on the *Brahma Sutras*. Of considerable importance also are his commentaries on ten Upanishads, particularly the *Chandogya* and the *Brihadaranyaka*, a commentary on the *Gita*, and a more systematic treatise called *Upadeshasahasri* ("A Thousand Teachings"). The various philosophical schools based on Vedanta all regarded the *Brahma Sutras* as condensations of the teachings of the Upanishads, and the differences of opinion arose about the meaning of the *sutras* and the Upanishadic texts to which they refer. Shankara did not originate the *Advaita* position, which was already rather well worked out by his teacher's teacher Gaudapada. Gaudapada, however, was explicitly dependent on the Madhyamika and Vijnanavada systems of the Buddhists, while Shankara harshly rejects such formulations even though he was accused of being a "crypto-Buddhist." *Advaita* continued to develop after Shankara, his followers splitting philosophical hairs in an attempt to perfect his system.

Coming to the Metaphysical questions, the basic question to be considered here has to do with the nature of *Brahman*. *Brahman*, or Ultimate Reality, is pure consciousness devoid of all attributes (*nirguna*) and devoid of all categories of the intellect (*nirvishesha*). There is no distinction between *Atman* and *Brahman*. *Brahman* is nondual (*advaita*), transcending the distinctions between knower, knowledge, and known. And since there is ultimately no duality, *Brahman* alone is ultimately Real. Transcending all categories, *Brahman* can best be described in negative terms. Positively the best one can do is to say that *Brahman* is pure consciousness, pure existence, and pure bliss. By stating the matter this way, one is denying that *Brahman* is a substance that has such qualities in favour of the position that existence and consciousness and bliss are one. In *Brahman* all intellectual distinctions end.

Associated with *Brahman* is its potency, or *maya*, which allows *Brahman* to appear as qualified Lord (*Ishvara*) who is the creator, preserver, and destroyer of the world, which is his appearance. In this state one often refers to *Saguna Brahman*, or *Brahman* with qualities as distinct from *Nirguna Brahman*, without qualities. *Nirguna Brahman* is ultimately a designation, which describes a state of immediate experience of the plenitude of Being rather than being a mere concept.

In much Indian thought one must get used to thinking in terms of levels of being rather than in terms of whether something is real or unreal. Some entities are more real than others, and this is ultimately determined by their degree of participation in *Brahman*, *Brahman* alone being ultimately Real. Shankara's system can be understood in terms of three such levels.

1. Reality (*sat paramarthika*). The whole truth and the sole Reality.
2. Appearance (*vivarta*). Illusory and characterized by change.
    a. Phenomenally real (*vyavaharika*). Ordinary waking experience. Religiously speaking it is the theistic religious experience.
    b. Illusory existent (*pratibhasika*). The illusion of dreams and other illusory experience.
3. Unreality (*asat*). The level of logical contradictions.

These levels are to be understood in terms of the principle of devaluation (*badha*, or contradiction). This is the process whereby we devalue a previously approved object in light of new experience. In this scheme the levels of appearance are not unreal (*asat*), since they do not consist in logical contradictions, but neither are they Real, since they can be devalued by experience of the Real. They have the level of appearance or phenomenal "reality" but ultimately they can be devalued. The level of appearance does not in fact have an objective counterpart, but the level of *asat* cannot in principle have a counterpart. The world is appearance (*vyavaharika*). It has a practical reality, but does not qualify for the designation "Real" since it can be devalued. It is real only so long as we are in a state of ignorance and so long as knowledge does not dawn. In describing the relationship of the world to *Brahman*, several terms are used which are almost identical in meaning. It is based on ignorance, *adhyasa*, in that it is a superimposition such as when one mistakes a rope for a snake at dusk, and *vivarta* in that it is merely appearance. In this ignorance, man takes the world for what it is not—the Real.

Ultimately the doctrine of *maya* is inexplicable. *Maya* itself is not Real, for it exists on the level of appearance and has no existence apart from *Brahman*. On the other hand, one cannot say it is unreal, since it projects the world of appearance. Such conflicts led Nagarjuna to ultimate silence and the rejection of all logic. Shankara, by holding that *maya* has only a phenomenal and relative character, is saying nearly the same thing, and the similarity led to the accusation of his being a "crypto-Buddhist." When right knowledge appears, ignorance and *maya* are removed. Shankara held to the view that the cause alone was real and that the effects were false (satkaryavada). This is the view of causation, which states that the effect (*karya*) is existent (*sat*) in the material cause and is not a novel thing. The process of the imaginary attribution of something where it does not exist is *adhyasa* (superimposition). As Nagarjuna, Shankara rejected the view that things arise by chance. But since *Brahman* alone is Real, he was forced to take the view that there is no change in substance and hence no change in Reality. Change belongs to the level of appearance. While we must, on this level, live as though things change, when knowledge dawns, we will see that such views are due to our ignorance.

To consider the psychological questions, the levels of the phenomenal and the Real are equally relevant for an examination of human nature. To begin with, there is the supreme *Atman* (*paramatman*). *Atman* fits into the level of the Real, and hence is pure, undifferentiated, self-shining consciousness. *Atman* transcends all such distinctions as subject and object, time, space, or thought. *Atman* cannot be an object knowable by the mind or perceivable by the senses, since thought functions only through forms and multiplicity. Thought is a process, while *Atman* is a state. *Atman* is not different from *Brahman*, which means that in the depth of man's being, he is not different from Reality.

On the phenomenal level is the *jiva*, which represents the individual human person, the phenomenal self which is a combination of reality and appearance. *Jiva* is reality to the extent that *Atman* is its ground, but it is appearance since it is finite, conditioned, and relative. Hence the individual self is empirically real for it is part of our experience, but it is transcendentally unreal for the only Real is the *Atman* which is not different from *Brahman*. Unlike the Pali tradition, man's problem is not that he holds to permanence when all is change, but that he identifies the change, of which the *jiva* is a part, with the Real. The consciousness of human limitation is grounded in ignorance. The *Atman* is essentially unlimited and Real.

As regards the epistemological questions, reason does not occupy a primary place in the system of Shankara. The value of reason is that it is a necessary tool for assisting us to understand *Shruti*. The ultimate truth cannot be known by reason alone since it transcends reason, which is part of the realm of appearance. What one debater shows to be reasonable can be shown by a more expert debater to be false. The ultimate truth is found in *Shruti*. This means that Shankara was not compelled to show that his metaphysical system was completely and compellingly rational. Its truth depended on *Shruti*. If his position could be shown to be faithful to *Shruti* and if its apparent contradictions could be explained away without flying in the face of experience, there was little more for him to do. In the final analysis, his position would only be convincing to those who had achieved realization. As one moves up the levels of being and has the corresponding experiences, thus devaluing lower levels of existence, he becomes more convinced of the truth of the formulation. Absolute certainty comes only at that point at which the request for certainty is meaningless. In the final analysis, it is realization, which clinches the matter. But, one must hasten to add, when that occurs, Shankara's entire system is devalued and seen for what it actually is—part of the level of appearance.

Lastly, about liberation and ethics, it is believed that perfection is possible in this life. When one comes to the realization that he is *Brahma*, he is a *Jivanmukta*, one who is liberated while living. Although living, the *Jivanmukta* does not identify himself with the body, which he realizes is only appearance. The world still appears for him, but he is not deceived by it. He is not affected by the world's misery and has desire for the world's objects. The reason why one can be liberated and still continue a bodily existence is explained by distinguishing three kinds of *karma*. There is *karma* that has brought forth its effects, *karma* that still lies accumulated, and *karma* that is gathered in this life. Knowledge of Reality (*Jnana*) destroys accumulated *karma* and makes it impossible to gather more *karma* in this life. But the *karma* that has already borne its effects in having produced the body must run its natural course. This *karma* ceases when its force is exhausted just as the turning wheel of the potter comes to a full stop only when its momentum is spent. When the body perishes, the *Jivanmukta* is said to attain the disembodied state of liberation called *videhamukti*.

The role of ethics must also be placed in terms of the levels of being. If *Brahman* is beyond all distinctions, this includes ethical distinctions as well. The *Jivanmukta* is above all distinctions of good and evil. He is not susceptible to moral judgments. While he would probably not involve himself in the world of moral distinctions since he is not touched by sorrow or desire, neither would he be inclined to commit murder or other acts which would seem to presume egoism. On the lower level of the phenomenal world, moral distinctions are necessary for ordering existence. In general one might say that those actions which lead to the highest good, or *moksha*, and tend to minimize ego involvement are good. On the other hand, those acts that lead to ego involvement are bad. All the acts of the *jiva* are to some extent involved in selfish desire, a fact which makes ethical virtues desirable on the lower level. Shankara generally accepts the *Dharmashastras* for ordering the phenomenal world. Yet it must be admitted that in terms of the Real, all such distinctions could be devalued.

From the time of the *Gita*, and even before, one can see evidence of the growth of the *bhakti* movement. Alongside the *bhakti* movement was the development of an articulate *advaita* position based on the Upanishads and culminating in the thought of Shankara. Shankara systematized his position prior to the composition of the *Bhagavata Purana* which systematized the *bhakti* of that time. With arguments which convinced many, Shankara relegated *bhakti* to the lower level of appearance. His view continues to dominate philosophy departments in India today. Nevertheless, *bhakti* was not easily relegated as merely preliminary to a nondual system. Many *bhaktas* did not find such a preliminary role for *Bhagavan* (the personal God and object of devotion) acceptable. The reaction against Shankara reached its peak in the writings of Ramanuja (1017-1137) which came to be known as *Vishishtadvaita*.

Intending to remain loyal to the theism of the *bhakti* sects, Ramanuja attempted to offer a sound philosophical basis, which claimed the Upanishads and *Brahma Sutras* for its authority. Ramanuja's position was furthered by the formation of a sect called 'Shri-Vaishnavism' or 'Shri Sampradaya.' This sect carried on many of Ramanuja's emphases. They developed the doctrine of *prapatti*, or submission to God, and opened Vedic knowledge even to Shudras (members of the lowest caste). Although in traditional fashion Shankara denied Vedic knowledge to those who were not of the twice born, Ramanuja admitted Jainas, Buddhists, Shudras, and even untouchables into his fold. Ramanuja also placed some emphasis on the use of images and included in his texts elaborate directions for the construction of temples and the various rituals associated with image worship. Ramanuja rejected Shankara's doctrine of levels of reality. This rejection carried implications, which made his view of Ultimate Reality, man, and liberation somewhat different from Shankara's. Ramanuja's view of Ultimate Reality is called *Vishishtadvaita*, or qualified nondualism.

For him the absolute is not distinction less, but is qualified by diversity. It is a whole, which consists of interdependent and interrelated elements. There is no undifferentiated pure consciousness. All knowledge involves distinctions. When the Upanishads speak of *Brahman* as devoid of qualities, they only mean that *Brahman* has no bad qualities and not that He has no qualities whatsoever. Having rejected Shankara's distinction of levels of reality, it follows that he would also reject the distinction Shankara made between *Brahman* and *Ishvara*. For Ramanuja, *Brahman* is no formless entity, but a Supreme Person qualified by matter and souls, which are sometimes called his body. Ramanuja considers three things as ultimate and real: matter (*achit*), soul (*chit*), and God (*Ishvara*). While all three are real, the first two are dependent on God. *Ishvara* is *Brahman*. God manifests himself in various forms for his devotees: as the immanent soul of the universe: as the transcendent personal Lord; as creator, preserver, or destroyer; as *avatara* in human or animal form; as images enshrined in temples so that his devotees can see him physically.

Shankara's interpretation of *avidya* and *maya* is also rejected. *Maya* is the real power of God whereby he creates the world. There is no illusion involved since the world is also real. This position leaves open to Ramanuja a view of causation in which the effect is as real as the cause. For him, change is not apparent but real, being contained in the cause. Just as curd is a real transformation of milk, so an effect is as real as a cause. Ramanuja spends considerable energy arguing against Shankara's view of *maya*. He asks, for example, where *maya* resides if it indeed exists? It cannot exist in *Brahman* without nondualism breaking down, nor in the individual self, which is mere appearance. Ramanuja concludes it is a pseudo-concept which exists in the mind of the *advaitin*. Furthermore, when Shankara maintains that *maya* is neither real nor unreal, he is merely engaging in intellectual gymnastics. Real and unreal are exhaustive and exclusive. A thing is either one or the other; no further alternative exists without the violation of well-established canons of logic.

Ignorance (*avidya*) is the cause of bondage, which means that the *jiva* wrongly identifies its reality with material objects such as the body. And, immediate intuitive knowledge is liberation. Souls are bound because of their ignorance and *karma*. While meditation is useful, it is subordinate to *bhakti* and is obtained by throwing oneself on the mercy of God. The highest *bhakti* only dawns by the grace (*prasada*) of God. Liberation is not the realization that ultimately there is no distinction between *Brahman* and *Atman*, but the intuitive realization on the part of the soul that it is a mode of God. The liberated soul never becomes identical with *Brahman*. It is always finite while God remains infinite, and the soul does not share God's power as creator, preserver, and destroyer of the universe. For Ramanuja there is no possibility of liberation while one lives (*Jivanmukta*). As long as the soul remains associated with the body, it is clear that *karma* persists and the soul cannot become pure.

Two centuries after Ramanuja, his followers divided into two schools. The *Vadagalai* (baby monkey) or northern school, held that one had to purify oneself in order to receive divine grace. It maintained the need for man's cooperation with God in salvation and came to be known as the 'monkey school.' Just as the monkey clings to the mother, so the devotee clings to God. When man casts himself entirely upon God, he does have to exert an effort to cling to him. The *Tengalai* (baby cat) or southern school, magnified the importance of divine grace in liberation, and held that no individual effort was necessary for divine grace to dawn. This position came to be known as the 'cat view.' As the mother cat lifts its kitten and carries it to a safe place without any effort from the kitten, so does God bestow his grace on man.

The classical presentation of *Yoga* is found in the *yoga sutras* of Patanjali. This sutra contains four parts which deal respectively with the nature and aim of concentration, the means for attaining realization, the supranormal powers which are by-products of this discipline, and the nature of liberation and the realization of the transcendent self (*purusha*). The *yoga* system has been closely connected with the *sankhya* system since it accepts, with minor modification, the epistemology and metaphysics of *sankhya*. It is basically a dualistic system witch distinguishes between *purusha* and *prakriti*. *purusha* is the eternal self witch is pure consciousness. It is changeless and omniscient. *Prakriti* is the principle, which accounts for everything that is physical, including matter and force. *Prakriti* is characterized by change. Because of the reflection of the *purusha* in the changing states of the mind (*chit*), one is led, however erroneously, to believe that it is the Self (*purusha*), which is responsible for performing the functions that we often attribute to the Self (*purusha*). Essentially, the *chit* is not conscious, but is merely a transformation of *prakriti* which is attributed with consciousness because of the reflection of the *purusha*. Chandradhar Sharma's explanation on the subject is enlightening, the following are a few lines from it:

> *Chit*, therefore, is the physical medium for the manifestation of the spirit, just as in a red-hot iron ball, formless fire appears spherical and cold iron appears hot, similarly on account of its reflection in the *Chit*, *Purusha* appears changing and *Chit* appears conscious. Just as the moon appears as moving when seen reflected in the moving waves, and waves appear as luminous, similarly *Purusha* appears as undergoing modifications and *Chit* appears as conscious due to *Purusha*'s reflection in it (158).

Unlike *Advaita*, the world of change and matter is real. The *purusha* is also real. Liberation (*moksha*) comes when one ceases to confuse the activities of the *chit* with the unchanging *purusha*. It is not the *purusha* which suffers and undergoes rebirth, but the phenomenal self or *jiva* which is the *purusha* as reflected in the *chit*. Liberation is effected through a carefully worked out discipline for which *Yoga* philosophy is most commonly remembered. But the word "*yoga*" has numerous meanings. Sometimes it simply means "method." On other occasions, as in *advaita*, it refers to the spiritual union of *Atman* and *Brahman*. "In Patanjali's system, *Yoga* does not mean union, but only effort, or, as Bhoja says, separation (*viyoga*) between *Purusha* and *prakriti*" (Baird and Bloom 76). The goal of *yoga* is the cessation of mental modifications after which one will no longer identify the *purusha* with the modifications of the *chit*. The eight steps of this discipline enumerated in Patanjali's *Yoga Sutras* are *Yama* (restraint), *Niyama* (observances), *Asana* (posture), *Pranayama* (breath control), *Pratyahara* (control of senses), *Dharana* (attention), *Dhyana* (meditation) and *Samadhi* (concentration). Up to the point of *samadhi*, one is engaged in a negative process of distinguishing the *purusha* from *prakriti*, but in the final state of realization, the positive nature of the eternal *purusha* manifests itself untainted by *prakriti*.

Each step toward *samadhi* is attended by supranormal powers. *Yogin*s are said to be able to tame the most ferocious wild beast, see through solid objects, and pass through them as well. They can appear and disappear at will. They can know the past, present, and future immediately. It is tempting to be sidetracked by such "rewards" for one's diligence, but the texts continually warn that these are really hindrances to the ultimate realization, since they have the power to become ends in themselves. Delight in such powers will prevent the *yogin* from reaching the goal. As Radhakrishnan points out, "They are by-products of the higher life. They are the flowers which we chance to pick on the road, though the true seeker does not set out on his travels to gather them. Only through the disregard of these perfections can freedom be gained" (1923: 367).

In each of the above cases the system is religious because it is a systematic articulation of what is held as man's ultimate goal. The first two systems considered (*Advaita* and *vishishtadvaita*) are largely philosophical explanations of the spiritual reality while the third system discussed (*yoga*) presents an integral view of man's ultimate destination along with his physical mental and spiritual means of reaching there.

2.8 Interdependence of Philosophy and Poetry

Having briefly surveyed the different facets of Indian philosophy, let us now explore the age-old method of its broadcast, that is through poetry. The relationship between philosophy and poetry is akin to the relationship between the soul and the body. Poetry is an apt embodiment or medium for expression of philosophy. Between religion and philosophy in their essence, and the arts, there is not only a historical coincidence in time, but an inevitable co-operation. Poetry, the oldest of the arts, has always been the favorite medium for expression of philosophical thought in every age and culture for it makes an abstract concept more lively, tangible and palatable.

The *Rig Veda* is a collection of poetic hymns sung by sages in praise of deities worshipped by them. The Vedic poet employed meter and skill, added sound effects and end rhymes and gave brilliant descriptions of his deities, many of whom were personifications of natural phenomena, the Sun, the dawn, the wind, etc. The Rig-Vedic poet reveled in figures of comparison and could give graphical, natural descriptions and had a gift for bodying forth abstract speculations in sublime words. The Veda was thus the foundation of Indian poetry, not merely of Indian religion and philosophy, points out *Princeton Encyclopedia of poetry and Poetics* (384). What is known through philosophy is to be disseminated and established by the word of the poem, as Heidegger puts it:

> Poetry is the act of establishing by the word and in the word. What is established in this manner? The permanent. But can the permanent be established then? Is it not that which has always been present?
>
> No! Even the permanent must be fixed so that it will not be carried away. . . .
>
> The poet names the gods and names all things in that which they are. . . . when the poet speaks the essential word, the existent is by this naming nominated as what it is. So it becomes known as existent. Poetry is the establishing of being by means of the word. (qtd. Iyengar 183)

Poetry is a term derived from the Greek, meaning 'to make.' A poem is made by a poet in the form of imaginative literary expression using sound and a language replete with imagery. Poetry or verse is often characterized by meter, rhythm, pitch, connotation, metaphor, symbolism and other sensory appeals. According to Johnson, Poetry is "metrical composition and the art of uniting pleasure with truth by calling imagination to the help of reason." Carlyle calls it "Musical Thought" while Wordsworth refers to poetry as the "breath and finer spirit of all knowledge," and defines it as "the spontaneous overflow of powerful feelings: it takes its origin from emotions recollected in tranquility." For Shelley "Poetry is the record of the best and happiest moments of the happiest and best minds" (qtd. Chandra and Sebastian 10). These definitions imply some subtle connection with the object of man's philosophical endeavor.

Philosophy is nothing but a habit of the human consciousness to formulate within itself some conception of the universe of which it found itself a part, and of its own relationship thereto. As Vijayasree puts it, "To see Beyond, in fact, has always been the vital preoccupation of human thought and the mysterious power behind the multifarious manifestations of the universe has always stimulated the human imagination" (166). Such conception it has also been a habit of the human consciousness to throw into expression, for the purpose of exchange, confirmation or correction.

To express a thought, the medium should take us to the heart or mind of things. Arts like painting or sculpture can take us up to the surface of form of a given object. Music can reach up to emotion but its appeal varies from race to race and may also disregard the accurate articulation of the word writes James. H. Cousins and adds that the vehicle for the expression of conscious thought is found in the literary arts, more so in poetry (184). The problem with prose-writings of philosophy is that they fail to arouse emotional interest or to make personal appeal as poetic-writings can, because they try to state the fact or concept as impersonally and as objectively as possible. At best they lean on parables or mythology, but can never achieve the dramatic element of a poem. There are two clear advantages of conveying philosophical thought through poetic medium:

i) Involvement of all the human faculties, including emotion, ensures longer and deeper attention, thus leading to better understanding or illumination.
ii) The realization of the divine is the central pivot of all philosophy. This path of Ascent is wrought with emotional, mental and spiritual experiences—guided by tested prac-

> tice and conceptual knowledge. Normally, such experiences are highly subjective and beyond logic. It is only through the poetic form with all its paraphernalia that these experiences can ever attain expression and articulation as T.S. Eliot had declared in his famous statement "Poetry is a raid on the inarticulate."

Perhaps, for these reasons, the ancient sages have always 'sung' of the Divine. In fact, as James H. Cousins recounts, in the ancient symbolism of the West, philosophy and poetry are figured as twin serpents, mutually destroying yet nourishing one another, and Hermes (Mercury) the bearer of the twin serpents was regarded as the guardian divinity of the seers on the one hand, and of the artists on the other; and therefore as the foe of those who would withhold from religion and philosophy the comradeship of beauty, or deny to the arts the fecundation and inspiration of the soul (184). In the East, particularly in India, one finds that. most of the Upanishads are in verse form in accordance with standard Vedic meters. Only some like the *Mandukya*, the *Taittiriya* are written in prose, while some others have a mixture of prose and poetry. The other great philosophical texts of India like Vedas, and the *Gita* are also in the poetic form. Owing to this medium, these treatises are embellished with beautiful similes, metaphors and imagery—which render their teaching easily intelligible and interesting. As Swami Harshananda points out, the simile of two birds (the *Jivatman* and the *Paramatman*) perching on the same tree (the human body) occurs in several Upanishads: *Katha* (1.3.1.); *Shvetashvatara* (4.6.) and *Mundaka* (3.1.1.). Both the *Gita* and the *Katha* Upanishad (6.1) compare the world to an inverted tree and the human body to a city with nine gates (5.1) and also to a chariot where the senses are likened to the horses, the mind to reins, the intellect to the charioteer and the *atman* to the owner of the chariot (3.3 and IV of *Katha*, and *Gita* respectively qtd. Harshananda 40).

The poetic style of these scriptures is not only simple and elegant but also quite powerful. Armed with the *mantric* potential, the philosophical concept seeps deep into all the realms of human consciousness. Thus philosophy appears to be the soul of poetry.

While analyzing the constituents of a poetic composition, James H. Cousins writes:

> In the unity of the Absolute is repose, and the end (as also the beginning) of the arts. Their fullest literary expression is in that fusion of the three great qualities of '*Satva,*' '*rajas*' and '*tamas*' (spirit, mind and body) whereby the image is made not merely intelligible to the mind but evocative to the inner realms. Apart, however, from this enlargement of mental and emotional scope, it is within the power of philosophy on its psychological and psychical sides to give to the arts in general, and to poetry in particular, a much needed enrichment through the extension and intensification of the instruments of consciousness, and through opening a clean way into the super-realms of nature and humanity (205).

The core of a (philosophical) poem is its intellectual or spiritual element which may be considered as its *satvic* component. That aspect of the poem which elicits or appeals to emotion is its *rajasic* constituent. And the skeletal part of the poem which lays the ground by a description of the immediate or the empirical which sustains the above two aspects and possibly also the poem's linguistic structures which make up the physical aspect are its *tamasic* elements. The fusion of these three qualities is precursor to all creation and equally to the poetic creation. In other words, poetry deals with thought as a vital process, not as a statement; as an act of creation, not as an answer to a sum. "It is therefore necessary that the thought which must be the hidden basis of the poem should be vitalized by feeling, and so be expressed musically; but it must also possess the static qualities of sculpture and painting; that is, it must show symmetry and imagery" Opines James H. Cousins while stating that a mere versification of the sublimest truth is not necessarily poetry. He emphasizes the necessity of all the three components thus:

> The black cloud of ignorance, sometimes grandiloquently called agnosticism, is not the air to nourish the poet. He needs the uplift of the heal on a mountain-side; the call of blue distance across waters; he needs frayed edges, indeterminate outlines all the symbols that open out from the little sharp circle of his separate life to One Life that ensphere all. But, while leading outward, subjective Philosophy also

> leads inward; teaches indeed the great truth that the path to knowledge of the outer is only safely and surely trodden when eye and foot are bent resolutely towards one's own spiritual centre. Hence the inspirational centre will not reside in the universe of things, and produce derivative verse, but will operate from the illimitable source in the poet's deeper consciousness, and produce authentic poetry (211-12).

It is necessary to lay stress on this point because during the gradual development of philosophical thought, there is the danger of subtle drawing away from the inner light through an externalized enthusiasm for the new teachings which renders the poem a mere rhymed statement of some occult or metaphysical fact. Sri Aurobindo expresses categorical opinions on the way poetry is sometimes used to convey a philosophy. When used thus, poetry often turns out to be prosaic, "one should be careful and see that the poetry is not flat or heavy when one is philosophizing" (*Letters on Poetry* 297). All great poets at one time or the other try to philosophize, and there is a difference between spiritual poetry and philosophical poetry. To produce a poem of lasting interest it should have the three elements which Sri Aurobindo considers essential in creation of poetry:

i) The original source of inspiration;
ii) the vital force of creative beauty; and
iii) the transmission of the outer consciousness of the poet.

The direct vision or experience of the Divine is the source and sustenance of the poem which can then convey a philosophical concept. Sri Aurobindo seems to corroborate this stand when he traces the origin of poetry as coming from "some subtle plane through the creative vital and uses the outer mind and other external instruments for transmission only" (*Letters on Poetry* 291). Such use of poetry would be no untried innovation, but simply a reversion to the method of the Vedas and the Psalms of David. One finds an obvious interdependence between poetry—the medium of expression and philosophy—the spiritual and intellectual experience of mankind. Expression is but the natural demand of experience and experience itself is the essential substance of expression.

In the modern Indian English poetry, this symbiosis of philosophy and poetry is well illustrated in the poetic compositions of Swami Vivekananda and Sri Aurobindo. Today, under the imposition of European ideals over practically the entire globe, "we are eating the Dead-Sea fruit of intellectual stagnation," writes Cousins, which, he says, "is the natural fruition as thought unfertilized by the spirit, thought devoid of poetry, with its equally sinister companion, poetry devoid of thought, both crying out for what each can give the other, yet both condemned to an arid celibacy through the blindness of more worldly seer ship, and the folly of the worldly wise" (195-196.). While, however, at the present stage of the world's evolution we may not advance the extreme claim for the complete fusion of religious or philosophical thought and poetry, we can at least profitably study some considerations that may lead to a "rapprochement" of both, and the enrichment of each, particularly through the poets of the renaissance in India like Swami Vivekananda and Sri Aurobindo who keep close to tradition in inspiration and language, or others like, Rabindranath Tagore, Swami Ramananda Tirtha, Sarojini Naidu and her younger brother Harindranath Chattopadhyay, who sing of the ancient spiritual ecstasy of India in English verse of fine quality.

As C. Vijayasree aptly observes, Swami Vivekananda's poetry teems with the touches of cosmic consciousness, revelations of greater spiritual life and suggestions of the Infinite. She says, "His rhapsodies reflect the vision of his soul and of his people. His poetry becomes the consecration of his deeper convictions and contains the whole truth of his religion" (173). The gospel of universal love, service to mankind and devotion to the Infinite are the three chief motifs that run through his philosophical poems which radiate from the central concept of *Advaita.* This non-dualistic Vedanta, one of the three schools of Vedanta, which upholds the doctrine of the identity of the individual soul with the supreme spirit. *Advaita* for Swami Vivekananda was not merely a philosophical position but the way of living itself. Many of his poems thus spring from a certain spiritual experience caused by a vision, or an experience of oneness with the Divine. "The Song of the Free," "A

Song I Sing to Thee," "The Cup," "No one to Blame" etc., contain the essence of his metaphysical insights. For example:

> Thus, day by day, till *karma*'s power spent
> Release the soul forever. No more is birth
> Nor I, nor thou, nor God, nor man. The "I"
> Has all become, the All is I and Bliss
>
> Know thou art That, Sannyasin bold, say—
> "Om, Tat Sat, Om!" ("The Song of the Sannyasin")

Here in "The Song of the Sannyasin" he weaves the concepts of *Advaita*, the law of *Karma* and life of renunciation into lucid poetry. The realization of this all encompassing Self leads to spiritual humanism and universal religion of Swami Vivekananda:

> Where seekest Thou friend, God
> leaving aside those before you in myriad forms?
> He indeed serves God who loves God in all living beings.

All the rational, metaphysical and theological principles should culminate in this highest wisdom that the service of man is the service of God. The outlines of this neo-Vedantic philosophy have been drawn from Shankara's *Advaita* and its practical application in the life of his master Sri Ramakrishna.

Sri Aurobindo also rejects the imperfect materialist affirmation like Swami Vivekananda, but he rejects the ascetic denial of life as well. He evolved out of his study of the Vedas and the Upanishads and especially his own experience, a philosophy which harmonizes the two ends of existence—Spirit and Matter. As Parthapritam Ray states clearly, "his Integral *yoga* not only aims at ascent of world to the Divine, but also seeks to transform the external world through the descent of the Divine into it" (30-35). In Sri Aurobindo's view, '*Satchidananda*' is involved through descending series of the Supermind, mind, life and matter and naturally evolution is going on through an ascending series of matter, life, mind, Supermind and '*Satchidananda*.' Moreover '*Satchidananda*' was involved even in the darkest inconscience before the beginning of evolution. This thought-provoking theme binds its shape in "The Miracle of Birth" as:

A spark of the eternal fire, it came
To build a house in matter for the Unborn
The inconscient sunless Night received the flame,
In the brute seed of things dumb and forlorn.

In the poem "Evolution," the ascent of the soul (ancient force) is picturized in more ornamental language with mystical touches:

I passed into a lucent still abode
And saw as in a mirror Crystalline
An ancient force ascending serpentine
The unhasting spirals of the aeonic road.

Sri Aurobindo's sonnets "The inner Sovereign," "Light," "The Silver call," and others like the ones given below reveal chiefly his divine transformation, which he aspires for all mankind as well as for all creation:

He who would bring the heavens here
must descend himself into clay ("A God's Labour")
Still by slow steps the miracle goes on,
The immortal's gradual birth mid mire and stone. ("Nirvana")

His ideas on overhead poetry, poetry of the *Mantra* and his background of Indian spiritual heritage, his knowledge and belief in the Vedas, the Upanishads have added a unique Indian touch to the themes and symbolism of Sri Aurobindo's philosophical poetry writes Syamala Kallury (13).

Besides gnostic poems, Sri Aurobindo has also written some poems addressed to a personal deity with subtle devotional tones, though in his Integral *yoga* these three lines of approach (*Jnana, bhakti & Karma*) meet and coalesce thoroughly. For example, "Rose of God" traces the path of realization through devout self surrender and self-dedication points out S. Krishna Sarma (25). Poems on Krishna and Shiva celebrate a mystical unison with God. While Sri Aurobindo revels in resplendent colours and forms of *Brahma*, Swami Vivekananda dares to love Kali. The Goddess of love and life is also looked upon as the Goddess of wrath and death. The intention of this two dimensional love is explained in an ecstatic poem "Kali the Mother":

Who dares misery love,
And hug the form of Death,
Dance in destruction's dance,
To him the Mother comes.

The poet exhorts us to rise above the dualities of life and death and misery and joy for attaining the Mother signifying *Brahma*. Other devotional poems of Swami Vivekananda like "And Let Syama Dance There," "Shiva's Ecstasy," "My Play is Done" are born out of spiritual vision that emerged from the churning of his soul.

Philosophical poetry, like mystical poetry, is difficult to achieve, but not impossible. Confronted by the crisis in expression, the great poet 'can' master it and safely come through as illustrated by Swami Vivekananda, Sri Aurobindo, and others before them.

Besides taking forward the *mantric* poetry in English, which was inaugurated by Swami Vivekananda, Sri Aurobindo appears to be the spiritual heir of Sri Ramakrishna and Swami Vivekananda. It would be of interest to take into account the interrelationship between the two poets (interaction at spiritual level, intellectual influence, etc.). Indeed, the *Yoga*s promulgated by both Swami Vivekananda and Sri Aurobindo are very comprehensive in nature which aim for the collective uplift of the humanity as a whole. To take the message in brief, the philosophy of Swami Vivekananda is an exhortation for renunciation and service, while the aim of Sri Aurobindo's philosophy is spiritual transformation. Swami Vivekananda adheres to *Karma Yoga* for inner purification, while Sri Aurobindo's *Jnana Yoga* lays stress on gnosis and psychic awakening. *Karma Yoga* for Swami Vivekananda is performance of one's duties for social good in a spirit of perfect selflessness of dedication to the Lord. On the other hand, meditation in addition to a spirit of detached action assumes great significance at Sri Aurobindo *Ashram*. On a pamphlet, bearing the title *Visitor's Guide to Sri Aurobindo Ashram*, which is distributed at the *Ashram*, Sri Aurobindo's own words on his method of *Sadhana* have been published. A part of it reads thus:

> The *Sadhana* of this *Yoga* does not proceed through any set mental teaching or prescribed forms of meditation, *Mantras* or others, but by aspiration, by a self-concentration inwards or upwards, by self-opening to an Influence, to the Divine Power above us and its workings, to the Divine Presence in the heart and by the rejection of all that is foreign to these things. It is only by faith, aspiration and surrender that this self-opening can come.

While social and national regeneration are significant steps in the scheme of practical Vedanta of Swami Vivekananda, the inner spiritual awakening is the course to achieve a new and diviner race in the *Sadhana* of Sri Aurobindo. It is believed that Sri Aurobindo has continued the course of spiritual thought from the point where Swami Vivekananda had left it, interestingly at the latter's numinous direction. A significant spiritual instruction imparted by Swami Vivekananda has been recorded by Sri Aurobindo in the following words:

> I began my *Yoga* in 1904 without a *Guru*; in 1908 I received important help from a Mahratta Yogi and discovered the foundations of my *Sadhana*; . . . But in the jail I had the *Gita* and the Upanishads with me, practiced the *Yoga* of the *Gita* and meditated with the help of the Upanishads; these were the only books from which I found guidance; . . . It is a fact that I was hearing constantly the voice of Vivekananda speaking to me for a fortnight in the jail in my solitary meditation and felt his presence. . . . The voice spoke only on a special and limited but very important field of spiritual experience and it ceased as soon as it had finished saying all that it had to say on that subject.

Sri Aurobindo also recorded in his diary, the directions given by Sri Ramakrishna with respect to his *Sadhana* and the course of spiritual thought that the latter had indicated, in the following words:

> Diary Entry of Dec. 5, 1912: (Record of *Yoga*)
>
> . . . 18th October . . . . . the third and last message from Sri Ramakrishna was received. The first message was in Baroda, the "Arabindo, *mandir karo, mandir karo!*," and the parable of the snake *Pravritti* devouring herself. The second was given in Shanker

> Chetti's house soon after the arrival in Pondicherry, and the words are lost, but it was a direction to form the higher being in the lower self coupled with a promise to speak once more when the *sadhana* was nearing its close. This is the third message (18 Oct. 1912)
>
> "Make complete *sannyasa* of Karma.
> Make complete *sannyasa* of thought.
> Make complete *sannyasa* of feeling.
> This is my last utterance."
>
> (*Swami Vivekananda and Sri Ramakrishna in Sri Aurobindo's Writings* 7, 8)

The second direction given to Sri Aurobindo soon after his arrival in Pondicherry, to form the higher being in the lower self, appears to be an initiation into the concept of Transformation, which was developed greatly by Sri Aurobindo through the course of his *Sadhana*. Thus the philosophy of Sri Aurobindo is a continuation of the philosophy of Sri Ramakrishna and Swami Vivekananda.

The poems of Swami Vivekananda and Sri Aurobindo discussed in the ensuing chapters will demonstrate the fusion of philosophy and poetry, metaphysics and aesthetics. The examples will highlight the manner in which the apparently unrelated activities of religion or philosophy and poetry may be brought into a mutually beneficent unification.

Chapter 3

Philosophical Poetry of Swami Vivekananda

Swami Vivekananda's personal experiences as a *Sadhaka* and his familiarity with the ancient scriptures inform his literary productions, especially his philosophical poems. In this introductory section, a brief sketch of life, literature and philosophy of Swami Vivekananda have been discussed, with a view to comprehend his poems better. After this, the philosophical poems of Swami Vivekananda are discussed in the succeeding three sections under three broad heads: Descent to the Relative; Ascent to the Absolute; and Synthetic estimate of the concept of *Advaita*. The Scriptural background of these concepts is discussed after an elucidation of the poems.

3.1 Life, Literature and General Principles of Philosophy

Swami Vivekananda who was named by his parents as Narendranath Dutta, was born in Calcutta on January 12 1863, of an aristocratic kayastha family. His mother was steeped in the great Hindu epics, and his father, a distinguished attorney of the Calcutta high court, was an agnostic about religion, a friend of the poor, and a mocker at social conventions. Even in his boyhood and youth Narendra possessed great physical courage and presence of mind, a vivid imagination, deep power of thought, keen intelligence, an extraordinary memory, a love of truth, a passion for purity, a spirit of independence, and a tender heart. An expert musician, he also acquired proficiency in physics, astronomy, mathematics, philosophy, history, and literature. He grew up into an extremely handsome young man. Even as a child he practiced meditation and showed great power of concentration. Though free and passionate in word and action, he took the vow of austere religious chastity and never allowed the fire of purity to be extinguished by the slightest defilement of body or soul.

As he read in college the rationalistic western philosophers of the nineteenth century, his boyhood faith in God and religion was unsettled. He would not accept religion on mere faith; he wanted demonstration of God. But very soon his passionate nature discovered that mere universal reason was cold and bloodless. His emotional nature, dissatisfied with a mere abstraction, required a concrete support to help him in the hours of temptation. He wanted an external power, a guru, who by embodying perfection in the flesh would still the commotion of his soul. Attracted by the magnetic personality of Keshab, he joined the Brahmo samaj and became a singer in its choir. But in the samaj he did not find the guru who could say that he had seen God.

In a state of mental conflict and torture of soul, Narendra came to Sri Ramakrishna at Dakshineswar. He was then eighteen years of age and had been to college for two years. The master wanted to train Narendra in the teachings of the non-dualistic *Vedanta* philosophy. But Narendra, because of his Brahmo upbringing, considered it wholly blasphemous to look on man as one with his creator. One day at the temple garden he laughingly said to a friend: "How silly! This jug is God! This cup is God! Whatever we see is God! And we too are God! Nothing could be more absurd." Swami Nikhilananda narrates the succeeding events thus, in his introduction of the treatise, *The Gospel of Sri Ramakrishna*:

> Sri Ramakrishna came out of his room and gently touched him. Spellbound, he immediately perceived that everything in the world was indeed God. A new universe opened around him. Returning home in a dazed state, he found there too that the food, the plate, the eater himself, the people around him, were all God. When he walked in the street, he saw that the cabs, the horses, the streams of people, the buildings, were all *Brahma*. He could hardly go about his day's business. His parents became anxious about him and thought him ill. And when the intensity of the experience abated a little, he saw the world as a dream. Walking in the public square, he would strike his head against the iron railings to know whether they were real. It took him a number of days to recover his normal self. He had a foretaste

of the great experiences yet to come and realized that the words of the *Vedanta* were true (Gupta 58).

After Sri Ramakrishna's death in 1886, his disciples, under the leadership of Naren, formed what was later to be called the Ramakrishna Order of Monks. They gathered in a dilapidated house in Baranagore, midway between Calcutta and Dakshineshwar. Rejecting the traditional concept of pain-hugging, irritable ascetics, the monks under Naren's intellectual guidance transformed the monastery into a miniature university. Studies were undertaken to discover the essential spirit of history, sociology, literature, art and the sciences. Disputations on the philosophical theories of such philosophers as Kant, Mill, Spencer, and such schools as *Vedanta*, Buddhist and Christian, so honed Naren's debating skills that thereafter none was able to withstand his rhetorical power.

He infused a spirit of public rather than personal salvation into his *gurubhais* (brother disciples), by urging them to shorten their meditations and utilize the time saved by offering help to the famine-stricken villagers. This service has been a crucial feature of the Ramakrishna Order of Monks until the present day. The Hindu proverb, "like flowing water, the monk who is always on the move, remains pure," influenced Naren's next move—to become a *parivrajaka* (an itinerant monk).

"The Cyclonic Hindu"—a term given to Naren in America achieved his training in the whirlwind activities during the *parivrajaka* years (1887-1893). As an ochre-robed monk, carrying only a staff, possessing only one or two books wrapped in a blanket and a *Kamandalam* (water pot), Naren traveled the length and breadth of India, collecting the insights that were later to form the nucleus of his speeches and writings. The great poverty that he witnessed while visiting the sacred *Tirthas* (places of pilgrimages) stirred him to seek help for his fellowmen. After an intense fret, the solution suddenly dawned upon him at Kanyakumari. He decided to travel to America, earn money for India by way of lecturing, for a mutually beneficial exchange of spiritual enlightenment for financial help. The *parivrajaka* years initiated voluminous correspondence by which Naren guided his associates. The Maharaja of Khetri, a devotee and faithful supporter of Naren, gave him the name of Swami Vivekananda just prior to Naren's sailing for America. The name "Vivekananda" literally means, the "bliss of spiritual discrimination" and was inspired by Naren's perspicacity. The Parliament of Religions held in Chicago, 1893, introduced Swami Vivekananda to America, and the first five words of his speech—"Sisters and brothers of America"—established the tenor of his relationship with the West. Within the two years he stayed in the U.S., many Americans had become his "proclaimed disciples" points out the treatise, *The Life of Swami Vivekananda by his Eastern and Western Disciples* (349). The same great message by which Swami Vivekananda "aroused the foremost thinkers and representatives of American life and culture to a new order of thought and to a new spiritual outlook," was now taken to England, and met with immediate success. There also Swami Vivekananda was urged to set up classes to which people flocked, initially out of curiosity, but later with an ever increasing thirst for more knowledge (*LSVEWD* 371).

In the subsequent years, he established some important *Ashrams* and societies for a healthy give and take of ideas between the East and the West. "The Vedanta Society of New York,' established in 1896 with J.J. Goodwin as its secretary, is one of the prominent among such institutions. The mystical 'Mayavati Advaita *Ashrama*' in the Himalayas was established in 1899 and 'Shanti *Ashrama*' in California was founded in the year 1900. Right up to his passing away in 1902, Swami Vivekananda sowed the seeds of an interchange of ideas between the East and the West, to create "open doors as it were, through which the East and the West could pass freely back and forth, without a feeling of strangeness, as from one home to another" (*LSVEWD* 33).

Literature remained a significant part of Swami Vivekananda's life and mission. As Thomas Mannumel puts it, "The ancient heritage that had become alive in Sri Ramakrishna's life was cast to the four winds by this "cyclonic" disciple, Swami Vivekananda" (10). He did this mostly through public speeches, class lectures, private conferences, conversations and dialogues than through the medium of writing, though there are a few treatises which were written by a disciple at his dictation. Then there are numerous letters (five hundred and thirty nine, to be exact) which are in print at present in four series. The language he used was mostly English. The comparatively few works he wrote in his mother tongue, Bengali, or in Sanskrit were all collected, translated and published by his disciples in *The Complete Works of Swami Vivekananda*.

His first treatise, *Sangita Kalpataru* in Bengali, was written in 1887. This work brings out the "Theoretician' and musician aspects of Swami Vivekananda. In fact his literary contribution began with his address at the Parliament of Religions, Chicago. Here for the first time, all his speeches were recorded and noted down. Besides he wrote a paper on Hinduism himself and read it at the Parliament. After the Parliament, Swami Vivekananda undertook a series of "Apostolic campaigns' to spread the message of Sri Ramakrishna. Around June, 1895, he completed writing a treatise on *Raja Yoga* with the help of his amanuensis Miss S.E. Waldo (known as sister Haridasi later on). This book entitled *The Philosophy of Yoga* (*Raja Yoga*) was published from New York in 1896. The first publication during his lifetime, it brought him recognition from well known scholars like Russian novelist Leo Tolstoy, Indologist Max Muller, Philosopher William James, etc.

He later dictated two more treatises on *Bhakti Yoga* and *Karma Yoga*. *Jnana Yoga* comprises his lectures delivered in London and America. To the West, Swami Vivekananda gave India's ancient message in keeping with the spiritual needs of the contemporary West:

> The goal . . . of life . . . is to manifest the divine within by controlling nature, external . . . by science, technology and socio-political process . . . and internal . . . by ethics and religion . . . Do this and be free (*C.W.* 1: 124).

To awaken men and women everywhere to their divine birthright constituted Swami Vivekananda's mission. The one recurring theme in all his utterances revolved around man—his growth, development and fulfillment. He started the publication of three magazines: *Prabudha Bharata* in English *Udbodhan* and *Brahmavadin* in Bengali.

In June 1899, Swami Vivekananda set out upon his second journey to the West. He had delivered numerous lectures during this period. Some are published in *C.W.* but most of them remained unwritten in the absence of a 'second Goodwin'—Swami Vivekananda's secretary during his first visit (Khatri 15-19). There are nine volumes of *The Complete Works of Swami Vivekananda* (*C.W.*), the compilation of his works, which contain his original writings, lectures, exhorting epistles to his disciples and brother-monks, conversations and dialogues, questions and answers, poetic compositions—in Sanskrit, Bengali (translated into English) and English, (appearing in fourth, fifth, sixth and eight volumes) four *Yogas*, speeches and inspired talks among other items.

Among the thirty seven poems that Swami Vivekananda wrote, a number of poems like "Hold on Yet a While Brave Heart," "A Benediction," and "To an Early Violet" originally formed a part of the letters written by the prophet to his friends and disciples. Twenty two poems were written directly in English by Swami Vivekananda, while fifteen are English versions of the poems composed by him in Sanskrit, Bengali and Hindi. Poems like, "A Song on Samadhi," "And Let Shyama Dance There," and hymns written in adoration of Sri Ramakrishna, Shiva and the Divine Mother, etc., belong to the second category. Apart from these poems written by Swami Vivekananda, there is a collection of seven poems which are translated by him in verse form. The English titles of the poems are: "Rudra-Prayer," "Hymn of Sweetness," "Hymn of Creation," "Nirvanashtakam," "Renunciation Alone is Fearless," "Thy Love I Fear," "A Song of Suradasa." The original sources of these poems are given in detail in the anthology, *In Search of God and Other Poems*.

In his childhood Swami Vivekananda developed a love of poetry that never left him. As a child he spent many hours listening to his mother's recitation of stirring tales from ancient epics, and as a student, he came under the afflatus of the British Romantic poets. From a very early age, Swami Vivekananda began writing poetry and composing songs, all of which reveal the imprint of his early spiritual inspirations. As Carebanu Cooper puts it, "the Soul became his persona, the 'Reflector true—Thy pulse so timed to mine ("To My Own Soul"), that he constantly searched for the how and why of things, and was not satisfied with stereotypic answers, Vivekananda formulated his own responses based upon his meditations" (36). These answers were written in poetic form. Swami Vivekananda's poetry was spontaneous, expressing the immediate emotion of a spiritual experience.

Three broad themes run through Swami Vivekananda's poetry, the perceptions are disparate, yet inextricably interwoven. Swami Nikhilananda points out in his introduction that "they represent Swami Vivekananda's philosophy of life, which reflects Sri Ramakrishna's teachings of unity and Oneness that stretched from the lowly worms to the heavenly *devas* or gods" (Gupta 58). The three broad motifs in Swami Vivekananda's poetry are: the religious or metaphysical, the social or critical sentiments and the poems of prophecy. Swami Vivekananda's reputation as poet of note stemmed not so much from his prosody, but from the embedded concepts interwoven into the poems. Most of his poems, like his oratory, reveal an authority of *jnana* (self-knowledge), whose strength lies in their autobiographical nature. Hence, for the purpose of the present study, the thematic classification of Swami Vivekananda's poems is based on the principal Vedic-Upanishadic concepts of Involution/Descent and Evolution/Ascent.

Since very few of his poems are dated, the images Swami Vivekananda used and the feelings he evoked are universal. Like the great philosophical poets, Milton and Whitman, Swami Vivekananda used blank verse to convey his meaning. This form of poetry allowed him to attain an incredible range and flexibility in his verse.

Though Swami Vivekananda's poems are primarily addressed to someone or written for a particular occasion, they have a universal appeal, transcending the barriers of time and place. His ideas of *Advaita* and of chastity and charity have been woven through centuries of general and personal experience in a changing pattern. The very number of cultures, religions and languages and of associations with the experiences of other poets and mystics is enough to suggest its universality. For example the moral of "The Song of the Sannyasin" is true to all seekers of God in all ages. "Hold on yet a While Brave Heart" was written to the Maharaja of Khetri, but still works as a source of inspiration for all those who are the victims of this world of bondage. "To the Awakened India" was written in the context of pre-independent India to awaken the masses, but is still relevant to our age. "How can the message to be "strong and steady," "Blissful, bold and free," or of "Infinite Love" loose its relevance?" asks Khatri, while adding "Has not his appeal for the liberation of all colonies in "To the Fourth of July" kept them inspiring?" (112). Even the poetic value of this celebration is everlasting, just as man's quest for spiritual liberation—which is the true essence of the poem. Similarly "The Living God" was written to an American friend, "A Benediction" to Sister Nivedita, "Requiescat in Pace" on JJ. Goodwin's death, "My Play is Done" was written about himself. But they all are steeped in Vedantic ideology and thus attain spiritual and intellectual appeal. Vedantic as they are, they owe a great deal to his readings of the Vedas, the Upanishads, the *Gita* and the six systems or schools of thought, besides the two great epics and other Sanskrit and Bengali works of literature.

Before starting a detailed study of the poems written by Swami Vivekananda, let us take a brief overview of his philosophy. Swami Vivekananda considered himself an *Advaitin*, but attempted to make his position understandable beyond academic circles. He preceded Radhakrishnan in arguing that to say that the world is *maya* is not an outright rejection of the universe nor is it equivalent to saying that the world does not exist. To designate the world as world is *maya* is not to say that it is illusion, but merely to indicate its relative reality. *Maya* indicates that the world is full of contradictions and to that extent, can be considered unreal or illusory. But it is through *maya* that we come to the realization of Reality. Hence *Advaita* does not imply inactivity or an attempt to escape from the world, but proposes to use the world as a means of transcending it.

Once it is emphasized that *maya* does not mean that the world is nonexistent, the qualified reality of the world is in turn emphasized in order to make room for social concern and activity. "The man who says that he will work when the world has become all good and then he will enjoy bliss, is as likely to succeed as the man who sits beside the Ganga and says 'I will ford the river when all the water has run into the ocean' (Selections from *C.W.* 146).

While he held a place for *jnana yoga* (the way of knowledge), and although this experience transcended reason, Swami Vivekananda also held that no genuine inspiration contradicts reason. Inspiration sees things in flashes and is higher than reason, yet one must be on guard to distinguish inspiration from mere intellect or even deception. Swami Vivekananda was particularly cautious with regard to Occultism and Mysticism, but he had no doubts about the authenticity of Sri Ramakrishna.

Like many of those thinkers who have been characterized as 'neo-*Advaitin*,' Swami Vivekananda put considerable stock in science. Although he spoke out against Western materialism, he read in the sciences and not infrequently used scientific analogies to clarify and add weight to *Advaita* position. Swami Vivekananda nevertheless did maintain the distinction to be taken up by Radhakrishnan, that India's role had been to stress the spirit while the West had concentrated on unraveling the forces of nature. He felt that nationalistic expressions of his day, which attempted to lay the blame for India's ills at the door of religion were misplaced. India could not survive without religion since it had always been integrated with her destiny.

While an ardent defender of Vedanta, Swami Vivekananda was not beyond attacking certain practices that he held were irrational or sentimental. He felt that it was sometimes necessary to abandon custom. There were certain ideas about food that he ridiculed. As for bathing ritual, if its merits were to be accepted we should expect a fish to reach heaven before anyone else, since it bathes all the time (qtd. Naravane 101). Swami Vivekananda's

Advaita did not lead to inactive meditation, but was a call to action. He did not see knowledge, devotion, or action as three paths leading in different directions but as compliments reinforcing each other. He placed stress on practical work, for liberation was never an escape from the world. The critics of *Advaita* had contended that by declaring Brahma to be the sole Reality, a devaluation of human life had resulted. On the contrary, Swami Vivekananda held that if man is identical with God, he should work to abolish the indignities of the world, "Religion is the manifestation of the Divinity already in man" (*C.W.* 4 1962: 358).

Using Shankara's ultimate level in support of action on the relative level poses a difficulty, since ultimately such distinctions as 'the world' do not exist. But a shift in emphasis has taken place coupled with a reinterpretation of the *Advaitin* position. Two American authors, Robert D. Baird and Alfred Bloom have aptly pointed out in their book Indian and Far Eastern Religious Traditions that "Swami Vivekananda has attempted to make room for social concern and the dignity of the individual which is so commonly affirmed in the twentieth century" (113-14).

3.2 Poems on Descent or Involution

As one starts reading the poetry of Swami Vivekananda, one immediately notices a fine interweaving of symbols, of archetypal patterns of imagination in religious poetry and principles of *Advaita* philosophy. If one wishes to make a survey of his philosophy, one generally studies the prose texts of Swami Vivekananda. A perceptive survey of his religious poetry will yield a dependable insight into his philosophy as a spiritual experience. This is because Swami Vivekananda accorded very high importance to poetry, which he expresses in the following lines:

> Drama and music are by themselves religion; any song, love song or any song, never mind; if one's whole soul is in that song, he attains salvation. . . . If a man's whole soul is in that, his soul gets salvation. (qtd. Dasgupta 218)

The aesthetics of an apostle, of a Sannyasin who was concerned with the spiritual and moral questions of life, serve a very important purpose. The above opinion was expressed in one of his lectures reproduced in 'Notes of Class Talks and Lectures' as 'Fragmentary Notes on the *Ramayana*' included in the sixth volume of his *Complete Works*. Such a view breaks down the barrier between religious and secular literature. Its implication, as explained by R.K. Dasgupta, is that when a piece of literary work goes deep into the human soul, when it presents all the deeper concerns of life, it is a part of man's spiritual activity (218).

To Swami Vivekananda, the Upanishads are a great source of poetry. They are a treasure house of similes and metaphors and furnish sublime style of poetry. Like T.S. Eliot, he adored the 'Theory of Impersonality' and cited the Vedas and the Upanishads as its best example. The authors of these oldest scriptures of religion remain unknown. A striking feature of the poetry of Swami Vivekananda is its resemblance to the Upanishadic style of poetry. For example,

> The stars are blotted out,
> The clouds are covering clouds,
> It is darkness vibrant, sonant. ("Kali the Mother")

Swami Vivekananda himself illustrates a famous verse from Upanishad which is very similar to the above quoted lines, in the following passage, where he puts forth his idea on the poetic value of the Upanishadic texts:

> I want to bring to your notice one or two points in the study of the Upanishads. In the first place, they are the most wonderful poems in the world. If you read the Samhita portion of the Vedas, you now and then find passages of most marvelous beauty. For instance, the famous *Shloka* which describes Chaos—*tam aseet tamasa gudhamagre* etc., "when darkness was hidden in darkness," so on it goes. One reads and feels the wonderful sublimity of the poetry (*C.W.* 3: 329-30).

Swami Vivekananda's reverence to the ancient scriptures is equally fervent for their conception and comprehensiveness. After stating his idea of progress through evolution, he says that there is a process of evolution within the corpus of Upanishadic literature itself. He highlighted the incompleteness of the theories of evolution put forth by the modern science, saying, it was only one wing of the whole building when compared with the Vedantic Cosmogony. The evolution has a counterpart in Vedantism, namely the process of involution which science has not discovered yet, but will discover in a not distant future—believed Swami Vivekananda. Without it the explanation is like a one-winged bird; which needs the other wing to make it whole, to be able to fly steadily in the thought-world ("Soul, Nature and God" *C.W.* 2: 427).

Swami Vivekananda elucidates of the concept of 'Descent of the spirit to the Relative' in some of poems. The process of Creation is presented in these poems as Projection (*Sristi*) on the analogy of Exhalation. Inhalation therefore represents a return of this Creation into its Creator. The universe, explains Swami Vivekananda, is the result of the 'Projection' or manifestation of the Absolute and the Sanskrit word *Sristi* is to be translated as Projection and not as Creation. As to process of projection, he frequently offers an account of cosmogony which is rooted in *Sankhya*, without however admitting the *Sankhya* duality, and developed more or less in conformity with Upanishadic tradition (although there are different accounts of Creation in different Upanishadic texts). Swami Vivekananda says that all the Vedantists believe in *Kalpas* or 'Cycles' of evolution and involution of the cosmos. This cyclic process has its beginning and end in the "One Being manifesting itself." It is *Brahma*, "psychologically called *Mahat*" or "Cosmic Mind." The *Mahat* differentiates itself into *Akasa* and *prana*. "*prana* acting on *Akasa* is creating or projecting the universe." Everything that is material throughout the universe is the outcome of *Akasa*; and all force, whether gravitation, attraction or repulsion, or life is the outcome of the primal force unit, *prana*. At the beginning of a cycle, *Akasa* is motionless, unmanifested. It is in finer state than it would be later. Soon *prana* begins to act, "creating grosser and grosser forms out of *Akasa*—plants, animals, men, heavenly objects and so on ("The Vedanta philosophy *C.W.* 1: 360).

Thomas Mannumel explains that after an incalculable period this evolutionary action ceases and involution begins; everything is resolved back through finer and finer forms into the original *Akasa* and *prana*. But in this state *Akasa* and *prana* do not become extinct; they remain potentially quiescent for a period, ready to spring forth into another Creation (*Sristi*). When the moment comes, *Akasa* again begins to vibrate under the action of *prana*. When the vibration becomes intense, *Akasa* is lashed out anew into all these wave forms which men call sun, moon, plants, etc. (100). This use of the term 'Involution' is different from Sri Aurobindo's explanation of the term, which elucidates the process of Creation-as a result of descent of the spirit into the matter.

Swami Vivekananda employs nature-imagery, to illustrate this cyclic process in the poem "A Song I Sing to Thee." As C.L. Khatri writes, we find the recurrent theme of nature imaged and symbolized as Creatrix. "God to him was not only the Father immanent in the universe but also the Creatrix at play." For this reason, the poet consciously uses both feminine and masculine appellations to address the Supreme Power in the poem. Subscribing to the concept of *Lila*, the poet sets aside logic. C.L. Khatri further explains, "As a matter of fact, true spirituality springs from some such convictions that Creation is a sort of divine play and that God is not only *Sat* and *Chitta* but also *Ananda*" (106). The poet presents all these aspects of the divine as he sings:

> At the Beginning, I the Omniscient One,
> I am! The moving and the un-moving,
> All this creation comes into being
> By the unfoldment of My power supreme.
> Perforce of My command, the wild storm blows
> On the face of the earth; clouds clash and roar;
> The flash of lightning startles and rebounds;
> Softly and gently the Malaya breeze
> Flows in and out like calm, unruffled breath;
> The moon's rays pour their cooling current forth;
> The earth's bare body in fair garb is clothed,
> Of trees and creepers multitudinous;
> And the flower abloom lifts her happy face,

> Washed with drops of dew, towards the sun.
>
> ("A Song I Sing to Thee")

The alliteration of the / l / sound in close succession in 'clouds / clash,' 'flash / lightning,' 'softly / gently,' etc., produces a dramatic effect in the poem. The metaphor of 'flower abloom lifting her happy face . . . towards the sun' represents the aspiration of the created beings towards God. The Creator or *Brahma* is *Satchidananda*, Being-Consciousness-Bliss and all-pervading. The entire universe consisting of finite beings and nature is basically, identical with *Brahma*, which is one without a second, becomes many, that is to say the world of multiplicity.

In "Nirvanashtakam," the poet presents an artistic personification of *Brahma*—as experienced in the state of *Nirvana*. "Nirvanaṣhtakam" was written by Shankaracharya and translated by Swami Vivekananda in Bengali. As Carebanu Cooper rightly points out, though a poem that is taken out of one language and translated into another usually suffers great loss, Swami Vivekananda's "Nirvanashtakam" does not (44). On the other hand, the poet's experiences as a *parivrajaka* (an itinerant monk) and an *acharya* (teacher) facilitate his elucidation of the ungraspable *Brahma*:

> I am untouched by the senses, I am neither Mukti nor Knowable;
> I am without form, without limit, beyond space, beyond time;
> I am in everything; I am the basis of the universe, everywhere am I.
> I am Existence Absolute, Knowledge Absolute, Bliss Absolute
> I am He, I am He (Shivoham, Shivoham). ("Nirvanashtakam")

This parallels Whitman's vision which sees "The universe . . . in myself—it shall pass through me as a procession" (Complete Writings of Walt Whitman 49). Each verse of the literary ballad begins with the personified *Brahma* or the Supreme stating what it is not. The penultimate line is the resounding climax, intensified by a reversion in the usual order of sentence structure: "Existence Absolute, Knowledge Absolute, Bliss Absolute." In the last line, (the resolution), the riddle is solved when the Supreme (*Brahma*) declares itself positively, "Shivoham, Shivoham" (the Absolute God). The pattern of rising tone developing to a climax, then falling to a resolution, is repeated in the five stanzas. The first verse is built on the structure of a ballad:

> I am neither the mind, nor the intellect, nor the ego, nor the mind-stuff;
> I am neither the body, nor the changes of the body;
> I am neither the senses of hearing, taste, smell, or sight,
> Nor am I the ether, the earth, the fire, the air;
> I am Existence Absolute, Knowledge Absolute, Bliss Absolute—
> I am He, I am He (Shivoham, Shivoham). ("Nirvanashtakam")

In this first verse, the poet declares that *Brahma* is not a composite of physical traits like the body or its senses, neither emotional or moral values, nor is He limited by the time sequence of birth, life and death. The repeated words "I am neither" arouses the reader's curiosity as to what *Brahma* is, as opposed to the repeated statements of what He is not. What *Brahma* actually is, is revealed through the refrain of the last two lines in each stanza which commences with "I am." The last verse completely explicates *Brahma* as formless and limitless in space and time. He is everywhere—represented by Existence Absolute, Knowledge Absolute, Bliss Absolute—the '*Sat-Chit-Ananda,*' which according to the scriptures, is man's highest goal. Thus *Brahma* is "Shivoham" or Shiva-the Absolute God. The poet arrives at this realization as a result of his intense '*tapasyas*' or austerities and the revelations of the Supreme.

In other poems like "A Song I Sing to Thee" and "The Hymn of Creation" Swami Vivekananda reinterprets and elucidates the philosophy of the Supreme, Nature and *Maya*, which have been vividly explained in the *Gita*. The sage-poet says that as long as he was under the spell of worldly attachments he searched for God in vain "like a child in the wildest forest lost." When the veil of *Maya*, of senses, of worldly attachments was renounced after long years of sacrifice, the poet realized the Eternal within himself and felt oneness with all animate and inanimate objects:

> In rapture all my soul was hushed,
> Entranced, enthralled in bliss.
> A flash illumined all my soul,

The heart of my heart opened wide,
O joy, O bliss, what do I find!
My love, my love, you are here,
And You are here, my love, my all!
And I was searching Thee!
From all eternity you were there
Enthroned in majesty. ("In Search of God")

The poet felt His presence in soft moon light, sunlight, radiant stars, in the morning, noon, evening and night, in the sea and rivers, in the songs of birds, in the laughter of innocent children, in the mother's lap and her affectionate kisses. *Brahma* is in all, and all things are in him. All religions owe their existence to Him:

Thou wert my God with prophets old;
All creeds do come from Thee;
The Vedas, Bible, and Koran bold
Sing Thee in harmony.
"Thou art,' "Thou art' the soul of souls
In the rushing stream of life
'Om Tat Sat Om.' Thou art my God.
My love, I am Thine, I am Thine. ("In Search of God")

'In the rushing stream' of love the universal principle of oneness is spontaneously experienced and expressed by the poet. The verse is in contrast to the earlier poems of Swami Vivekananda, which record his struggle and longing to reach this communion with the Divine.

Creation or Involution of *Brahma* is explained as projection of the universe. The liberated soul or self "is the perfect saint' who, taught by likeness within himself, sees the same Self everywhere, the outer be pleasurable or painful." According to the *Gita*, the free self sees his own Self in all beings, and all beings in his own Self. He experiences the fundamental unity of life underlying the phenomenal manifestations. He looks on everything with impartial eye and realizes that the Supreme Self is birthless and timeless. This revelation of the *Gita* has been deftly poetized in poem after poem. For example, in "The Hymn of Creation," he sings:

One Mass, devoid of form, name and colour,
Timeless, devoid of time past and future,

> Spaceless, voiceless, boundless, devoid of all—
> Where rests hushed even speech of negation.
>
> From thence, down floweth the river causal,
> Wearing the form of desire radiant,
> Its heaving waters angrily roaring
> The constant roar, "I am," "I am."

The creativity and magnificence of *Brahma* are represented by the gushing waters of the river and mighty ocean respectively. Gradually, from the third stanza, the dynamics of creation begin to appear in the poem, as the unity of *Brahma* brings forth the multiplicity of the universe. The process of *Brahma*'s Involution into the material universe or Creation is picturized in a graphical manner thus:

> In that ocean of desire limitless,
> Appear shining waves, countless, infinite,
> Oh, of what power manifold they are,
> Of what forms myriad, of what repose,
> Of what movements varied, who can reckon?
>
> Millions of moons, millions of suns,
> Taking their birth in that very ocean,
> Rushing headlong with din tumultuous,
> Overspread the whole firmament, drowning
> The points of heaven in light effulgent.
>
> In it arise and reside what beings,
> Quick with life, dull and lifeless—unnumbered,
> And pleasure and pain, disease, birth and death!
> Verily, the Sun is He, His the ray,
> Nay, the Sun is He, and He is the ray. ("The Hymn of Creation")

The countless waves of the ocean symbolize 'forms myriad' and 'movements varied' of the universe. The poetic style of Swami Vivekananda is characterized by simplicity, gracefulness, picturesqueness, dramatic elements besides the pervasive 'Supramental Light' (in Aurobindonean sense of the term). That Creation is a part of the Absolute and is Real, which Sri Aurobindo also emphasizes, is vindicated in the Advaitic statement:

Verily, the Sun is He, His the ray,
Nay, the Sun is He, and He is the ray.

Therefore Swami Vivekananda, like Shankara, is opposed to a mere illusory conception of the universe. For him it is an appearance that cannot be properly defined, but is all the same a unique type of reality. "This *Maya* is not absolute zero, nor non-existence. It is (better) defined as neither existence nor non-existence" (*C.W.* 2: 363-64).

Thomas Mannumel explains that this power of *maya* cannot be distinguished from *Brahma* anymore than the burning power of fire can be from the fire itself. It is by his mysterious power that *Brahma* or *Iswara* (as we call *Brahma* in this creative capacity) projects on Himself the objects of the material world. In this sense the scriptures speak of Him as Great Magician who conjures up this world-show with its marvelous objects. Like the power itself the projection or superimposition (*adhyasa*) is not a separate entity any more than, let us say a clay pot is separate from the clay of which it is formed, gold ring from the gold. The clay pot is nothing but the clay, and the gold ring nothing but the gold; only the external name and form (*nama-rupa*) are different (106). This *Brahma*—the Absolute God who is personified as Shiva in "Nirvanashtakam" is adored as the World-Mother in "A Hymn to the Divine Mother."

Manifestations of Her glory show
In power of immeasurable might,
Throughout the universe, powers that swell
The sea of birth and death, forces that change
And break up the unchanged and changed again.
Lo! Where shall we seek refuge, save in Her?

("A Hymn to the Divine Mother")

The poet's initial contemplation on creation gradually transforms into an emotion of self-surrender—a longing for the mother's benevolent refuge. The superconscient, creative *Brahma* is personified here as the Mother. She, the supreme ruler and supporter of the universe is devoid of form, name and time, who sets forth the dynamic and turbulent creation of myriad forms, infinite movements, which are all subject to birth-death, pain-pleasure, etc. The poet is unable to fully comprehend the reason for Her ceaseless activity of creation as he attempts to grasp Her unbound magnificence through the finite intellect.

> *What Thou art, the Mother! the All. How praise?*
> My understanding is so little worth.
> 'Twere like desire to seize with hands of mine
> The sole Supporter of the universe!
> So, at Thy blessed feet—contemplated
> By the Goddess of Fortune Herself—the abode
> Of fearlessness, worshipped by service true—
> There, at those blessed feet, I take refuge! (*Ibid.*)

Isha Upanishad, which elaborates upon the proper utilization of physical life, seems to explain the phrase 'worshipped by service true.' The third part of the Upanishad (verses: 8-14) discusses how one enters the world of darkness at the time of death—because of an improper use of physical life or by an unnatural termination of it. In the continuation of this idea, the Upanishad later refers to the results that follow after the death of a person who has made the best use of his physical life and works. By surrendering his will in works to *Agni*, the Divine-will, his sins are removed and he becomes eligible for reaching the worlds of light and felicity when he passes out of the body. This is reflected in the prayer to *Agni* (verses: 17-18). On reaching the world of *Surya* or *purusha* by the good path, he is blessed with the vision of Truth and becomes one with the immortal person—*Sah aham asmi* (I am He). Surrendering one's will in works to the Divine and to become an instrument of His will, is the ultimate stage in *Karmayoga* (trans. Harshananda 17).

The creation abides by the law of the Mother's will. She is the *Vidhata*—who according to Shankara is the controller of all actions of men and dispenser of fruits of such actions. Swami Vivekananda puts it thus:

> *Incessantly distributing the fruits*
> Of actions done, guiding unceasingly
> All actions yet to come—bestow Her boon

> Of blessing on me, Her child, for evermore.
> I realize, I know, that it is Thou
> Who holdest in Thy hands dread Karma's rope. (*Ibid.*)

The Mother of creation is the source of all animate and inanimate creatures and is also their Supreme ruler. The law of *Karma* is the foundation of Her government. Besides this She is the primal guide and shelter of all beings. So the poet blissfully surrenders himself to the Mother just in the manner as Arjuna takes refuge in Sri Krishna—as a disciple, unconcerned with the results of actions—on the battlefield of Kurukshetra:

> *She, who has always through my life inspired*
> My understanding, She, my Mother, She,
> The All, is my resort, whether my work
> O'erflow with full fruition or with none.(*Ibid.*)

The poem is a unique blend of all the three *yogas*—Knowledge, Devotion and Action. *Karma-Yogi*'s renunciation is chiefly in the shape of giving up all the fruits of his action. The *Jnana-Yogi*'s task is more difficult, says Swami Vivekananda, for "he has to realize from the very first that the whole of this solid-looking nature is all an illusion" He has to tear himself away from all the bondage to nature by the sheer force of rational conviction. But of all the renunciations the one demanded of a *Bhakta* is the least difficult and the most natural. There is no violence in it. As one grows in love for God, everything else becomes distasteful to him and loses its hold on him. He slowly gives up and outgrows even those little things which helped him in the beginning. "Forms vanish, rituals fly away books are superseded; images, temples, churches, religions and sects, countries and nationalities—all these little limitations and bondages fall off by their own nature from him who knows this love of God" (*C.W.* 3: 71-72). In addition to the established modes of devotion, like *Vatsalya*, *Madhura*, *Dasya*, etc., Swami Vivekananda adds a strikingly different mode of worship and devotion. "The Living God," a poem written on July ninth, 1897, has for its central figure, both God and Man. In this poem as elsewhere, he promulgates the worship of the 'Living God'—the poor, the weak, the downtrodden, the wretched. He gave a clarion call for 'Eternal Love and Service Free.'

> *Ye fools! who neglect the living God,*
> *And His infinite reflections with which the world is full.*
> While ye run after imaginary shadows,
> That lead alone to fights and quarrels,
> Him worship, the only visible!
> Break all other idols!

The constant theme in Swami Vivekananda's poetry is the concept of "*Iswara-kalpa*" or the God-like quality of man, which assures humanity of immortality. C.L. Khatri sees this as a direct attack on the dualistic trend in religions and a favor for the Advaitic concept of God (117). A forceful command "break all other idols" as they lead to "fights and quarrels," emerges from the gentle guidance of,

> He who is in you and outside you, . . .
> Him worship, the only visible.

Written in blank verse, the poem makes for easy reading and offers therapeutic value to the reader, for the poet had consciously tapped the primordial being, God, older than the historical man and all forms of religion. According to Jung, it is possible to live the fullest life only when man is in harmony with this eternally living symbol, which Swami Vivekananda reveals in melodic verse:

> In whom is neither past life
> Nor future birth nor death,
> In whom we always have been
> And always shall be one,
> Him worship. Break all other idols. ("The Living God")

Coming back to the saga of Creation, Swami Vivekananda conceived of God or *Saguna Brahma* as the ground of world appearance and possessor of *maya* or wielder of *maya-shakti*. As Sanat Kumar Rai Chaudhuri explains, the determining and dynamic aspect of God stands out in the indeterminate background of the changeless static absolute (92). *Maya* is the power or tool in the hands of *Brahma*—using which He appears as many. In other words, it is by time, space and causation that the Absolute is seen as differentiated under various forms and names. This is *maya*.

At the Beginning, I the Omniscient One,
I am! The moving and the un-moving,
All this creation comes into being
By the unfoldment of My power supreme.
I play with My own Maya, My Power Divine.
The one, I become the many, to behold
My own Form. ("A Song I Sing to Thee")

Thus we are brought face to face with the elusive reality of the *Advaita* philosophy—*Maya*. "It was Shankara," remarks Swami Vivekananda "who first found out the idea of the identity of time, space and causation with *maya* (*C.W.* 1: 17). With the help of this notion Shankara in his *Bhasyas* endeavors to reconcile the opposing Upanishadic statements regarding creation of the world, taken in its literal sense, with those denying the world of multiplicity. *Brahma* as reality devoid of all assignable characteristics becomes unintelligible if His creatorship is real. Moreover, the Upanishads teach the disappearance of all Multiplicity on the realization of *Brahma*. Swami Vivekananda grasps this essential Upanishadic concept and restates it in the following verse:

When all the many movements of the mind
Are, by Thy grace, made one, and unified,
The light of that unfoldment is so great
That, in its splendor, it surpasses far
The brilliance of ten thousand rising suns.
Then, sooth, the sun of Chit reveals itself.
And melt away the sun and moon and stars,
High heaven above, the nether worlds, and all!
This universe seems but a tiny pool
Held in a hollow caused by some cow's hoof.
("A Song I Sing to Thee")

Here is the subjective and individualized aspect to *maya* and it is by transcending *maya* that man returns to the Absolute in the realization of his own true nature. The irony with man is that he is in ignorance of his divine birth-right. He considers himself as a part of nature with its limitations and imperfections. Thus *maya* also plays the role of an illusion-producing ignorance—besides being the instrument for Creation. As Mannumel puts it, "it has the double aspect of concealment (*avarana*) of the reality and of distortion (*vikshepa*) of it into something else." The real is only *Brahma*. Therefore whatever is real in man is also *Brahma*. But this truth remains concealed and man takes himself to be a limited self (*jiva*) confined to a body" (121-22). For being able to overcome the influence of *maya* and achieve that vision of Truth, the poet recommends a detached role-playing by dissociating oneself from the smaller identity and watching the ups and downs of worldly-life from a distance:

> If things go ill or well—
> If joy rebounding spreads the face,
> Or sea of sorrow swells—
> A play—we each have a part,
> Each one to weep or laugh as may;
> Each one his dress to don—
> Its scenes alternative shine and rain. ("Thou Blessed Dream")

Worldly life has a magical veil—*maya*, through which everything is perceived in a distorted manner. Such vision is symbolized in the poem by a couple of paradoxes like "desert in bloom" and "Harsh thunder" which sounds as a "sweetest song" only the curtain-fall of death will release the viewer from this delusive play.

> No magic but in thee!
> Thy touch makes desert bloom to life.
> Harsh thunder, sweetest song,
> Fell death, the sweet release. ("Thou Blessed Dream")

"My Play is Done" is another reputed poem which equates the worldly existence to a mere 'play.' The poet grieved for being forced to live on "this floating bubble earth" which like a bubble is hollow and ephemeral.

> *Alas for me, I cannot rest. This floating bubble, earth—*
> Its hollow form, its hollow name, its hollow death and birth—
> For me is nothing. How I long to get beyond the crust
> Of name and form! Ah, ope the gates, to me they open must

Open the gates of light, O Mother, to me Thy tired son.
I long, oh, long to return home! Mother, my play is done.

A skilful repetition of the word "hollow" makes us understand the poet's poignant cry. The theatrical imagery highlights the delusive mask-like nature of this life as compared to the eternal reality. Further references to "toys" and "dreams" intensify the unreal quality of the corporeal world. Swami Vivekananda is "inside" his poem and the readers identify with his emotions and passionate craving to never let "delusive dreams veil off Thy face from me." A subtle shift occurs in the above line wherein the poem is no longer personal, an undercurrent of something more emerges; it becomes the longing of entire mankind, an inexorable heartache which replaces serenity. The contracted and closely interlocked imagery gives a cumulative force to the agonizing desire "to return home." The controlling metaphor of the poem is the comparison of life to a play. Swami Vivekananda's verse springs from a profound personal emotion experienced during a traumatic period of struggle. The itinerant monk purifies his inner self and goes on to help others to come out of the darkness of *maya*'s veil by the way of preaching:

There is but One—The Free—The Knower—Self!
Without a name, without a form or stain.
In Him is Maya, dreaming all this dream.
The Witness, He appears as nature, soul. . . .
Then cease lament,
Let go thy hold, Sannyasin bold! Say—
"Om Tat Sat, Om!" ("The Song of the Sannyasin")

Again the world is being referred to as a "dream." "The Knower-Self" contains *maya* that deludes the soul which forsakes its true identity, and holds fast to the "rope" of the world. This would again be not understandable if the world were real. However, one can readily understand that real knowledge attained in realization would dispel unreal appearances. Could it then be that the world is such an unreal appearance? If the world is similar to an object in a dream, it is easy to understand one in the real awakening of realization it will disappear and the true Reality will appear in all its clarity.

> This is the reaching of the region which
> Beyond the plane of the external lies. ("A Song I Sing to Thee")

Here is an assertion of divine incomprehensibility and human impotence to fathom the motives of the actions of God to whom nothing can accrue. Like most Indian sages of old, writes Thomas Mannumel Swami Vivekananda "is at a loss to explain this baffling reality that is the world and so has recourse to the doctrine of *Lila*" (102). It would be of interest to recall here, a conversation of Sri Ramakrishna with some of his disciples on the subject of the *Lila* of the Divine Mother:

> The master said: "The Divine Mother is always playful and sportive. This universe is Her play. She is self-willed and must always have Her own way. She is full of bliss. She gives freedom to one out of a hundred thousand."
>
> A Brahmo devotee: "But sir, if She likes, She can give freedom to all. Why, then, has She kept us bound to the world?"
>
> Master: "That is Her will. She wants to continue playing with Her created beings. In a game of hide-and-seek, the running about soon stops if in the beginning all the players touch the 'granny.' If all touch her, then how can the game go on? That displeases her. Her pleasure is in continuing the game. Therefore the poet said:
>
> 'Out of a hundred thousand kites, at best but one or two break free; And Thou dost laugh and clap Thy hands, O Mother, watching them!'" (qtd. Gupta 136)

The allusion of this song is to the well known kite flying competitions in India. Several people fly their kites and try to cut one another's kite strings. Whosoever has his string cut loses his kite and quits the game. Another popular game alluded to is that of hide and seek, in which the leader, known as the 'granny,' bandages the eyes of the players and hides herself. The players are supposed to find her. If any player can touch her, the bandage is removed from his eyes and he is released from the game.

Similarly the title of Swami Vivekananda's poem "Who Knows How Mother Plays," implies that only a select few are chosen by the Mother who then intuit Her plans. The Mother unfolds various forms and events on the universal stage, which remain ungraspable for the common intellect. Whom and when does She select for the accomplishment of Her designs, is a mystery and the poet ponders:

> Perchance the shining sage
> Saw more than he could tell;
> Who knows, what soul, and when,
> The Mother makes Her throne?

The poet's constant search for the Mother made him feel that "perchance" the child had glimpses of divinity, hidden from the adult. Or, at the other end of the spectrum of maturity, perhaps it is the sage's soul that housed the Mother's throne or was the custodian of Her secrets. Corresponding to the Wordsworthian poem "My Heart Leaps Up," Swami Vivekananda states:

> To child may glories ope
> Which father never dreamt.

The poet endeavors to fathom the *Lila* of the Divine Mother using the extra-cognizant faculties, akin to a child's and a prophet's powers of perception:

> Perchance a prophet thou—
> Who knows? Who dares touch
> The depths where Mother hides
> Her silent failless bolts!
>
> Perchance the child had glimpse
> Of shades, behind the scenes, . . .

"The mind can disentangle itself from worldliness if, through Her grace, She makes it turn towards Herself. Only then does it become devoted to the Lotus Feet of the Divine Mother" explains Sri Ramakrishna and continues, "Men are deluded through Her *maya* and have become attached to the world" (qtd. Gupta 137). For this reason, Swami Vivekananda resorts to *prapatti* or total self-surrender and resignation at the Mother's Feet, accepting Her Will as the resistless law and Her freak as the greatest order! No laws or guidelines can bind Her freedom and Will.

> What law would freedom bind?
> What merit guide Her will,
> Whose freak is greatest order,
> Whose will resistless law?

It is through this loving and unconditional acceptance that the poet (*jiva*) elicits the supreme grace of the Mother, who is the remover of the bondage that binds one to the world.

The Scriptural background of the concept of *maya* and theory of Creation which Swami Vivekananda presents in the poems discussed above may briefly be surveyed here. Fundamentally, Swami Vivekananda's views regarding the universe seem to tally with that of Shankara. That it should be so is but natural since Swami Vivekananda had drawn largely, as studied in the second chapter, from the teaching of Shankara (Refer: 2.7). And theory of *maya* is so fundamental to Shankara's doctrine that his *Advaita-Vada* is identical with *maya-Vada.* To a disciple's question "Is *maya-Vada* different from *Advaita-Vada*?, Swami Vivekananda replies "No. They are identical. There is absolutely no other explanation of *Advaita-Vada* except *maya-Vada* (qtd. Mannumel 118). It is well known that Shankara's dialectical subtlety and logical skill reach a very high mark in his explanation of the world as the outcome of *maya.* In keeping with his theological method, he first carefully scrutinizes the scriptural testimony regarding *maya*.

Already in the *Rig Veda*, the god Indra is said to appear in many forms through powers of creating illusion—*maya.* This idea is accepted by *Brihadaranyaka* Upanishad when it declares "Indra by his magic powers (*maya*) goes about in many forms." Later in *Shvetashvatara* Upanishad, the origin of the world is attributed to clearly to God's subtle power (*maya*) over *prakriti* which is the material cause.

> This whole world the illusion-maker (*mayin*)
> Projects out of this (*Brahma*)
> And in it by illusion (*maya*) the other (i.e. the

individual soul) is confined.
Now, one should know that Nature (*prakriti*) is
illusion (*maya*)
And that the Mighty Lord (Maheshwara) is the
Illusion-maker (*mayin*)
(*Shvetashvatara* Upanishad 4-9-10. Trans. Harshananda 41)

Such scriptural testimonies furnish Shankara with sufficient clues to the problem of this world. There is no true reality but *Brahma*. The *Brahma Sutra* declares "But (the act of Creation) is mere sport (of the Lord) even as is seen in the ordinary world" (203). Ranade in his work, *Constructive Survey of Upanishadic Philosophy*, vindicates the notion that Shankara's conception of *maya* is based on Upanishadic teaching as follows:

> "When we consider that we have the conception of a veil (*Isha* Upanishad—15) of blindfoldness (*Katha* 1.2.4.5) of a knot (*Mundaka* II 1. 10), of ignorance (*Chandogya* 1.1.10), of not being, of darkness, of death, (*Brihadaranyaka* 1.3.28) of unreality and uncertainty (*Katha* II.4.2), of untruth (*Chandogya* VIII. 3, 1-3), of crookedness and falsehood, and illusion (*Prashna* I, 16) of power of God, of his power as identical with nature (*Brihadaranyaka* II. 5, 19 and *Rig Veda* VI, 47, 10 and *Shvetashvatara* IV. 5), of meshes (*Shvetashvatara* III, 1 and V.3), of semblance as it were and an appearance (*Brihadaranyaka* II 4.14) and finally of a world, a mode and the name (*Chandogya* VI, 1.14), let no man stand up and say that we do not find the traces of the doctrine of *maya* in the Upanishadic philosophy" (qtd. Mannumel 116-17).

3.3 Poems on Ascent or Evolution

In several of his poems like "Thou Blessed Dream," "My Play is Done," "The Song of the Sannyasin," etc., Swami Vivekananda's views regarding the universe seem to suggest that it is a tempting reality, an indefinable something that escapes our grasp. It is *maya*. As Swami Vivekananda puts it, "According to the *Advait*ists proper, the followers of Shankaracharya, the whole universe is the apparent evolution of God. God is the material cause of this universe, but not really, only apparently" (*C.W.* 1: 363-64). His term 'evolution' in the above lines is to be read as involution if one follows Sri Aurobindo's terminology. In fact, the aspiration for Supermanhood—by way of evolution, forms a pivotal part of the philosophies of both the sages. Swami Vivekananda wrote,

> Each one of us has come out of one protoplasmic cell, and all the powers we possess were coiled up there. . . . The energy was there, potentially no doubt, but still there. So is infinite power in the soul of man, whether he knows it or not. Its manifestation is only a question of being conscious of it. Slowly this infinite giant is, as it were, waking up, becoming conscious of his power, and arousing himself; and with his growing consciousness, more and more of his bonds are breaking, chains are bursting asunder, and the day is sure to come when, with the full consciousness of his infinite power and wisdom, the giant will rise to his feet and stand erect. Let us all help to hasten that glorious consummation. (*C.W.* 2: 340)

It is this 'being conscious of it' or Gnosis which makes all the difference; hastens the process of evolution. On the contrary, the ignorance of one's infinite nature leads to bondage. Swami Vivekananda unfolds this view of ascent in his poems as well. In "Angels Unawares," he explains how, the soul gradually identifies itself with the body under the spell of *maya*. Having traveled a great distance of time in this illusory universe, it becomes totally oblivious of its true nature. The poem consists of three sections which recount the spiritual discovery by *Satvic*, *Tamasic* and *Rajasic* men respectively. The dreary life of the protagonist in the first section which is devoid of a consciousness of the Divine or an emotional attraction towards It, is described as joyless and the poet laments:

> One bending low with load of life—
> That meant no joy, but suffering harsh and hard—
> And wending on his way through dark and dismal paths
> Without a flash of light from brain or heart
> To give a moment's cheer, till the line
> That marks out pain from pleasure, death from life,
> And good from what is evil was well-nigh wiped from sight
>
> ("Angels Unawares" part I)

Swami Vivekananda, like Shankara and all other Hindu thinkers through the centuries with the exception of the materialist Charvakas and some Lingayats, unquestioningly accepts the doctrine of transmigration. In the course of these transmigrations, the soul or self ensheathed in the subtle body carries with itself all the myriad impressions of its actions performed not only in the immediately preceding life, but in other lives. These impressions, the scars, as it were, or effects of actions good and bad, cause the indwelling self to continue to identify itself with material world-show and the part it plays therein. Under these conditions, the self is unable to realize its identity with the one Absolute reality and is, as it were, imprisoned in its own house. This situation is eloquently presented in the three parts of "Angels Unawares." We see a quick *Satvic* ignition in the protagonist of the first part—as soon as he receives the revelation. The second and third parts trace the spiritual awakenings of *Tamasic* and *Rajasic* men respectively. While in the dark, "the self never questions the why and wherefore of everyday life, or if so, only in a superficial way resulting at best in an intellectual understanding of the relationship between the individual self and Supreme self of the universe" ("Soul, Nature and God" *C.W.* 2: 424). It is only a faint glimmering an evasive thought, even when the imprisoned *jiva* perceives the Truth:

> Saw, one blessed night, a faint but beautiful ray of light
> Descend to him. He knew not what or wherefrom,
> But called it God and worshipped.
> Hope, an utter stranger, came to him and spread
> Through all his parts, and life to him meant more
> Than he could ever dream and covered all he knew,
> Nay, peeped beyond his world. ("Angels Unawares" part I)

But the worldly intellectuals, humorously called 'sages' here, are ever-sceptical regarding the transcendental Truth:

> The Sages
>
> Winked, and smiled, and called it "superstition."
> *But he did feel its power and peace*
> And gently answered back—
> "O Blessed Superstition." ("Angels Unawares")

Throughout the poem, spiritual knowledge and awareness of the Divine are symbolized as light, like 'beautiful ray of light' or 'flash of light from brain or Heart," etc. Likewise, the 'dark and dismal paths' indicate a course leading the soul away from God—a path devoid of self-knowledge. In several other poems also—like "The Song of the Free," "Hold on Yet a While Brave Heart," etc., Swami Vivekananda employs the symbol of light effectively to reflect on spiritual concepts.

In the poems of another renowned saint poet Rama Tirtha also, the symbol of light has been deftly used for spiritual knowledge, self-illumination and God. Darkness stands for sheer ignorance. The 'errands' of the Divine 'run like lightning fires.' God illumines all without any discrimination:

> The sun lights the gardens as well as the waste,
> Alike I do light all changes of fate.

In "Hallelujah" the poet says that spiritual light alone dispels the gloom of ignorance:

> As the golden lance
> Of the sun's sharp glance,
> I pierce the heart of flowers
> As the silver ray
> Of the full moon gay.
> I hook up the sea to my bowers. ("Hallelujah" by Rama Tirtha)

The raciness, simplicity and spontaneity of the style, language and versification of the *Gita*, also influenced the language and style of Swami Vivekananda and Rama Tirtha. Soaked in the philosophy of the *Gita*, they caught not only its spirit but also the subtleties of its style and diction. Like the *Gita*, they too ransacked the treasure of nature for apt symbols, images, similes and metaphors. Flash, light, sun, taper etc. are used for the radiant light of knowledge which dispels the darkness of ignorance as per the *Gita*. Swami Vivekananda uses these symbols for the light of knowledge. He indicates a way to attain this light: "When you think you are a body, you are apart from the universe; when you think you are a soul, you are a spark from the great Eternal Fire; when you think you are the *Atman*, you are All" (*C.W.* 5: 409). It is our 'thinking' or perception, which changes our state of being. Swami Vivekananda repeatedly urges the indwelling self to persist on the stand of non-dual reality and not to get confused because of the worldly distracters:

> Know these are but the outer crust
> All space and time, all effect, cause.
> I am beyond all sense, all thought.
> The witness of the Universe!
> Not two nor many this but one. ("The Song of the Free")

The movement of the verse is not harsh; rather there is a smooth gliding movement of the verse. The musical effect, in these rousing poems, is achieved through alliteration, assonance and consonance:

> Speed forth, O Soul! upon thy star-strewn path
> ("Requiescat in Pace")
> The goal so shadowy seems and dim,
> Yet plod on through the dark, brave heart,
> With all thy might and main. ("Hold on Yet a While Brave Heart")

He cautions the spiritual aspirants of the pitfalls of *maya* and exhorts them to steadfastly anchor themselves to the Real:

> Let darkness go; the will-o'-the-wisp that leads
> With blinking light to pile more gloom on gloom
> This thirst for life, for ever quench; it drags
> From birth to death, and death to birth, the soul.
> He conquers all who conquers self. Know this
> And never yield, Sannyasin bold! Say—
> "Om Tat Sat, Om!" ("The Song of the Sannyasin")

"The Song of the Sannyasin" is a brilliant summing up of renunciation and complete identification with God. One of his disciples writes about the occasion of the composition of this poem:

> There were three of us and it seemed as if Pentecostal fire descended and touched the Master. One afternoon, when he had been telling us of the glory of renunciation, of the joy and freedom of those of the ochre robe, he suddenly left us, and in a short time he had written his

> "Song of the Sannyasin," a very passion of sacrifice and renunciation (qtd. Cooper 47).

It is a spontaneous overflow of powerful spiritual feelings. The pure and detached know the Supreme truth about self. Besides internal rhyming, the use of present participle and of above mentioned poetic devices not only give a cadence to verse but also reinforce the meaning and add a colour to it—feels C.L. Khatri (122-23). Coupled with proper use of diction and varied range of images, they provide structural unity and cohesiveness to the poem. Swami Vivekananda does not seem to be very particular about a uniform metre. Feet keep on changing in a poem. But there are a few poems like "Requiescat in Pace" and "The Song of the Sannyasin" in iambic and trochaic pentameter.

In many of his poems, Swami Vivekananda emphasized the last line of each stanza, a continuous reading of which reiterates the message of the title. For example in the poem "Hold on Yet a While Brave Heart" which is quoted above, the last lines read thus:

> The victory is sure to come . . .
> Be steady then and brave . . .
> With all thy might and main . . .
>
> *No good is ever undone . . .*
> Heed none and gently guide . . .
> To thee may all come right!

Having achieved victory over *maya*, the soul would ascend into the realms of freedom through the renowned paths of Knowledge, Devotion and Action. Here are some poems of Swami Vivekananda which sing of these three pathways:

Jnana-Yoga in the poetry of this monk-poet is presented as the light of knowledge. Swami Vivekananda frequently uses the symbol of Light to represent the quest for Knowledge and a realization of the Oneness in the apparent multiplicity. There seems to be a passionate craving after this Light, which finds a frequent expression in his writings—as in the prose work quoted below:

> He who sees in this world of manifoldness that One running through all, in this world of death, he who finds that One Infinite Life, and in this world of insentience and ignorance, he who finds that One Light and Knowledge, unto him belongs eternal peace. Unto none else, unto none else (*C.W.* 2: 117).

The poem "To the Fourth of July" opens with the same foreboding images that characterize "Hold on Yet a While Brave Heart": "dark clouds . . . gloomy pall," but a "magic touch" transforms them into the jocund illustration of "high noon . . . shackles broken . . . in springing joy their life renewed!" This "magic touch" as a symbol for Spring, "awakens . . . the world to a 'new life' of love and freedom" while the Sun "Lord of Light" emerges from behind the "gloomy pall" of dark clouds, recalling the similar image of hope and triumph which dominates the poem "Hold on Yet a While Brave Heart."

> Behold, the dark clouds melt away
> That gathered thick at night, and hung
> So like a gloomy pall above the earth!
> Before thy magic touch, the world Awakes.
>
> ("To the Fourth of July")

"To the Fourth of July" that celebrates the anniversary of America's freedom, indicates that the freedom of the nation will come through individual freedom. This poem is also an invocation to the Sun-God: "Move on, O Lord, in thy resistless path" and echoes the invocation contained in 'Gayatri' *Mantra*: *Om bhur bhuva Svaha tatsaviturwarenyam bhargo devasya dhimahi dhiyo yo na prachodayat!* It is both *Mantra* and prayer rolled into one to lead, not only the person offering prayers, but also mankind as a whole, from darkness to light. The last stanza of the poem bursts into joyful prayer for man's release from bondage.

> Move on, O Lord, in thy resistless path!
> Till thy high noon o'erspreads the world,
> Till every land reflects thy light,
> Till men and women, with uplifted head,
> Behold their shackles broken, and
> Know, in springing joy, their life renewed!

The metaphor "high noon" represents light and knowledge, which the poet aspires, should spread all over the world—releasing the imprisoned souls from their limitations (physical and mental), thus renewing life. Thus, "To the Fourth of July," which is written in blank verse, represents a near-perfect integration of image and idea with symbol and thought. Similarly, the symbol of light has been aptly used in "The Song of the Free" too. When "a flash" illumines all his soul, darkness of ignorance vanishes and he realizes the presence of God in him and in the multitudinous objects of the phenomenal existence:

> The flame stirred up doth blaze . . .
> the cloud puts forth its deluge strength
> When lightning cleaves its breast,
> When the soul is stirred to its inmost depth
> Great ones unfold their best! ("The Song of the Free")

The poet prays to God to "Open the gates of light" to illumine the dark and dreary path of "the struggling, crying, laughing throng" in "My Play is Done." The radiance of the Divine is hidden behind the veil of *maya*, the allurements and temptations of physical existence, as the sun is hidden behind the clouds:

> If the sun by the cloud is hidden a bit,
> If the welkin shows but gloom,
> Still hold on yet a while, brave heart,
> The Victory is sure to come. ("Hold on Yet a While Brave Heart")

Light also symbolizes hope and redemption from the darkness of phenomenal existence. In "Angels Unawares" the poet says that man "wends on his way through dark and dismal paths" of pleasure and pain, life and death but when he understands the hollowness of name, fame and pelf "a faint but beautiful ray of light" descends to him. The poet hails God as the most radiant Light in the poem "A Song I Sing to Thee" because He alone illumines all:

> When all the many movements of the mind
> Are, by Thy grace, made one, and unified,
> The light of that unfoldment is so great
> That, in its splendor, it surpasses far

The brilliance of ten thousand rising suns.
Then, sooth, the sun of Chit reveals itself. ("A Song I Sing to Thee")

In the lines quoted above, Swami Vivekananda poetically sums up the culmination of spiritual evolution, which can be reached after steadying the mind by conquering *maya*. The brilliance of spiritual knowledge is symbolized by "ten thousand rising suns" and *Chit* stands for Absolute Knowledge. The "many movements of the mind" are symbols for evanescent material and emotional attachments which fetter man's self. In the mind of a seer, who is detached, the delusive clouds of passion are cast away and the effulgent and luminous Sun of self-knowledge shines bright.

On the other hand, water and its various synonyms like 'river,' 'sea,' 'ocean,' 'stream' etc. are used for the fleeting and ever changing aspects of material existence. For example, 'God is the soul of souls "in the rushing stream of life," "Ever rising, ever falling with the waves of time, still rolling on I go / From fleeting scene to scene ephemeral, with life's current ebb and flow"; the earth is "a floating bubble," the world is "seething, surging sea of passions strong and sorrows deep." ("My Play is Done"). Written in spring of 1895 in New York, "My Play is Done" explains the agony of earthly existence and the bliss one is supposed to embrace at the time of release. As Akhouri Rajendra Prasad points out, Swami Vivekananda is, "like the mystic poets of Persia—Khayyam, Rumi and Hafiz, standing 'on little life's high, narrow bridge,' watches 'the struggling, crying, laughing throng' but fails to understand the purpose of this unending show" (78). The meaning and message that he is able to decipher tells him to "Go, mix with them and drink that cup, / and be as mad as they" because "Who dares to know but comes to grief." But the hollow form, the hollow name' with 'its hollow death and birth' is nothing more than 'delusion's toy' with 'false hope as motor, desire nave; grief and joy' as spoke, he prays to the merciful Mother to rescue him from the show of floating desire called the world. 'Dream' and 'darkness' stand for ignorance and delusions. Cup, in the lyric "The Cup" is full of the 'dark drink' of miseries and sorrows. In fact the Cup of life, containing the dark brew of one's own *karma*, working as the guiding motive of one's existence, also compels him to surrender unconditionally to the Divine Mother. The voice of the Mother, contained in the silent whispers of the soul, tells him not to enquire but to surrender.

> But you, My child, must travel here.
> This is your task. It has no joy nor grace,
> But it is not meant for any other hand,
> And in my Universe hath measured place,
> Take it. I do not bid you understand.
> I bid you close your eyes to see My face. ("The Cup")

By undergoing all struggles and pitfalls of life does one arrive at the ultimate peace, and not by insulating oneself from the world. The protagonist in the third part of the poem "Angels Unawares," a typical *Rajasic* man, with good health and renown, is given to emotions. For long, he watches others struggling with their lives. Standing aloof, he thinks that he is 'safe' and untouched by those troubles:

> Beheld that he was safe, whilst others long
> And vain did struggle 'gainst the surging waves.
> ("Angels Unawares" part II)

But then his mind is not insulated from *maya* or nature from within. It seeks the 'bad' and falls headlong.

> Then Fortune smiled on him, and his foot slipped. That ope'd his eyes for e'er, and made him find
> That stones and trees ne'er break the law,
> But stones and trees remain; that man alone
> Is blest with power to fight and conquer Fate,
> Transcending bounds and laws.

Only after his 'fall' into the worldly life does he realize its necessity for the evolution of the inner being; of the soul (the soul does not evolve in vacuum). His horizons of experience expand and gradually, he glimpses the abode of eternal peace. The passive existence like 'stones and trees' will never elevate the self.

> From him his passive nature fell, and life appeared
> As broad and new, and broader, newer grew,
> Till light ahead began to break, and glimpse of That

Where Peace Eternal dwells—yet one can only reach
By wading through the sea of struggles—courage—giving came.
Then looking back on all that made him kin
To stocks and stones, and on to what the world
Had shunned him for, his fall, he blessed the fall,
And with a joyful heart, declared it. ("Blessed Sin!")

The path of Action (*karma yoga*), which is the sum and substance of the message of the *Gita*, has been expressed poetically in the poetry of both the great saint poets being studied in this work. Sri Aurobindo in his poem—"To the Sea" accepts the challenge of the 'rough' world to pass through it because

On the safe land
To linger is to lose what God has planned
For man's wide soul,
Who set eternal godhead for its goal.
("To the Sea" by Sri Aurobindo)

The world which is symbolized by the great sea, for him, is but a means to attain godhead:

That man may grow
King over pain and victor of o'erthrow
Matching his great
Unconquerable soul with adverse Fate.
Take me, be
My way to climb the heavens, thou rude great sea. (*Ibid.*)

Karma yoga is detached action through enlightenment and the *Gita* is a clarion call to action to meet the obligations and duties of life, but always keeping in view the spiritual background and the larger purpose of the universe. Inaction is condemned, and action and life have to be in accordance with the highest ideals of the age, for these ideals themselves may vary from age to age. The *yugadharma* the ideal of the particular age, has always to be kept in view. Swami Vivekananda mildly rebukes his countrymen to redeem themselves from sloth and inaction and to follow the time honored path of desireless action in "To the Awakened India"

Awake, arise, and dream no more!

This is the land of dreams, where Karma
Weaves unthreaded garlands with our thoughts,
Of flowers sweet or noxious, and none
Has root or stem, being born in naught, which
The softest breath of Truth drives back to
Primal nothingness. Be bold, and face
The Truth! Be one with it! Let visions cease,
Or, if you cannot, dream but truer dreams,
Which are Eternal Love and Service Free.

Man can accomplish desireless action only when he renounces love of phenomenal life, wealth and power and 'emotions strong and deep,' and cultivates tolerance, perseverance, purity and true knowledge of self. In short when man is free from passion and ignorance and attains purity, which have been discussed in detail in chapter fourteen of the *Gita*, he is capable of desireless action. In the above verse, Swami Vivekananda points out that the nature of *Karma* is not absolute. It does not have "root or stem" and even the "softest breath of Truth" will drive it "back to Primal nothingness." In other words, the actions of men do not have any absolute significance; they fly away lightly before the Truth. But the *Karma* performed in ignorance of its real nature would bind its doer. Recourse is to perform the liberating *Karma* of "Service Free." This solution of the poet appears to be within the grasp of any ordinary intellect. In several of his poems, Swami Vivekananda points out that the wise man accomplishes selfless action. In his lyric "Peace" he enumerates the qualities of the pure and detached mind:

It is joy that never spoke
And grief unfelt, profound,
Immortal life unlived,
Eternal death unmourned.
It is not joy nor sorrow,
But that which is between,
It is not night nor morrow,
But that joins them in. ("Peace")

The heart of the pure is full of love and kindness for all. To him Love is God. To him Renunciation is God. To him Selfless Service is God:

> Thy service true complete thy sacrifice,
> Thy home the heart of love transcendent find;
> Remembrance sweet, that kills all space and time,
> Like altar roses fill thy place behind!
> Thy bonds are broke, thy quest in bliss is found,
> And one with That which comes as Death and Life:
> Thou helpful one! unselfish e'er on earth,
> Ahead! still help with love the world of strife. ("Requiescat in Pace")

The elegy, "Requiescat in Pace" honoured the memory of the poet's deceased friend Goodwin. Mr. J.J. Goodwin had been Swami Vivekananda's faithful companion and scribe in their travels. Echoing Tennyson's "In Memoriam" Swami Vivekananda's poem also contains a variation of the standard elegy pattern. An entire thought is expressed in the first three lines of each quatrain, with a comment or summary in the fourth line. The first quatrain reveals the soul speeding on its way to "where time and space no longer mist the view." The next commends Goodwin's "service time" and the third verse reveals the soul's unity with the Divine "which comes as Death and Life." The last lines of each quatrain not only sum up the three lines preceding it, but form another verse:

> Eternal peace and blessings be with thee! . . .
> Altar roses fill thy place behind! . . .
> Ahead! still help with love the world of strife. (*Ibid.*)

The poem places universal love and service above personal salvation. Lamentation and exultation are intertwined in the condolence letter Swami Vivekananda wrote to Goodwin's mother:

> Those who think that they have been helped by any thought of mine ought to know that almost every word of it was published through the untiring and most unselfish exertions of Mr. Goodwin. In him I have lost a friend true as steel, a disciple of never-failing devotion, a worker who knew not what tiring was, and the world is less rich by

> the passing away of one of those few who are born, as it were, to live only for others (qtd. Nikhilananda 138).

Swami Vivekananda conceived that India's greatness had been built upon the concepts of Renunciation and Sacrifice, and saw the necessity to add another criterion, Service, to bring India in line with the modern age. The gospel of universal love, service to mankind and devotion to the Infinite culminate in this highest wisdom that the service of man is the service of God. The outlines of this Spiritual Humanism have been drawn from Shankara's *Advaita* and its practical application in the life of his master Sri Ramakrishna. In the poem "The Living God," Swami Vivekananda teaches his readers to recognize the divine indweller in every visible, living form around themselves and exhorts them to worship God through these forms rather than through idols:

> He who is in you and outside you,
> Who works through all hands.
> Who walks on all feet.
> Whose body are all ye,
> Him worship. . . . ("The Living God")

If we compare with other poets, writes C.L. Khatri, the pantheism of Swami Vivekananda is more sublimated than that of Shelly. "Shelly could not develop any systematic philosophy" (115). Swami Vivekananda says that when a man realizes the all pervadingness of God through any of the four paths *Raja*, *Karma*, *Bhakti* or *Jnana-Yoga*, he sees "The One in All' as he writes:

> The living God is within you, and yet you are building churches and temples and believing all sorts of imaginary nonsense. The only God to be worshipped is the human soul in the human body. Of course all animals are temples too, but man is the highest, the Taj Mahal of all temples. If I cannot worship in that, no other temple will be of any advantage. The moment I have realized God sitting in the temple of every human body, the moment I stand in reverence before every human being and see God in him—that moment I am free from bondage, everything that binds vanishes, and I am free (Teachings of Swami Vivekananda194).

Like the Romantics, for Swami Vivekananda too adoration of Nature has been a favorite medium to express *Bhakti*. There is unity in diversity everywhere. Man's contact with Nature, which is the radiant manifestation of God, will enable the *yogi* or spiritual aspirant to understand reality. To Swami Vivekananda, like Swami Rama Tirtha and Wordsworth, Nature is the sanctuary of peace and joy which are untraceable in the world. He felt a fair and abiding companionship with nature.

> The moon's soft light, the stars so bright,
> The glorious orb of the day,
> He shines in them; His beauty—might—
> Reflected lights are they.
> The majestic morn, the melting eve,
> The boundless billowy sea,
> In nature's beauty, songs of birds
> I see through them, It is He. ("In Search of God")

Swami Vivekananda feels a mystic kinship with nature in whose realm peace and joy reign Supreme. These *Vibhuties* or glorious manifestations of the Divine, like the Sun, the Moon etc., kindle a direct emotional bond between the *Antaryami* and the *Bahiryami*—the self within the embodied *Jiva* and the self residing in the manifestations of the cosmos.

> Lo! the sun, the moon,
> The moving planets and the shining stars,
> Spheres of abode by myriads in the skies;
> The comet swift, the glimmering lightning flash;
> The firmament, expanded, infinite—
> These all, observant watchful eyes behold. ("A Song I Sing to Thee")

Various objects of Nature proclaim God's glory in "A Song I Sing to Thee." The fire of love burns the veil of *avidya* completely away and the *Bhakta* "feels that he has become absolutely merged in the object of his worship" Nothing is left but unity and oneness. In the embrace of the Divine, the soul finally finds itself, the return to the Absolute is complete! Human mind due to its inherent limitations fails to grasp how the Absolute has become mingled with the finite world, the mind, the relative. Swami Vivekananda replies, "It has never mingled. You are this Absolute Being, you have never changed. All that changes is *Maya*, the screen held between the real Me and you. The end, the very object of life, of all human evolution, of the unceasing ascension of Nature from the lowest order where dawns existence—is the gradual elimination of the screen" ("BhaktiYoga" *C.W.* 3: 100). When the screen will be removed by virtue of true insight, sacrifice and love we know our true self and nothing remains but the Absolute or *Brahma*.

Let go your vain reliance on knowledge,
Let go your prayers, offerings, and strength,
For Love selfless is the only resource;—
Lo, the insects teach, embracing the flame!

The base insect's blind, by beauty charmed,
Thy soul is drunken with the wine of Love;
O thou Lover true, cast into the fire
All thy dross of self, thy mean selfishness. . . .
From highest Brahma to the yonder worm,
And to the very minutest atom,
Everywhere is the same God, the All-Love;
Friend, offer mind, soul, body, at their feet. ("To a Friend")

The poet maintains that our attempts at finitization of the infinite can not escape contradiction. As Sanat Kumar Rai Chaudhuri rightly puts it, "Our moral conception and logical method cannot but be transcended to realize the essence of infinitude of God who is verily super-moral and super-rational" (91).

Thus Swami Vivekananda seems to believe that each of the *yogas* is capable of taking man to his final goal. They are equally effective and therefore one cannot speak of a 'high road' and a 'low road' among them. "You must remember that freedom of the soul is the goal of all *yogas*, and each one equally leads to the same result. By work alone men may get to where Buddha got largely by meditation and Christ by prayer. Buddha was a working *jnani*; Christ was a *Bhakta*" ("KarmaYoga" *C.W.* 1: 55). In this context Sanat K. Rai Chaudhuri writes:

Swami Vivekananda truly imbibed from his great teacher Sri Ramakrishna nay the fountainhead of the Upanishads, the essence of spiri-

> tuality that transforms and transfigures the individual into self-enlightened, ever-blissful universal plane. The end of spiritual evolution is to eliminate the false ego, caged in the narrow frame of body and mind and elevate it to the vastness of the universal spirit. (96)

Swami Vivekananda preaches that all human beings are potentially perfect and free. This is to be realized through *Tyaga* and *Prema* or Renunciation and Love. Rolling water symbolizes the limitless freedom of the seer. For example, "Like rolling river free / Thou ever be, Sannyasin bold" ("The Song of the Sannyasin"). Flowers are symbolic of joy. Violet in "To an Early Violet" is a beautiful symbol for renunciation and sacrifice:

> Change not thy nature, gentle bloom,
> Thou violet, sweet and pure,
> But ever pour thy sweet perfume
> Unasked, unstinted, sure.

Every path has its own problems and difficulties. Only the strong and the persevering can win the prize. Despite this, the heart of the poet spontaneously chooses the path of *Bhakti* as it is natural, easier and 'richer' than the other three, namely, *Jnana*, *Karma*, or even *Raja Yoga*.

> Listen, friend, I will speak my heart to thee;
> I have found in my life this truth supreme—
> Buffeted by waves, in this whirl of life,
> There's one ferry that takes across the sea [the sea of *Samsara*]
>
> Formulas of worship, control of breath,
> Science, philosophy, systems varied,
> Relinquishment, possession, and the like,
> All these are but delusions of the mind—
> Love, Love—that's the one thing, the sole treasure. ("To a Friend")

Coming to the Scriptural background of the pathways for ascent, the Hindu scriptures, especially the *Gita* and the Upanishads, have outlined four methods or *Yogas* for God-realization. Swami Vivekananda has given a coordinated and systematic account of them all in his works. When these four *Yogas* are explained individually one feels the need for their coordination.

Jnana Yoga aims at the discrimination of the real from the unreal, to distinguish appearance as against Reality. The real is *Brahma*, and the *atma* is identical with it, and through lack of discrimination we are ignorant of the identity-consciousness. *Bhakti Yoga* consists of the cultivation of love and adoration towards the Supreme reality, and it culminates in the final integration of the individual with God through the supreme power of love. The personal God is the Absolute for the devotee (*bhakta*). *Karma Yoga* is the selfless God-dedicated, egoless activity which makes man a pliable instrument in the hands of the Lord to work out His purposes. *Raja Yoga* is the psycho-somatic training outlined in great detail by sage Patanjali to gain an immediate apprehension of the Supreme, through the purification of the *citta*, i.e. mind (Ref.: 2.7).

All these *Yogas* are intertwined, none can be practiced independently and exclusively of the other, which is the verdict of the *Gita*. The four *Yogas* are at heart one. In the manner of the *Gita*, but with great force and clarity, Swami Vivekananda has reinterpreted the four *Yogas*. P. Nagaraja Rao, in his concise treatise, Contemporary Indian Philosophy, writes that this integration of the four pathways is Swami Vivekananda's "most significant intellectual achievement and contribution to Hinduism" (43).

3.4 Poems of Advaita: General Estimate of Advaita

On the basis of the Upanishads and worked out more or less in accordance with Shankara's system, Swami Vivekananda has presented us with a synthetic doctrine of the Absolute. The Absolute according to him, is incomprehensible, trans-objective, simple, Omnipresent, self-existent and transcendent Spirit. He is essentially subsisting Knowledge and Bliss. In spite of Swami Vivekananda's enthusiasm for the idea of evolution, he saw clearly that a changing God would be no God at all. Like Shankara conceiving action as necessarily implying instrumentality and change, Swami Vivekananda preferred to consider the Absolute as actionless. Yet on this question Swami Vivekananda's stand is certainly more conventional than that of Sri Aurobindo whose God is essentially a Being-Becoming integrality. But, "Swami Vivekananda's preference for the description of the Absolute as '*Satchidananda*' is certainly commendable" writes Thomas Mannumel as he cites similarity of the term to the Christian mystery of Holy Trinity (168). There are two processes by which one comes to know the Absolute according to Swami Vivekananda:

> One is positive, and the other negative. The positive is that, through which the whole universe is going—that of love. If this circle of love is increased indefinitely, we reach the one universal love. The other is the *neti*—"not this," "not this"—stopping every wave in the mind which tries to draw it out; and at last the mind dies, as it were, and the Real discloses Itself. We call that *Samadhi* or superconsciousness (*Selections from C.W.* 92).

Swami Vivekananda designates this experience sometimes by the term *Samadhi*, sometimes super-consciousness perception and more frequently as realization in his interactions with his disciples. Further, *Samadhi* is of two types: *Savikalpa Samadhi* (with modifications) and *Nirvikalpa Samadhi* (without modifications). In the former, along with the perception of *Brahma* there is an awareness of oneself, of the universe and of the process of contemplation. In the poem, "A Song on Samadhi," Swami Vivekananda presents both the experiences in the order of their attainment. The song begins with the experience of *Savikalpa Samadhi*:

> Lo! The sun is not, nor the comely moon,
> All light extinct; in the great void of space
> Floats shadow-like the image-universe.
> In the void of mind involute, there floats
>
> The fleeting universe, rises and floats,
> Sinks again, ceaseless, in the current "I"

This state is similar to the dual-consciousness involved in seeing a clay elephant wherein there is a simultaneous awareness of clay as well as the elephant. In one of his inspired talks, Swami Vivekananda clarifies the matter and briefly sums up, "There are two kinds of *Samadhi:* I concentrate on myself, then I concentrate and there is a unity of subject and object" (*Selections from C.W.* 406). In

Nirvikalpa Samadhi, there is the experience of *Brahma* only, the other two aspects of awareness (of oneself and of the process of contemplation) being transcended. So the poet continues to sing thus:

> Slowly, slowly, the shadow-multitude
> Entered the primal womb, and flowed ceaseless,
> The only current, "I am," "I am."
>
> Lo! "Tis stopped, ev'n that current flows no more,
> Void merged into void—beyond speech and mind!
> Whose heart understands, he verily does.

"The paradoxes of mystical language are resolved when they are taken over into vital consciousness" says Radhakrishnan in his introduction of the seminal text *The Principal Upanishads* and adds:

> Man must be surpassed. There are different regions in the realm of spirit in which the consciousness of man freed from the finitude of self and enlarged finds fulfillment. In other religions too, we have these varieties of mystic experience. There are some who wish to establish contact with God regarded strictly as a person and live a life in ever complete accord with the divine will and at long last reach the most intimate union with God. There are others who wish to go beyond union to unity, a state of consciousness which is above subject-object relationship (Introduction 143).

"Nirvana," a poem written by Sri Aurobindo presents a very similar account of the experience of the dissolution of the "I" as presented in "A Song on Samadhi"

> Only the illimitable Permanent
> Is here. A peace stupendous, featureless, still,
> Replaces all,—what once was I, in It
> A silent unnamed emptiness content
> Either to fade in the Unknowable
> Or thrill with the luminous seas of the Infinite.
>
> ("Nirvana" by Sri Aurobindo)

Sri Aurobindo describes the state of *Nirvana* where the soul is dissociated from the world around, the mind is released from thought and heart is left without a trace of grief. It is a state of perfect contentment which transcends both ignorance and knowledge. "Featureless" is an apt word chosen to describe the unfathomable peace of self-transcendence. Having reached the threshold of that consciousness, Sri Aurobindo wonders about the true nature of the Absolute and the final destination of the soul. It is said that, doubts of this nature and on the very existence of God dog the footsteps of the aspirants even at some advanced stages of *sadhana*. The journey to God-realization is long and arduous. The advice of an apposite spiritual guide will lighten the task and ensure that the devotee does not stray from the correct path. As Talari Anantha Babu rightly points out, "with rare exceptions, an enlightened *Guru* (teacher) is essential to achieve success in this endeavor" (83). The role of the *Guru* is an integral part of the effort to reach God.

Swami Vivekananda explained several times, the significance of the preceptor in the lives of spiritual aspirants, in his lectures and writings. In the following example, he emphasizes the necessity of the *Guru*:

> There is nothing higher and holier than the knowledge which comes to the soul transmitted by a spiritual teacher. If a man has become a perfect yogi it comes by itself, but it cannot be got in books. You may go and knock your head against the four corners of the world, seek in the Himalayas, the Alps, the Caucasus, the desert of Gobi or Sahara, or the bottom of the sea, but it will not come, until you find a teacher. (*Teachings of Swami Vivekananda* 101)

Swami Vivekananda's idea of Indian religious thought is rooted in his understanding of the life and teachings of his Master Sri Ramakrishna. In stressing the point it may be worthwhile to refer to Swami Vivekananda's Sanskrit *sloka* on Sri Ramakrishna, which is his *pranama* or salutation and supplication to his Master "*sthapakaya cha dharmasya sarvadharma swarupine*." Here Sri Ramakrishna is said to represent all religions. To understand Swami Vivekananda's life and work, and to realize fully the uniqueness of his message to his countrymen and to the world at large, it is important for us to understand the nature of his relationship with his Master Sri Ramakrishna. "There is something in that relationship which is a great deal more than the relationship between a Master and his disciple" writes R.K. Dasgupta in his article, "Swami Vivekananda and his Master Sri Ramakrishna" and adds that "the relationship between the two has certain very special features which we do not find in any instance of such discipleship in the world's spiritual history" (148-49). Swami Vivekananda wrote three ardent hymns to worship his Master Sri Ramakrishna apart from his tributes in prose. Two of the hymns were composed in Sanskrit entitled "A Hymn to Sri Ramakrishna" while one was written in Bengali, whose translated version bears the title, "A Hymn to the Divinity of Sri Ramakrishna."

Swami Vivekananda's presentation of Vedanta philosophy as he understood it through his Master has its own unique approach. His Vedantic ideals are not just echoes of the voices of the great commentators like Shankara and Ramanuja although he had great respect for them. And Sri Ramakrishna was not an interpreter of Vedanta: he was, as Christopher Isherwood very precisely says "Vedanta's greatest human exemplar." In "A Hymn to Sri Ramakrishna," Swami Vivekananda hails the Master as an embodiment of Truth; a confluence of *Jnana*, *Bhakti*, and *Karma:*

> Hail, O Lord of Men! Victory unto you! I
> surrender myself to my Guru the Man-God, the physician
> for the malady of this Samsara (relative existence), whose
> mind ever dwelt on the non-dualistic Truth, whose
> personality was covered by the cloth of Supreme Devotion,
> who was ever active (for the good of humanity) and whose
> actions were all superhuman.
> Hail, O Lord of Men! Victory unto you!

The first stanza of the hymn refers to Sri Ramakrishna as Sri Rama and the second as Sri Krishna and the refrain "Naradeva Deva Jaya Jaya Naradeva" supports and sustains the main contention of the poem. The second hymn beginning with "Om Hrim ritam tvamacalo gunajita gunedyo" is more in the nature of a supplication. "The emphasis of the poem is on Swami Vivekananda's personal limitation and the omnipotence of Sri Ramakrishna" writes

Akhouri Rajendra Prasad in his article "The Poetical Corpus of Vivekananda" (81).

> Om! Hrim! Thou art the True, the Imperturbable
> One, transcending the three Gunas and yet adored for Thy virtues!
> Inasmuch as I do not worship day and night, with yearning,
> Thy compassionate lotus feet which destroy all ignorance, therefore,
> O Thou friend of the lowly, Thou art my only refuge.
>
> "A Hymn to Sri Ramakrishna"

The use of both the sacred syllables Om and Hrim in the hymn is significant. As Sri Ramananda Saraswati explains in *Tripura Rahasya*, "Om is well known as the sacred syllable signifying the Highest Being in the abstract; so also 'Hrim' is the sacred symbol of the same as Goddess". Introduction 9). In answer to Nachiketa's third question, Yama had explained to him that *Brahma* can be understood through the understanding of this one letter "Om." And Rajendra Prasad further elaborates in his article "What is 'Om' for the Vedas is 'Hrim' for the Tantras, and Swami Vivekananda's use of 'Om' and 'Hrim' for Sri Ramakrishna represents both manifested and unmanifested aspects of *Brahma*" (81-82).

The idea of the spiritual commonwealth of man may be considered here to understand why Swami Vivekananda looked upon Sri Ramakrishna not only as an *Avatar*, but as the greatest of all *Avataras*. This idea finds an exuberant expression in the poem, "A Hymn to the Divinity of Sri Ramakrishna." It is consistent with Swami Vivekananda's idea of a man's spiritual progress or evolution towards a greater and higher goal.

> O Lord of the world, through Thy Yoga power
> Thou shinest as the Incarnation clear
> Of this our time. O thou of strict restraint,
> Only through Thine unstinted grace we see
> The mind in Samadhi completely merged;
> Mercy Incarnate! austere are Thy deeds.
>
> Thou dealest to the evil of Misery
> Destruction. Kali's [of the iron age] binding cords
> Are cut by Thee asunder. Thine own life
> Thou gavest freely, O sweet Sacrifice,

O best of men! O Saviour of the world!
("A Hymn to the Divinity of Sri Ramakrishna")

Beginning his work in the last decade of the nineteenth century Swami Vivekananda thought that the time was a turning point in man's spiritual and moral history. The East and the West were then meeting for the first time in a multidimensional cultural encounter. There was the pressing need for a spiritual unity of mankind and Swami Vivekananda discovered in his Master Sri Ramakrishna a living symbol of that unity. In the course of a conversation at the Cossipore Garden House Swami Vivekananda said "in the present age, it is to bring into coalition both these civilizations that *Bhagavan* Sri Ramakrishna was born." Swami Vivekananda did not find this universalist attitude in any other founder of religion. When in a letter to his brother disciples written from the USA in the summer of 1895 he said: "Our Lord was the greatest of all *Avataras*" he did not mean to make a chauvinistic claim on behalf of his country and religion. It was his conviction as he said in his historic letter to the members of the Alambazar Math dated 27 April 1896: "in point of character Paramahamsa Deva beats all previous records; and as regards teaching he was more liberal, more original, and more progressive than all his predecessors. In other words, the old teachers were rather one-sided while the teaching of this new Incarnation or Teacher is that the best point of *Yoga,* devotion, knowledge and work must be combined now to form a new society" (qtd. Dasgupta 158). Obviously, by new society Swami Vivekananda meant a new human society. This dream is distinctly presented in the concluding stanzas of "A Hymn to the Divinity of Sri Ramakrishna" which reads thus:

Fearless art Thou, and past all gloom of doubt;
Thy mind is wrapt in its own firm resolve;
Thy lovers, whose devotion mounts above
The realm of reason, who renounce the pride
Of caste and parentage, of name and fame—
Their safe refuge art Thou alone, O Lord!

My one true treasure is Thy blessed feet,
Reaching which the whole universe itself

Seems like a puddle in the hollow made
By hoof of passing cow. O bestower
Of Love! O Seer of equality
In all! O verily, in Thee the pain
And evil of this mortal world escapes,
And vanishes, O cherished One, in Thee!
("A Hymn to the Divinity of Sri Ramakrishna")

We may now ask how far has Swami Vivekananda's understanding of Sri Ramakrishna touched the modern mind? We may think that Swami Vivekananda's view of Sri Ramakrishna as the greatest of all *Avataras* is an ecstatic exaggeration in the tribute of a disciple to his Master. "But Swami Vivekananda gives this high status to Sri Ramakrishna after a close analysis of the works of all the great teachers of the world in man's spiritual history. And he makes this analysis in terms of his idea of man's spiritual and moral progress in a grand process of human evolution" asserts R.K. Dasgupta in his article, "Swami Vivekananda and his Master Sri Ramakrishna" (161).

Swami Vivekananda believed that in the nineteenth century there was the need for a teacher who would assimilate in his wisdom the finest things in man's spiritual tradition, absorbing the teachings of all the major religions of the world and keeping in view the condition and the spiritual needs of his age and then would summon all mankind to an ideal for the universal man. He found in Sri Ramakrishna such a teacher, and what struck him most in him was that his love of God was indistinguishable from his love of man. This he thought was the essence of *Advaita*. Swami Vivekananda discovered that his Master's spirituality was not a world-negating and a life-negating spirituality. He was amazed by his Master's dismissing the whole idea of *Samadhi*, the *summum bonum* of spiritual life as but a luxury of the soul, but at the same time he realized that his Master was saying this at a time when his country and mankind as a whole was waiting for redemption. This was a great lesson for the founder of the Ramakrishna Order, the lesson that liberation of mankind was more important than private salvation.

As a *Guru* himself, Swami Vivekananda with his call for action aroused the *Advaitins* to an active life. He injected activism into the minds of his disciples and Indians at large. As Jawaharlal Nehru said: "Vivekananda came as a tonic to the depressed and demoralized Hindu mind and gave it self-reliance and some roots in the past" (15). Swami Vivekananda demonstrated to the world through his word and deed that an ascetic, a practicing *Advaitin*, can lead a life of activity and social service. He showed that the philosophy of *Advaita* "can be brought from caves to family and society," as he himself put it and he showed that the principles of *Advaita* can be translated into a life of vigorous action. He exhorted all to see God in the poor, to look upon the poor and needy as *Daridra-Narayanas* and serve them respectfully. "Basing himself on the *Advaitic* doctrine of the Oneness of beings, he provided a rational basis for active life, and preached a religion of equality and universal brotherhood thus infusing self-reliance into the minds of his hearers" hails Jacob Kattackal in his note "Swami Vivekananda and the call for practical Vedanta" (228). In this way he established that the *Advaitic* doctrines can be converted into practical religion and ethics. Like his Master Sri Ramakrishna, Swami Vivekananda used to remind the youth of their worldly duties. "A Benediction" written to sister Nivedita is a fine piece of poetic benediction written in short span of eight lines in which Swami Vivekananda has distilled the essence of religion and spiritual attainment:

> The mother's heart, the hero's will
> The sweetness of the southern breeze,
> The sacred charm and strength that dwell
> On Aryan altars, flaming free;
> All these be yours, and many more
> No ancient soul could dream before
> Be thou India's future son,
> The mistress, servant, friend in one.

The "sweetness of the southern breeze" referred to in the poem itself gets distilled in the sweetness of tone and temper of the person offering benediction. The reference to "Aryan altars, flaming free" not only conjures up the spirit of *Vedic* times but also includes the freedom of spirit like the freedom of fire. Freely flaming spirit is what a person achieves by burning the impurities of passion and providing it with requisite strength to ascend the difficult path and become one with *Param Padam*. Use of words "son" and "mistress" suggests rejection of sexual difference, the only real obstruction to the difficult ascent, and thus prompts sister Nivedita to become the servant and friend of India. Akhouri Rajendra Prasad recounts an interesting anecdote that took place between Sister Nivedita and Swami Vivekananda, a few days before the Master left his body:

Three days before his *Mahasamadhi* "on an Ekadasi day, he fed Sister Nivedita with his own hands, though he himself was fasting. At the end of her meal he helped her wash hands by pouring water for her, and then he dried them with a towel." Sister Nivedita naturally felt puzzled and protested by saying that in normal course of things it was her duty to serve the Swami and in no case he was supposed to serve her. But Swami Vivekananda's reply to her protest was even more startling than his behavior. He had quipped: "Jesus washed the feet of his disciples." This inevitably brought the idea that in case of Jesus it was the last supper but she could not utter her thoughts. Here also in case of Swami Vivekananda it was for the last time. (80)

Swami Vivekananda's love for India and desire to help its people motivated his ministry and trip to the West. Sister Nivedita, who was Miss. Margaret Noble prior to her coming to India, was a twenty eight year old school headmistress in London. She was one of the many westerners who joined Swami Vivekananda in his expeditions and enrolled themselves as members of the 'Ramakrishna Mission' which he was to found shortly. Miss. S.E. Waldo (later Haridasi), Miss. Greenstidel of Detroit (later "Sister Christene"), Miss. Marie Louise (Abhayananda), Miss. Josephine McLeod, Mr. and Mrs. Francis Leggest of New York and Mr. Wright, a Professor of Harvard, were some of the Western followers of the Master. In the treatise, *Reminiscences of Swami Vivekananda by his Eastern and Western Admirers*, Josephine

McLeod—an American disciple, is mentioned to have asked him, "Swami*ji*, how can I best help you?," his succinct answer was, "Love India" (250).

The regeneration of India and fond adoration of the motherland are recurring theme in Swami Vivekananda's thought and poetry. "On The Sea's Bosom" is a short poem of four stanzas which expresses the emotional attachment and romantic love of the poet towards his motherland. The foreign seas fail to appease the traveling poet who is watching the cloud formations during the sunset aboard a ship. Swami Vivekananda composed this poem in Bengali during his return from his second trip to the West. At the time of writing it, he was probably crossing the eastern Mediterranean as indicated in the footnote of the poem (*C.W.* 6: 180).

> Below, the sea sings a varied music,
> But not grand, O India, nor ennobling;
> Thy waters, widely praised, murmur serene
> In soothing cadence, without a harsh roar. ("On the Sea's Bosom")

The poem also reveals Swami Vivekananda's lyricism and his technique of visualization which illuminates the meaning of the verse. We see the cloud formations and recognize their ephemeral nature at once.

> The wind blows as it lists, a hurricane
> Now carving shapes, now breaking them apart;
> Fancies, colours, forms, inert creations—
> A myriad scenes, though real, yet fantasy
>
> There light clouds spread, heaping up spun cotton;
> See next a huge snake, then a strong lion;
> Again, behold a couple locked in love.
> All vanish, at last, in the vapoury sky. ("On the Sea's Bosom")

The shapes and scenes presented by the cloud formations are metaphorical of the short lived creatures and relationships of the world. The monk-poet often denounces the worldly relationships and allurements, in his campaign for *Vairagya* and the path of detached action. For example, in the poem "And Let Shyama Dance There," he describes the worldly bondages as "captivity."

What stirring of emotions! How many
Hot sighs of Love! And warm tears coursing down!
The *Bimba* [a kind of fruit of a rich red color]—red lips of the youthful fair,
The two blue eyes—two oceans of feelings;
The two hands eager to advance—love's cage—
In which the heart, like a bird, lies captive.
("And Let Shyama Dance There")

The universal human predicament is explored and its weaknesses are sorted out. The principles of true *Sannyasa* like detachment and renunciation are offered as the cure to the malady of *Samsara*. The message is set forth in the following intrepid and unambiguous lines:

Free thyself from the mighty attraction—
The maddening wine of love, the charm of sex.
Break the harp! Forward with the ocean's cry!
Drink tears, pledge even life—let the body fall.
Awake, O hero! Shake off thy vain dreams,
Death stands at thy head—does fear become thee? (*Ibid.*)

The poem is a classic presentation of breaking of bonds and tearing of maya through disinterested discharge of duty. And its message is no vain preaching; the poet exhorts his followers to be heroic and ascend the heights of dispassion which he himself has ascended to. His Master Sri Ramakrishna, often hailed Swami Vivekananda for his high spiritual stature during his conversations with his other disciples. The following is one of such conversations, which took place in February, 1882:

> Pointing to Narendra (Swami Vivekananda) the Master said: "You all see, this boy . . . Narendra and people of his type belong to the class of the ever-free. They are never entangled in the world. When they grow a little older they feel the awakening of inner consciousness and go directly toward God. They come to the world only to teach others. They never care for anything of the world. They are never attached to 'woman and gold.'" . . .
>
> After Narendra leaves the room, the Master continues: "You see, Narendra excels in singing, playing on instruments, study, and

> everything. The other day he had a discussion with Kedar and tore his arguments to shreds" (qtd Gupta 88).

Swami Vivekananda exhorts the feeble-minded worshippers of the Mother Kali to be true heroes by completely eliminating their fright of death and misery. The brave heart never clings to worldly allurements and desires. Just as a soldier cuts all worldly bonds and love for the body to march ahead—unaffected and unconcerned with victory or defeat in the battlefield, the human soul has to conquer worldly entrapments and cultivate equanimity of mind in order to transcend *Samsara*. The poet strongly admonishes those men who hanker after worldly pleasures:

> O thou insane! Thou but cheatest thyself,
> Thou dost not turn thy head lest thou behold,
> Ay, the form terrible of the Mother.
> Thou courtest hardship hoping happiness,
> Thou wearest cloak of Bhakti and worship,
> With mind full of achieving selfish ends.
>
> ("And Let Shyama Dance There")

Just as a cremation ground with burning funeral pyres, is like a temple for the soldier, the true temple of Shyama for a spiritual aspirant is the burning ground of his heart where the little-self, false hopes, and name etc., are destroyed.

> Constant defeat—let that not unnerve thee;
> Shattered be little-self, hope, name and fame;
> Set up pyre of them and make thy heart
> A burning-ground.
> And let Shyama dance there. (*Ibid.*)

The misery and terror of one's privation are the "burning-ground" whereupon one's egoistical self is burnt to ashes, and through the sorrow does one achieve Spiritual awakening. Swami Vivekananda often told disciples:

> Learn to recognize the Mother as instinctively in . . . terror, sorrow and annihilation as in that which makes for sweetness and joy. . . . The Mother Herself is Brahma. . . . The heart must become a crema-

> tion ground, pride, selfishness, and desire all burnt to ashes. Then, and then alone, will the Mother come! (qtd. *LSVEWD* 596)

We are to uproot our frailties and cultivate strength and vision to face trials and ordeals of life with heroic calm and determination. "If we are *Advaitists*," says Swami Vivekananda, "we must think from this moment that our old self is dead and gone, they were mere superstition and what remains is the ever free, the ever strong, the almighty, the all knowing. That alone remains for us and then all fear vanishes from us" (qtd. Cooper 88). Achievement of such state and the stages of understanding that the self passes through to reach there have been graphically presented in "No One to Blame." Written at New York on sixteenth of May, 1895, the poem "No One to Blame" is a scientific exposition of the Law of *Karma*, the building up and dissolution of one's personality—which leads to the dawning of Wisdom or the state known as *Nirvana*.

> I am my own embodied past;
> Therein the plan was made;
> The will, the thought, to that conform,
> To that the outer frame;
> No one but me to blame. ("No One to Blame")

The *Jiva* acquires mind and *Samskaras* (tendencies) around itself and then the physical body through its own *Karma*. This individuation is the estrangement from the spiritual center. The *Jiva* can re-unite with the center by undoing the mind and burning up of *Samskaras*. This puts an end to death and privation:

> I give up hate, I give up love;
> My thirst for life is gone;
> Eternal death is what I want,
> Nirvanam goes life's flame;
> No one is left to blame. ("No One to Blame")

Realization is native to the soul and not a derivative object. It is not the attainment of a distant object. The mystic formula of *Advaita* is "Thou art that" and not that "Thou will become that." In the supreme stage of spiritual realization the finite limited being sheds his individuality to enter into the indeterminate. In "No One to Blame," the poet looks back at his past life which is the cause of his present state. The same thought has been explained in one of the well known essays of Swami Vivekananda, "The Secret of Work," where he writes:

> Every work that we do, every movement of the body, every thought that we think, leaves such an impression on the mind-stuff; and even when such impressions are not obvious on the surface, they are sufficiently strong to work beneath the surface, subconsciously. What we are every moment is determined by the sum total of these impressions on the mind. What I am just at this moment is the effect of the sum total of all the impressions of my past life. This is really what is meant by character; each man's character is determined by the sum total of these impressions. If good impressions prevail, the character becomes good; if bad, it becomes bad (*Selections from C.W.* 20).

Since these impression-forming thoughts and deeds are done by oneself in one's past, there isn't anyone else to be blamed for one's present state. The law of *Karma* thus emerges to be the supreme regulation which cannot be overcome unless one gives up both good and bad tendencies which together constitute any given action. The poem projects bipolar stance of the universe; the good is wedded to the bad, love always goes with hate, pleasure cannot be without pain and joy is forever coupled with sorrow. So also life comes hand-in-hand with death. These pairs of opposites are inseparable. An aspirant of liberation has to give up both and rise to neutrality for being freed from the *Karmic* cycle of rebirth.

> One only man, one only God, one ever perfect soul,
> One only sage who ever scorned the dark and dubious ways.
> One only man who dared think and dared show the goal—
> That *death* is curse, and so is *life*, and best when stops to be.
> Om Nama Bhagavate Samabuddhaya
> Om, I salute the Lord, the awakened. ("No One to Blame")

Removal of disparate tendencies leads to renunciation of action, which in turn confers liberation from the little-self; The "life's flame" or the soul attains *Nirvanam* with this unwinding of personality and thus, "No one is left to blame."

Action guided by the illumined mind of *Buddhi*, enlightened by true self, which is the self of all, becomes steady, purposeful and worthy. All true action finds its consummation in illumination—an accomplishment which is recorded in the poem, "Light." This single stanza poem forms a part of the letter written to Miss MacLeod, in December 1900. Swami Vivekananda in a retrospect of his life, writes in a tone of satisfaction thus

> I look behind and after
> And find that all is right,
> In my deepest sorrows
> There is soul of light. ("Light")

When spiritual consciousness, pervades man's life and activities, he attains the serenity and equilibrium—which stand by him through moments of crisis and his "deepest sorrows." Life gradually expands and becomes transfigured in universal plane after transcending the little-self. "He who sees every one in himself and himself in everyone, thus seeing the same God living in all, he becomes sage, no more he destroys the Self by the self" says Swami Vivekananda. This is the central truth of the *Advaita* Vedanta epitomized in the *Gita* (qtd. Chaudhuri 94-95). The *Advaita Sadhana* prescribes that one should realize one's own self in others, and it is the surest way of suffusing the world with love. Our false identification with the body and mind breeds attachment and fear. Once we realize our true nature, the birthless, deathless soul, all our mortal fear vanishes. Knowledge is the foundation of inner strength and power. The *Kena* Upanishad says (11, 4): *Atmana vindate viryam*, "Strength comes from the Knowledge of the *atma*" (Trans. Harshananda 19).

In the light of the above discussion on Swami Vivekananda's concept of *Advaita* it logically follows that there is no difference between man and man. All souls living on this earth have got essential identity and affinity among themselves because each soul is the manifestation of the same reality—the Absolute *Brahma*. This conviction forms the genesis of Swami Vivekananda's spiritual humanism, where he exhorts his followers to serve *jiva* (individual soul) as Shiva (the Absolute) Himself. On the basis of the teaching of the *Advaitic* ideal of oneness of existence, he also tried to solve social problems of India. He vehemently criticized the practice of untouchability, priestcraft, etc. prevalent in India in his time. He felt much for the downtrodden people of India. As Shail Kumari Singh feels Swami Vivekananda's religious and moral philosophy is rationalistic, spiritualistic, liberal, dynamic and all-embracing. "The feeling of oneness of existence is the basis of his entire philosophy" (222). Swami Vivekananda's adherence to the concept of *Advaita* is mostly due to the magnetic influence of his Master Sri Ramakrishna, the "Seer of Dakshineshwar" writes Thomas Mannumel and further adds "It is the personality of this ascetic, and, perhaps, to his mysterious powers that the youth Narendranath owed that personal conviction which was to make of him the great Swami Vivekananda" (172-73).

Thus, Swami Vivekananda's poems of *Advaita* reflect his philosophical conceptualization in four important ideas, namely, the Absolute, dissolution of the "I," the significance and need for a *Sad-Guru* on the journey of self-realization and detached action as a result of spiritual humanism.

A detailed exposition of various aspects of the doctrine of *Advaita* has been presented in the second chapter (refer 2.7). The philosophy of Swami Vivekananda is basically an admixture of the teaching of his master Sri Ramakrishna and *Advaita* Vedanta of Shankaracharya. From his master, he received the message of rendering selfless service to human beings, serving *jiva* as Shiva through the unique power of love. He was inspired by Shankaracharya as well as the messages like "*Tat tvam asi*" (Thou art that) or *Jiva Brahmaiva naparah*. Swami Vivekananda has synthesized these two great teachings in his own unique way, giving the name "Practical Vedanta." The topics like *Sannyasa*, Activism, *Samadhi* and *Sad-Guru*, which figure prominently in the *Advaita* poetry of Swami Vivekananda, have got sound scientific explanations in the ancient Indian scriptures. A few of such sources may be discussed here.

To start with *Sannyasa*, *Tapas* and *Nyasa* (renunciation) are the two leading doctrines of the Upanishads. Jacob Kattackal in his article, "The mystical outlook and the religio-ethical doctrines of the Upanishads" notes that *tapas* in the forest was the forerunner of *Vanaprastha*; and renunciation of everything was the forerunner of *Sannyasa-ashrama* (23). In the *Chandogya* Upanishad, *tapas* or ascetic life is raised to a special vocation (*dharma-skanda*). In the *Brihadaranyaka* Upanishad, translated into English by Swami Harshananda, we find men like Yajnvalkya departing to the solitude of the wilderness for doing *tapas* and contemplation of the *atma*. The *Chandogya* describes the *tapas* of Upakosala, the *Brahmachari*. The same Upanishad speaks of *tapas* as very important (*prathamas tapa eva*) (21-23, 54-55).

As regards Activism, The *Isavasya* Upanishad tells us that a man should try to spend his life span of one hundred years (*jijiviset satam samah*) in the constant performance of actions (*kurvan eva iha karmani*). The *Isa* (*Isavasya* Upanishad) seems to be attempting a reconciliation between *karma* (action) and inaction or asceticism in verses 9-11: "Into blinding darkness enter those who worship ignorance (i.e. who perform feverishly actions), and those who delight in knowledge (*vidya*, mysticism, quietism) enter into still greater darkness," says the *Isa*, verse 9. Mere action and bare contemplation are discountenanced by the *Isa* (Trans. Harshananda 12-13).

The peace and bliss enjoyed in *samadhi* are described by the *Advaitins* in glowing terms. Obtaining this essence (*rasa, Brahma-jnana)* man becomes perfectly happy" (*Taittiriya* Upanishad. 2.7.1). "Reaching this state, man considers himself to be supremely blessed" (Vidyaranya in his Panchadasi, last chapter). "Enjoying this unity experience, all sorrow and delusion are gone" (*Isavasya* Upanishad. 7). "Know *Brahma* through your own experience; the knower is delivered from all fears and worries, fetters and doubts" (*Taittiriya* Upanishad. 2.4.1; *Mundaka* Upanishad 2.2.9). And this bliss is inexpressible: "While attempting to express it, words as well as thoughts fail" (*Taittiriya* Upanishad. 2.9.1). "This blissful experience is beyond the reach of words and thoughts; one simply does not know how to impart it" (*Kena* Upanishad. 1.3 qtd. Kattackal 233).

The Hindu scriptures eulogize the *Sad-Guru* as God Himself and declare that spiritual wisdom is impossible of attainment without his grace. Shankara, following the Upanishads, lays great stress on the three processes, namely, *sravana*, *manana* and *nidhidhasana* as necessary steps to *Brahma-jnana*. *Sravana* etymologically means "hearing" or "attentive listening." In *Advaitic* parlance, *sravana* connotes the devout and patient hearing of the esoteric doctrines from a guru who himself has experienced *Brahma-sakshatkara*. The *Kathopanishad* proclaims: "The experiential knowledge of the *atma* (*anubhava-jnana*) cannot be obtained by taking instructions from an unqualified teacher; the reason is that various and curious notions are being held by many about the *atma*" (*Kathopanishad* 1.2.8). Commenting on this verse of the *Kathopanishad*, Shankara writes: "Thus when an *acharya* (spiritual teacher) possessing the traditional wisdom, presents the *paramatmam* to the aspirant as being non-different from himself, the *paramatmam* is well comprehended by the aspirant"—*eavam survijneya—atma agamavadacharyena ananyataya proktah.* Shankara expresses the same idea in his commentary on the *Gita* also: "Only the instructions imparted by the teachers who have realized the Truth in their own experience, are effective" (*Gita-Bhasya* 4.34 qtd. Kattackal 122, 128).

Chapter 4

Philosophical Poetry of Sri Aurobindo

This chapter offers a critical analysis of Sri Aurobindo's philosophical poems highlighting the fusion of philosophy and poetry in the work of this great seer. In achieving this fusion Sri Aurobindo has actually laid foundation for a new kind of poetry, the *mantric* poetry. A brief discussion of Sri Aurobindo's life and oeuvre precedes the critical analysis since his personal experiences as a *Sadhaka* deeply inform the spiritual verse of Sri Aurobindo. After this, the poems of Sri Aurobindo are discussed under three broad heads: Involution or Descent, Evolution or Ascent and Transformation in three sections respectively. The scriptural background of the concepts discussed is presented in each section after an elucidation of the poems.

4.1 Life, Literature and General Principles of Philosophy

Born on 15 August, 1872 in Calcutta to Krishnadhan Ghose and Swarnalatha Devi, Aurobindo Ghose belonged to a highly cultured family of Bengal. Krishnadhan Ghose wanted his children to be educated in England, as he himself was educated in London. All his three sons were sent to England for higher studies. At first Aurobindo Ghose studied privately under Rev. William Drewett and his wife. He was admitted in the St. Paul's for regular study later, where he won a scholarship. From there he proceeded to the King's College, London. He acquired a mastery over English, French, Greek and Latin. He successfully completed his I.C.S. examination, though he finally opted out of it. He stayed in England for fourteen long years and returned to India.

Aurobindo Ghose was a total stranger to his own mother land when he joined the Baroda State Service in 1893. He joined as

Professor of English in Baroda College and started his life, political as well as literary. His articles began to appear in *Indu Prakash* from 1893 itself. They however, had to be stopped as they were not received well by the then Congress Party. It was at this time that he came into contact with Bankim Chandra Chatterjee whom he called a *Rishi*, for having given the Mantra 'Bandemataram' to the nation. As soon as he settled down to life in India he began to learn and master Gujarati and Marathi besides refreshing his knowledge of Sanskrit and Bengali. His mastery over the English language and the technique of his English poetry also began to be recognized. In the beginning, like most other Indo-Anglican writers, he tried his hand at translations. He translated the Upanishads into English during this period. He also wrote articles on the *Ramayana*, the *Mahabharata*, on Vyasa and Valmiki and on Kalidasa. In addition to these he translated Kalidasa's *Vikramorvasiyam* into English. *Urvasie* and *Love and Death* were his original writings of this early period.

He shifted over to Calcutta's National College from Baroda State Service. He took up the editorship of the magazine *Bande Mataram*. He began to combine political activity with literary work. The glimpses of the spiritual glory that was to visit him in his later life were beginning to be noticed at this time. He started contributing regularly to Karmayogin. He was involved in the famous Alipore bomb case about this time and was effectively defended by Sir C.R. Das. He had his first *darshan* (i.e. Vision) of Narayana while in Alipore jail. His Uttarapara speech describes this experience in a grand and graphic way:

> I looked at the jail that secluded me from men and it was no longer by its high walls that I was imprisoned; no, it was Vasudeva who surrounded me. I walked under the branches of the tree in front of my cell but it was not the tree, I know it was Vasudeva, it was Sri Krishna whom I saw standing there and holding over me his shade. I looked at the bars of my cell, the very grating that did duty for a door and again I saw Vasudeva. It was Narayana who was guarding and standing sentry over me. Or I lay on the coarse blanket that were given me for a couch and felt the arms of Sri Krishna around me, the arms of my Friend and Lover. . . . I looked at the prisoners in the

> hall, the thieves, the murderers, the swindlers, and as I looked at them I saw Vasudeva, it was Narayana whom I found in these darkened souls and misused bodies (Sri Krishna: Words of Sri Aurobindo and the Mother 38).

In 1910 after receiving a command from above, he left Calcutta and his political life, and went to Chandernagore, where he stayed for a short time. Later in the year he left for Pondicherry after another command from above and there he lived a life of complete seclusion and spiritual striving. *Pravartah* a Bengali magazine was started in 1914 and *The Standard Bearer* in 1920. They contained most of his political, literary and spiritual writings.

Pondicherry, a seat of Vedic culture, was once called Vedapuri. It is said that sage Agasthya lived here. This place became, quite fittingly, the final abode of Sri Aurobindo. The first years were marked by intense meditation and persistent *yogic* practices. Many eminent people of the time visited the *Ashram*, and among them were the celebrated French couple Paul Richard and Madame Mirra Richard. Madame Richard, later came to be known as the Mother, came back to Pondicherry in 1920 and lived there till her passing away in 1973. She was his collaborator in the task of accelerating the supramental manifestations on earth and offered guidance to scores of disciples in the *Ashram* and showered her love upon them. *Arya*, another magazine, was started in 1914 and was run till 1921. It contained many of Sri Aurobindo's philosophical and spiritual writings, discourses and discussions. His well known works, *The Life Divine*, *The Secret of the Veda*, *The Ideal of Humanity*, *The Human Cycle*, *The Future Poetry* and *The Foundations of Indian Culture*, were all first serialized in *Arya*. On 24 November, 1929, he was said to have experienced the descent of Lord Krishna into his physical body; and eventually the descent of the Supermind as a result of persistent *Sadhana* and *yogic* practices. After this he gave public utterances only twice, during the Second World War and when India attained her independence. On 5th December, 1950 he left his body and attained *Mahasamadhi*. The body was said to have remained intact for four and a half days.

Thus, in a span of seventy-eight years, Sri Aurobindo lived the life of a *Purna Purusha* (a complete man). A brilliant student, an inspiring teacher, a great patriot, a fiery revolutionary, a versatile writer and finally a *yogi* and seer par excellence—these were the incredible facets of his multi-splendoured personality.

It is mainly as a writer of rare achievement that the present study is concerned with Sri Aurobindo. As mentioned above, *Indu Prakash*, *Bande Mataram*, *Karma Yogin*, *Pravartah*, *The Standard Bearer* and *Arya* were the magazines in which his political, literary and spiritual writings were published. "Urvasie," "Love and Death," "Ahana" and a host of short poems and sonnets were written and began to be published right from 1890 onwards. In addition to all his poetical writings, he wrote many verse dramas like *The Rishi*, *Perseus the Deliverer*, *Vasavadatta*, *Khaled of the Sea*. "Chitrangada," "Uloupie" and "The Tale of Nala" were some of his longer poems. The information on Sri Aurobindo's literary output and some of the biographical details have been taken from Syamala Kallury's *Symbolism in the Poetry of Sri Aurobindo* (7-10).

In all these writings Sri Aurobindo stands out as a great spiritual messenger and a fervent exponent of the Indian spiritual heritage. His *Life Divine*, *The Synthesis of Yoga* and *The Foundations of Indian Culture* testify to this. He prophesied that Asia would ultimately lead the world by bringing about a new awakening and a new Supramental consciousness.

His philosophy is a reinterpretation of certain traditional themes in the light of modern thinking (Western and Eastern). A coherence is achieved by the joint concepts of "involution" and "evolution." While Sri Aurobindo is most interested in evolution and in the possible developments for humanity in the future, he believes that no evolution is possible without previous involution. Involution refers to the divine descent even to the world of matter. The absolute transcendental Eternal Spirit is beyond all description but it nevertheless descends into the lower realms of being and then by evolution ascends until it returns to its source. In this descent the Supermind is the transition from the original unity to the multiplicity of the phenomenal world. The Supermind stands between the Supreme where there are no distinctions and the human mind which perceives all the distinctions and mutations in existence.

Matter the lowest level of being, is virtually devoid of consciousness, yet it is not merely what is appears to be, but is a low form of the Supreme. The characteristic stage of evolution reached by humans is Mind, which is preparatory to the Supermind. Robert D. Baird and Alfred Bloom observe in their note on Sri Aurobindo's philosophy that "Mind, however, interprets the truth of universal existence for practical purposes and since it is a fall from the Supermind, its salvation lies in returning to its original state" (122). The doctrine of *karma* points to the means whereby the soul grows through rebirth and the evolutionary process, rather than a series of rebirths where penalties from previous existences are experienced. The determining factor in the spiritual evolutionary process is not the law of *karma*, but the Spirit, which uses *karma* for its progressive upward development.

The doctrine of resurrection of the body is rejected by Sri Aurobindo, since death implies in the evolutionary scheme, that the soul has outgrown the present body. Such a view is a divination of the present life rather than and escape from it. Further, for Sri Aurobindo the doctrine of *maya* does not imply that the world is illusion, but refers to the power of differentiation, which gives form and shape to all phenomenal existence as it arises out of the indivisible unity of *Brahman*. Through the agency of *maya*, the world of the One becomes the world of the many. Hence the phenomena are not unreal, but a substantial form of Truth.

The practice of *yoga* is a method for awakening the potentiality for self-perfection which is latent in man. *Yoga* is not occult, but merely the intensification of Nature's ways for the perfection of man. The *Yogi* need not renounce the world. *Hathayoga* may perfect the body, but neglects the social sphere. *Rajayoga* aims at perfecting the senses, emotions, the mind, but puts too much emphasis on abnormal trances. The purpose of *yoga* should be to make the "spiritual life and its experiences fully active and fully utilizable in the waking state and even in the normal use of the functions." Integral *Yoga* is the synthesis of all other *yoga*s and aims at the divinization of the total life of man. This involves three steps as explained by Baird and Bloom: (1) surrendering oneself completely into God's hands; (2) watching with detachment the working of the divine in one's life—that is, the recognition that one's progress is not due to personal efforts, but to the Shakti (i.e. Power) working within; and (3) seeing the divine vision of the personal deity in everything. God's power manifests itself in the human life and man realizes that a "great power, not of our own, is thinking for us, feeling for us, acting for us, and that our heart and mind are being moved and motivated by it rather than ourselves" (121-23).

Historically, evolution proceeded from matter up to the present state of the Mind. But a thin veil separates the Mind from the Supermind, and when that veil is removed, through the descent of the one, the ascent of the other is achieved. Thus a higher level of humanity is attained whereby a newly constituted Gnostic being is created who will be involved in action but indifferent to its fruits. The life of such a one is not governed by external laws but by the Divine Life within. This higher level of humanity will begin when groups of Gnostic beings grow in different parts of the world. The number of such Gnostic communities will gradually increase until humanity itself reaches a new level of human existence. Sri Aurobindo *Ashram* at Pondicherry is a place where men and women of differing cultures live together to achieve that gnostic experience which Sri Aurobindo envisaged.

Sri Aurobindo rejects the idea of illusory nature of the Universe. He evolved out of his study of the Vedas and the Upanishads and out of his own experience, a philosophy which he thought would harmonize the polarities of existence Spirit and Matter. His Integral *yoga* not only aims at ascent of the world to the Divine, but also seeks to transform the external world through the descent of the Divine into it. In Sri Aurobindo's view, *Satchidananda* is involved through descending series of the Supermind, mind, life and matter and naturally evolution is going on through an ascending series of matter, life, mind, Supermind and *Satchidananda*. Moreover *Satchidananda* was involved even in the in-conscience before the beginning of evolution.

Thus the philosophy of Sri Aurobindo viz., the Integral *yoga* can broadly be summarized into three headings:

1. Involution/Descent
2. Evolution/Ascent and
3. Transformation

The above concepts have been studied in the selected poems of Sri Aurobindo under these three parts. The Scriptural background of these concepts is discussed after an elucidation of the poems.

4.2 Poems on Involution or Descent

The idea of evolution with the pressure of the force from above, the double line of ascent represented by prayer or aspiration from below and the descent from above is very fundamental to the philosophy of Sri Aurobindo. The process of evolution, is made possible by the process of involution. It is because of the descent of the Spirit into Matter, Life and Mind, that these can ascend to the higher regions of the Spirit. S.K. Maitra explains that the process of creation "is initially a plunge of the Spirit into Ignorance" (43). From the study of Sri Aurobindo's philosophy and its explanation by various scholars, including S.K. Maitra, Madhusudhan Reddy, R.S. Srivastava, Prema Nandakumar, Rishabhchand, etc., it is understood that the terms of Involution or Descent have been used in three contexts to explain three related concepts. Firstly, it is the Involution of the Spirit into Matter, which results in creation. Secondly, it is the special form of Descent of the Spirit as *Avatara*, with the dual purpose of upholding *Dharma* (i.e. righteousness) and presenting the goal of evolution before mankind. Finally, it is the Descent of Supermind into the world which results in transformation of Nature into Supernature and the human being into the gnostic being. This third concept of the Descent of Supermind, is the unique feature of Sri Aurobindo's philosophy, within the concept of Involution or Descent. For this reason, poems containing this concept have been discussed more elaborately in this section as compared with those dealing with the first two concepts of creation and incarnation or *Avatara*.

The poems on Involution, which are discussed in this section are "Shiva the Inconscient Creator," "God," "Krishna" on the first two concepts and "The Pilgrim of the Night," "A God's Labour," "In the Moonlight" "The Rose of God," "The Hidden Plan," "The Golden Light," "A Strong Son of Lightning," "Descent," "The Inconscient Foundation," "Light," "O Pall of Black Night," "The Vedantin's Prayer," "Bride of the Fire," on the third concept of Descent of Supermind.

First of all, Spirit completely involves Itself in Its complete negation and opposition in the Inconscience of Matter, as R.S. Srivastava sums up that Matter is the veiled Spirit (58). This phenomenon is beautifully presented in the poem "Shiva the Inconscient Creator":

> This was the closed mute and burning source
> Whence were formed the worlds and their star-dance;
> Life sprang a self-rapt inconscient Force,
> Love, a blazing seed, from that flame-trance.
>
> ("Shiva the Inconscient Creator")

The creative Inconscient is personified in Shiva, to quote Sri Aurobindo's own explanation:

> The Inconscient as the source and author of all material creation is one of the main discoveries of modern psychology, but it agrees with the idea of a famous Vedic hymn. In the Upanishads, *Prajna*, the Master of *Sushupti*, is the *Ishwara* and therefore the original creator out of a Superconscient sleep. The idea of the poem is that this creative Inconscient also is Shiva creating here life in matter out of an apparently inconscient material trance as from above he creates all the worlds (not the material only) from a Superconscient trance. The reality is a supreme Consciousness, but that is veiled by the appearance on one side of the Superconscient sleep, on the other of the material Inconscience. Here the emphasis is on the latter; the Superconscient is only hinted at, not indicated, it is the Infinity out of which comes the revealing Flame (*Collected Poems* 579).

The matted hair of Shiva, the still light of moon upon the blue and pale forehead of Shiva and His tranquil face portray His Superconscient trance. The cold mountain peaks, the lifeless air and vast emptiness symbolize the Inconscience of matter. These two constitute the 'veil' of the Supreme Consciousness (Shiva) that is torn apart by the dynamics of creation.

> Light—spear-tips revealed the mighty shape,
> Tore the secret veil of the heart's hold;
> In that diamond heart the fires undrape,
> Living core, a brazier of gold. ("Shiva the Inconscient Creator")

In the process of creation, this supreme Consciousness raps Inconscience around Itself for involving into matter and also originates Life and Love which sustain this creation. In another poem, "God," Sri Aurobindo adores this principle of Love as the essential nature of God above all other powers. "Not only does God descend into and fill all the worlds and the obscurest figures of Nature, He also animates them with the Divine presence. God is certainly power, knowledge, infinity and omnipresence, but He is even more essentially Love" explains Srinivasa Iyengar (1972: 146).

> Thou who pervadest all the worlds below,
> Yet sitst above,
> Master of all who work and rule and know,
> Servant of Love! ("God")

It is this Love that compels Him to give Himself to His creation. Besides His transcendence, He is one with 'all the worlds' and does not disdain to dwell in the clod and the worm.

> Thou who disdainest not the worm to be
> Nor even the clod,
> Therefore we know by that humility
> That thou art God. ("God")

The inversion 'the worm to be' instead of 'to be the worm' was perhaps necessary in the interests of the rhyme, points out Srinivasa Iyengar as he asserts that there is no ambiguity about the meaning otherwise (1972: 146). The main idea of the poem is, as

Sri Aurobindo puts it, "the vast impartiality shown in this humility is itself the very sign of the greatness of the Divine" (*Collected Poems*. 579). This is significantly the identifying feature of God. Scriptural source of Involution of the Spirit into Matter, resulting in creation has been discussed along with that of the concept of Evolution.

The ordinary form of descent of the Spirit has been discussed so far, the descent through ignorance, which is responsible for the creation, as well as the maintenance of the world-process. But the world-process sometimes requires a special form of descent of the Spirit. This is the descent as *Avatara*, which is mentioned in the *Bhagavad Gita*. S.K. Maitra explains that "the peculiarity of this descent is that it is a descent in human form of the whole of the Divine personality" (40). The *Gita* declares that the Divine incarnates at times when *dharma* is on the wane. Sri Aurobindo underscores the other 'more important' purpose of an *Avatara*: the Divine incarnates as man to guide mankind by leading an exemplary life and exhorting them to ascend to the Life Divine. Sri Aurobindo points out that the Divine consents to *Avatarahood* out of love for man. It is certainly no joke for the Divine to compress its *Viswarupa* into the miniature form of man (lower nature) elucidates Prema Nandakumar in her article "Sri Aurobindo's The Mother" (310). But the Lord willingly does so to save His creation.

While Sri Aurobindo's *Essays on the Gita* deals with all the implications of *Avatarahood* and his *Savitri* presents a unique symbol of an *Avatara*, there are also many shorter poems and brief tracts which deal with the theory of incarnation. "A God's Labour" is an illustrative lyric on this subject. The Divine when he wants to be the golden bridge between the human and the Transcendent has perforce to descend himself into the sordid clay of earth atmosphere, as the poem points out:

> Coercing my Godhead I have come down
> Here on the sordid earth,
> Ignorant, labouring, human grown
> Twixt the gates of death and birth.

I have been digging deep and long
Mid a horror of filth and mire
A bed for the golden river's song
A home for the deathless fire. ("A God's Labour")

The *Avatara* has to face insult, jeers and indifference from the multitude. "Why, ungrateful, purblind man gets ready even to slay his redeemer" exclaims Prema Nandakumar in her above mentioned article 'Come, let us slay him and end his course!'—they decide. But "the *Avatara* never despairs," she writes and quotes (310):

On a desperate stair my feet have trod
Armoured with boundless peace,
Bringing the fires of the splendor of God
Into the human abyss. ("A God's Labour")

In the *Gita* it is stated that as man falls more and more deep in the pit of sin and darkness, his redemption and ascent to light by the incarnation of God also approaches nearer. God takes birth on earth when darkness reaches its utmost limit. The "periods of transition when we are on the threshold of a brighter world or 'the transformed world'" writes Jagdish Saran Agarwal, "are always marked by the height of darkness and turmoil" (62). Sri Aurobindo sings of the glorious descent of the *Avatara* in such a gloomy situation in the poem "In the Moonlight":

He rises now; for God has taken birth.
The revolutions that pervade the world
Are faint beginnings and the discus hurled
Of Vishnu speeds down to enring the earth.

The old shall perish; it shall pass away,
Expunged, annihilated, blotted out;
And all the iron bands that ring about
Man's wide expansion shall at last give way. ("In the Moonlight")

"The Divine," says Sri Aurobindo, "works behind indeed and governs its special manifestation through this outer and imperfect consciousness and will, but is itself secret in the cavern, *guhyam*, as the Veda puts it, or as the *Gita* expresses it, 'in the heart of all existences the Lord abides turning all existences as if mounted on a machine by *Maya*.' This secret working of the Lord hidden in the heart from the egoistic nature-consciousness through which He works, is God's universal method with creatures. Why then should we suppose that in any form He comes forward into the frontal, the phenomenal consciousness for a more direct and consciously divine action? Obviously if at all, then to break the veil between Himself and humanity which, man limited in his own nature, could never lift" (Essays on the *Gita* 225). Sri Aurobindo sums up this vital purpose of an *Avatara* of leading the course of evolution thus:

> This is man's progress; for the Iron Age
> Prepares the Age of Gold. What we call sin,
> Is but man's leavings as from deep within
> The Pilot guides him in his pilgrimage. ("In the Moonlight")

Sri Aurobindo's Conception of *Avatara* is primarily drawn from the *Bhagavad Gita*. Sri Aurobindo says that upholding of *dharma* is not the only object of the descent of the *Avatara*, for it is not in itself an all-sufficient object, but is only "the general condition of a higher aim and a more supreme and divine utility." "For" he says "there are two aspects of the divine birth; one is a descent, the birth of God in humanity, the Godhead manifesting itself in the human form and nature, the eternal A*vatara*; the other is an ascent, the birth of man into the Godhead, man rising into the divine nature and consciousness, *madbhavam agatah*; it is the being born anew in a second birth of the soul. It is that new birth which *Avatara*hood and the upholding of the *dharma* are intended to serve. For Sri Aurobindo, therefore, the main significance of the conception of *Avatara* is the birth of man into the Godhead, and not merely the preservation of *dharma*. The *Avatara* is born, in his view, in order to show man what he is capable of becoming. It is to give him an ocular and practical demonstration that he can also become God without even leaving his body. This is what the *Gita* also says. Thus Sri Aurobindo points out, "that the *Gita* contains as its kernel this second and real object of the *Avatara*hood" as is evident from the fourth and ninth chapters of the *Gita* (*Essays on the Gita* 216).

The creative immanent *Satchidananda*, in Its aspect of Supermind, involves into the principles of mind, life and matter of the cosmos which are kept separate from each other by thick veils. The thickest veil is between the Supermind and the mind. When this veil is lifted, the illumination of Divine consciousness pervades the world.

> In a downpour of supernal light it reads
> The black Inconscient's enigmatic script—
> Recorded in a hundred shadowy screeds
> An Inert world's obscure enormous drift;
> All flames, is torn and burned and cast away.
> Here slept the tables of the Ignorance,
> There the dumb dragon edicts of her sway,
> The scriptures of Necessity and Chance.
> Pure is the huge foundation now and nude,
> A boundless mirror of God's Infinitude.
>
> ("The Inconscient Foundation")

On the descent of the Supramental Power, the present life of earth which is painful, would necessarily be filled with Joy. Sri Aurobindo describes this descent of Supermind frequently through the metaphors of Light or Dawn and sometimes of Music. He personifies it as the Mother, calling Her as Mahalakshmi, Shakti, etc. Sri Aurobindo uses the symbols of light and darkness suggesting that the light of Divine knowledge illumines the dark abodes of the human heart.

To consider a few examples, "The Pilgrim of the Night" presents man as traveling through the world of Night. He walks through a dim and blind vastness carrying God's immortal Light in his breast. He woos the dark and dangerous heart of the Night. He is not afraid of it as he carries in himself the Light of God. After a long walk which seemed to have no end the poet has lost the lustrous Godhead and cannot hear the voice of his celestial friend. He derives consolation from the fact that his foot-prints will ultimately lead him back to the path of Immortality.

> And yet I know my footprints' track shall be
> A pathway towards Immortality. ("The Pilgrim of the Night")

Dark, dim and blind as the path is, the poet is confident that the light and power of human soul will ultimately lead the soul to the deathless land of the Divine. At present the human mind is blind to the concealed symphonies of life. Man can be conscious of them only when he rises above the mind and opens himself to the Divine touch. Thus Sri Aurobindo prays to the Rose of God to:

> Transform the body of the mortal
> like sweet and magical rhyme. ("Rose of God")

The same thought continues with a greater vigour in "The Hidden Plan." However, long in the Night's hour, the poet asserts:

> I will not dream
> That the small ego and the person's mask
> Are all that God reveals in our life-scheme. ("The Hidden Plan")

He feels confident that a greater presence works in the soul's darkness of the Night and illuminates it. One day it will burst out of its limitations and reveal the magnificent hidden plan which conceals "the world-wide and immortal spirit in man." The light as the light of Divine knowledge is further strengthened in his sonnet "The Golden Light" where Sri Aurobindo says that it "is a calm illumination and a flame."

> Thy golden Light came down into my heart
> Smiting my life with Thy eternity

The light comes down to his brain and brings a calm illumination. It touches the throat and song breaks out in divine tunes. It descends on his heart and the heart turns into a temple where all its passions point only to the divine light. It finally comes down into his feet and the entire earth becomes the playfield of God. Image after image in this poem describes the vision of the poet in an awe-inspiring way.

"Light" is another sonnet in which Sri Aurobindo says that life's ignorant gulfs give up their secrecies at once as soon as the Light of Divine Knowledge touches them. The Divine Light opens the mysterious doors of the holy land:

> Light in its rapture leaping through the nerves!

> Light, brooding Light! Each smitten passionate cell
> In a mute blaze of ecstasy preserves
> A living sense of the Imperishable. ("Light")

The poet exclaims ecstatically,

> I move in an ocean of stupendous Light
> Joining my depths to His eternal height. ("Light")

The depth of the poet's conscious being rises to the height of God's grandeur with this light. "O Pall of Black Night" though short gives an equally strong image of Night painted with still gold stars. But this night is not a permanent feature.

> Then slumber shall come swinging the unseen
> Gates, and to lands guarded by a screen
> Of strange light. ("O Pall of Black Night")

And this light sets the human soul free and man then reaches the white light of eternity.

> Set free my soul charioted in a swift dream,
> From earth slipping into the unknown gleam,
> The Ray white. ("O Pall of Black Night")

The light becomes a strong lightning in the poem "A Strong Son of Lightning." The "strong son" comes down with swift feet of fire and splendidly engulfs the entire human frame. Then it will be like

> All the Gods in a mortal body dwelt bore a single name. . . .
> Man's soul was again a bright charioteer of days
> hired by God's impetuous bold,
> Hurled by one of His storm-winged ways, a shaft aimed
> at heights sublime. ("A Strong Son of Lightning")

The old grandeur returns to man. He rises to sublime heights and his white existence changes and

> Divine voices spoke on man's lips, the heart woke to white dawns of gleaning wonder,
> Air a robe of splendor, breath of joy, life a Godlike game.
> ("A Strong Son of Lightning")

The symbol here is more complicated and suggestion is deeper than in the earlier poems. Thus Light and darkness and the related symbols of dawn and night present a unified and single pattern as one clearly sees an advancement in the depth and intensity of the symbols as the meaning unfolds in poem after poem and Light dawns upon the dark abyss of the human mind and illumines it.

Like the lyre of Light, Sri Aurobindo also speaks of the lyre of music. The entire cosmos with all its diverse notes has always one rhythm. A day will come when it will resolve all the discordant notes into perfect harmony and the Nature will be filled with 'strange felicity' as this celestial Music draws nearer.

> Nearer and nearer now the music draws,
> Life shudders with a strange felicity;
> All nature is a wide enamoured pause
> Hoping her lord to touch, to clasp, to be.
> For this one moment lived the ages past;
> The world now throbs fulfilled in me at last. ("Krishna")

God's lyre is the harmony of the supramental consciousness which by its descent will evolve the concealed harmony of the aspiring earth. As Sri Krishna's flute releases the melody of the earth, His touch will totally transform her being.

The beauty in every outward act or movement which is the rhythm of the world forces, implies that there must be harmony and beauty of thoughts and feelings, for thought always precedes action. The goddess of beauty is said to descend in a heart which is stainless, which has rooted out all hate, selfishness, despondency and all the gross passions. As Sri Aurobindo writes about Mahalakshmi in his treatise *The Mother*: "But all that is ugly and mean and base, all that is poor and sordid, all that is brutal and coarse repels her advent" (qtd. Agarwal 140). And in an earlier poem, "The Vedantin's Prayer," he prays for the Divine help to transcend the human frailties. The Divine Shakti always plays Her music but we are deaf to hear it. It can be heard only in the quietness of the soul.

> These clamours still;
> For I would hear the eternal voice and know

The eternal Will.
This brilliant show
Cumbering the threshold of eternity
Dispel,—bestow
The undimmed eye,
The heart grown young and clear.

The poet therefore, to be an embodiment of perfect Beauty, wishes to become pure:

Remove my sullied centuries, restore
My purity.
O hidden door
Of Knowledge, open! Strength, fulfil thyself!
Love, outpour! ("The Vedantin's Prayer")

In another poem, "Bride of the Fire" it is the beauty of Light that the poet prays to:

Beauty of the Light, surround my life

This preliminary preparation of rejecting all evil is to be made before She will descend upon us. "The ugliness of life is attributed not to God's cruelty and indifference" explains J.S. Agarwal and points out that human beings have not made themselves "fit receptacles for the divine light and beauty" (140-41). At present the 'robe of the world' though transparent is black, but on the evolution of the Supermind it will be transformed into a "raiment of gold and blue":

I shall leave my dreams in their argent air,
For in a raiment of gold and blue
There shall move on the earth embodied and fair
The living truth of you. ("A God's labour")

God cannot thrust his greatness upon man. Man has to be a good receiver first. The idea of God's injustice is therefore quite foreign to Sri Aurobindo. Milton also sought to justify the ways of God to man but his justification, says Agarwal, sounds like the intellectual pleading of a religious zealot rather than a scientific view of the relations between the transcendent and the individual (142). In his treatment of love also, Sri Aurobindo, considers it necessary for the love to be moulded into the image of the beloved before there can be a complete union. He never loses sight of the great importance of human action and endeavor which should be a means of opening ourselves to the Divine love and beauty. Thus Mahalakshmi is also represented as a shy goddess. Unlike Kali she does not force her way into the hearts of the people. She consents to abide in their hearts only when the demand of this enchanting power is met as Sri Aurobindo writes in *The Mother*:

> A Divine disgust seizes upon her and she withdraws for she is not the one who insists; or veiling her face, she waits for this bitter and poisonous devil's stuff to be rejected and disappear before she will found anew her happy influence (64).

Let us now take a glance at the scriptural background of the concept of the Supermind as Sri Aurobindo himself points out that it is not an entirely new invention of modern philosophy. As early as the Vedas, there was its vision as *Satyam Ritam Brihat* (i.e. the True, the Right, the Vast) and it was symbolized as the Sun of knowledge in the highest heaven. "But the realization of the Supermind's significance and intention, is Sri Aurobindo's contribution to spiritual experience" writes K.D. Sethna and adds that the systematic and detailed exposition of them is his contribution to philosophy (5). Sri Aurobindo however elucidates the scriptural source of his conception of the Supermind in some of his prose treatises like: *The Life Divine*, *Essays on the Gita*, *The Synthesis of Yoga*, etc., the following are a few excerpts:

In the Veda, the Supermind is the Divine consciousness as self-knowledge and creative will. As explained in *The Life Divine*, it is *Satchidananda* "not indeed in its absolute self-existence but in its action as the Lord and Creator of its won worlds" (123). Its existence, Sri Aurobindo asserts, is spoken of, though in a concealed manner, in the *Rig Veda*. There the many gods are but the powers of the Supermind, "born in it, seated in it as in their proper home" (116). The Vedic name for the Supermind is, says Sri Aurobindo, *rita-chit* or the "truth-consciousness," "which means the consciousness of essential truth of being (*satyam*), of ordered truth of active being (*ritam*) and vast self-awareness (*brihat*) in which alone this consciousness is possible" (109).

Another scriptural support of Sri Aurobindo's conception of the Supermind is undoubtedly to be found in his interpretation of the third verse of the fourteenth chapter of the *Bhagavad Gita*: "My womb is the *Mahat-Brahma*; into that I cast the seed; thence spring all beings" (*Essays on the Gita* 379-81). As Sri Aurobindo understands this verse, the *Mahat-Brahma* or "womb" of *Brahma* is the infinite "ideal-being" *Mahat* made pregnant by infinite "ideal-force" (*vijnana*) (*The Synthesis of Yoga* 553). Conscious-force (*chit-shakti*) dwelling in concentration upon its infinite existence (*sat*) generates that idea or knowledge of Being and the idea energized by Conscious-force or will is the Supermind. The idea which is the substance of the Supermind is the "Truth-consciousness" of Being, *Satchidananda*; it contains all the infinite possibilities of existence, possibilities realized in the temporal-spatial universe by ideal-force (*chit-shakti*) or the divine will. The universe is then for Sri Aurobindo ontologically 'real' being the manifestation in time and space of *Satchidananda* as the Supermind, everywhere equally present and operative, realizing universal and individual existences according to the eternal truth of Being, "In the process of cosmic creation the Supermind differentiates Existence (*sat*), Consciousness (*chit*), and Bliss (*ananda*) as three distinct principles of the Infinite establishing a trinity of the indivisible unity of *Brahma*, and manifests the many and various self-determinations of the Divine, *Isvara*, *atma*, *purusha*, *shakti*, *maya*, *prakriti*" (*The Life Divine* 120 qtd. Sullivan 208-09).

Thus based on Scriptural knowledge, Sri Aurobindo's *Yoga* aims for an inner self-development by which, each one who follows it can in time discover the One Self in all and evolve a higher consciousness than the mental, a spiritual and supramental consciousness which will transform and divinise human nature.

4.3 Poems on Evolution

Sri Aurobindo's The Life Divine is an exposition of his metaphysical vision of evolution, which has been laid down by the ancient Indian scriptures. In this prose treatise, he explains at length that if the *Brahma* is involved in matter, then Its attributes of *Sat*, *Chit* and *Ananda* are also involved or hidden in matter. Each level of evolution progressively reveals the nature of *Brahma*; that is, each evolutionary level—from matter to plants to animals to human beings and ultimately to supramental being—expresses more and more the qualities of *Sat*, *Chit* and *Ananda*. The *Rig Veda*, appears to be the foundational text of not just the concept of evolution but also its poetic expression by Sri Aurobindo. To quote a few lines from The Secret of Veda,

> Our sacrifice is a journey, pilgrimage and a battle, a travel towards the Gods and we also make that journey with Agni, the inner flame, as our path-finder and leader. Our human beings are raised up by the mystic Fire into the immortal being, into the Great Heaven, and the things divine come down to us (Arya: 5 Ch. IV qtd. Agarwal 188).
> Sri Aurobindo

Evolution is the movement which is the reverse of the movement of Involution or creation. Because the Spirit in creation has involved itself in Matter, Life and Mind, therefore Matter, Life and Mind feel an impulse to rise to their source. Madhusudhan Reddy aptly calls this tendency for evolution 'a sort of home-sickness of the Spirit' in his article "Sri Aurobindo's Philosophy" (21). Sri Aurobindo presents these dual movements in a pictorial and graphical manner in his poems, which trace the sequential steps in evolution. The progress in evolution has been studied under four categories in this section, which correspond to four levels in evolution: 1) Nature's steps, 2) Freedom from desire, 3) Voyage to the other shore, and 4) The flight of the bird. In the following poems, we find a chronological course in the sketch of evolution.

If one watches the steps of Nature, one finds that all existence is a movement from inconscience to superconscience. At first there was only sea of force "huge somnambulist Intelligence" which was in an inconscient sleep and therefore without any forms.

> Out of a seeming void and dark winged sleep
> Of dim inconscient infinity

A power arose from the insentient's deep,
A flame-whirl of magician Energy.

Some huge somnambulist Intelligence
Devising without thought process and plan
Arrayed the burning stars' magnificence,
The living bodies of beasts and the brain of man. ("The Inconscient")

Having evolved matter, life and mind now the aim of nature is to take us from the lower world of matter, life and mind to the superconscious. This evolutionary movement of nature is imaged in the poetry of Sri Aurobindo as a huge Serpent:

It rises from the dim inconscient deep
Upcoiling through the minds and hearts of men,
Then touches on some height of luminous sleep
The bliss and splendour of the eternal plane. ("The Witness Spirit")

Man's life is a journey from the netherworld of darkness i.e. *Dityahood* to the immortality of *Aditihood*, from 'Matter's sleep' to the 'Spirit's Light.'

And man but a half-dark half-luminous sign
Of the transition of the veiled Divine
From Matter's sleep and the tormented load
Of ignorant life and death to the Spirit's light. ("Evolution")

This process of evolution is completed in the course of three steps: 1. bodily life which is the basis of our existence here in the material world, 2. a mental life into which we raise the body to higher uses and enlarge it into a greater completeness and 3. a divine existence which is at once the goal of the other two and returns upon them to liberate them into their highest possibilities. In the *Rig Veda* these are spoken of as the three strides of Vishnu who has gone aboard triply extending in the superconscient bliss (comprising of triple heaven *trin'i rochana*—the three luminous summits of *sat*, *chit* and *ananda*) in the heaven of mind, in the earth of the physical consciousness: "Of Vishnu, now I declare the mighty works, who has measured out the earthly worlds and that higher seat of self-accomplishing. He supports the wide-moving, in the threefold steps his universal movement" ("Hymn to Vishnu,"

Hymn of Dirghatmas Auchitya, qtd. Agarwal 188-89). The first two steps result in the creation of the lower world. Nature's aim is to lead man to the highest step, the summit which is the abode of the transcendent. The *Rig Veda* further says "three times, Vishnu paced and set his step uplifted out of the primal dust; three steps he has paced, the Guardian, the Invincible and from beyond He upholds their laws. Scan the workings of Vishnu and see from whence He has manifested their laws. That is His highest which is seen ever by the seers like an eye extended in heaven, that is illumined, the awakened kindle into a blaze, even Vishnu's supreme step" (1.22, 17-21 trans. Harshananda.2000: 5).

Sri Aurobindo seems to have identified the Supreme God Vishnu of the *Rig Veda* with cosmic force of evolution and His paces with steps or the rhythms of Nature.

> I have seen the vision of a happier fate
> Brightening thy form.
> Confident of His grace, expect His will;
> Let Him lead; though hidden be the bourne,
> See Him in all that happens; that fulfil
> For which thou wert born. ("To R—on her Birthday")

'He' essentially signifies the transcendent Supreme which can be denoted equally well by names of Vishnu or of Shiva (also known as Rudra). As Sri Aurobindo points out in his commentary on Hymn to Vishnu in *The Secret of the Veda* that the description of Vishnu in this language "He is like a terrible lion that ranges in the difficult places, yea, His lair is on the mountain tops" hints at His essential identity with the terrible Rudra (qtd. Agarwal 188-89). Man raised to that above is uplifted from the alloying taints and storms of the lower world and released from his bondage. For this reason Lord Shiva is hailed as:

> Majestic, mild, immortally august,
> In silence throned, to just and to unjust
> One Lord of deep unutterable love,
> I saw Him, Shiva, like a brooding dove
> Close-winged upon her nest. ("Epiphany")

Man living in the lower world is fettered by the triple chains of body, life, and mind but Lord Shiva is 'fetterless.'

> The God of Wrath, the God of Love are one,
> Nor least He loves when most He smites. ("Epiphany")

A true comprehension of God's plan of creation and destruction frees man from the fear of death. Once freed from this primal fear he can behold both Shiva and Rudra in a single form. Becoming this united Supreme is the final destination of man's evolution:

> Then freed from mortal breath
> He feels the joy of the immortal play;
> Grief, pain, resentment, terror pass away.
> He too grows Rudra fierce, august and dire,
> And Shiva, sweet fulfiller of desire. ("Epiphany")

The *Rig Veda* refers to the all-pervading God freely as Indra, Upendra, Shiva, Rudra, and occasionally as Viṣhnu. The kinetic aspect or Power of God, especially with reference to Shiva is known as Shakti. Freedom from desire is a necessary condition for allowing this kinetic aspect to work from within. The Divine Shakti or the cosmic force of evolution is leading all to the goal, the summit of evolution but this becomes swift only when we identify ourselves with Her consciousness, follow Her footsteps instead of stumbling in the dark pits of our egoistic desires. For this reason the poet expresses his wish in "Musa Spiritus" thus:

> Let my heart-beats measure the footsteps of God.

Shakti or the "World-Mother" as Sri Aurobindo prefers to address, awaits such an aspiration to awaken in man so as to lead him further in the evolution. The poem, "The Stone Goddess" unveils Her ways:

> The great World-Mother and her mighty will
> Inhabited the earth's abysmal sleep, . . .
> Hiding until our soul has seen, has heard
> The secret of her strange embodiment

The transformation needed in a man's ordinary life is best expressed in the poem "Transformation":

> My breath runs in a subtle rhythmic stream.

This breath is not physical breath but *prana* the nervous and vital energy which carries forward all our action. It is imaged as being yoked like a horse to the chariot of our body and mind. It is ever moving forward and is led by the divine consciousness who is the charioteer.

> My thoughts for the tramp of His great steads' course.
> 'My acts for the grooves of His chariot-race.' ("Musa Spiritus")

In the *Gita* also Lord Krishna as the charioteer of Arjuna symbolizes the *Shakti* of the *Purushottama* leading the human soul from the lower world to the supramental bliss. He is 'Time's charioteer' Who ever wheels on 'the children of time' to the summit of immortality. In the *Rig Veda* also, as Sri Aurobindo points out in his commentary on the "Hymn to Vishnu," He is spoken of as "the violent one who leads the upward evolution of the conscious being; His force battles against all evil, smites the sinner and the enemy; intolerant of defect and stumbling He is the most terrible of the gods, the one of whom alone the Vedic Rishis have any real fear" ("Selected Hymns" *Arya*: June 1915: 670). The same idea is suggested in "Rose of God."

> Rose of God, damask force of infinity, red iron of might,
> Rose of Power with thy halo piercing the night!

The life of ordinary consciousness in the lower world of body, life and mind is man's dream. He is fully awakened only when the charioteer leads him to the superconscious. The steps of dawn, said to have been heard by the waking ear of Nature, (*Savitri* I-1) are symbolical of the footfalls of the unborn power i.e. Shakti, who will build new luminous reality upon the earth when Nature will be roused from her inconscient sleep of darkness and the dreams built by life and mind. This idea which celebrates the emergence of Superman, is expressed in the following lines:

> A might no human will nor force can gain,
> A knowledge seated in eternity,
> A bliss beyond our struggle and our pain
> Are the high pinnacles of our destiny. ("Evolution")

The poet envisions a bright future for the mankind, i.e. through the appearance of Superman. He exhorts his fellow humans to aim and work for such an Ascent:

> O Thou who climbest to mind from the dull stone,
> Face now the miracled summits still unwon. ("Evolution")

This movement is also visualized as a voyage across the stormy sea of the lower hemisphere, from the one shore of the inconscient to the other shore of the supramental truth. The stormy sea is a metaphor for the challenging world, an essential route to immortality, which should not be escaped:

> On the safe land
> To linger is to lose what God has planned
> For man's wide soul,
> Who set eternal godhead for its goal. ("To the Sea")

The mysteried shore is the "harbour home," the dawn of infinite light as the poet sings in "Moon of Two Hemispheres":

> The illumined star-thought sloops leading
> To the Dawn, their harbour home, to the Light unsealed.
> ("Moon of Two Hemispheres")

The other shore is also distinguished by its absence of sorrow.

> But now I listen to a greater Word
> Born from the mute unseen omniscient Ray:
> The Voice that only Silence' ear has heard
> Leaps missioned from an eternal glory of Day.
>
> All turns from a wideness and unbroken peace
> To a tumult of joy in a sea of wide release.
> ("The Word of the Silence")

Referred to as "An Everlastingness cut off from time" in *Savitri* III-1, the human evolution at present is in the mid-voyage and therefore one cannot see the lofty coast ahead though perpetually moving towards it.

> I strain my eyes but cannot see
> The lofty coasts ahead,
> But still behold waves' sapphire glee

And the sky with ocean wed. ("Mid-voyage")

It is the nameless coast which has not been reached by anyone, so far:

Hosting billows glide to shore-
Waves that break in phantom thunders,
Sands which feel no footprint-score. ("Moon-Script")

But though unseen by anyone, its echoes always flee to us on the sea. God is the captain who is steering the human vessel towards the shore. As Sri Aurobindo writes in "To R—on her birthday":

We, too, by the Eternal Might are led
To whatsoever goal He wills.
Our helm He grasps, our generous sail outspread
His strong breath fills.

Man should not fear the violent storms for the captain is always leading him and the latter is destined to reach his goal.

Rejoice and fear not for the waves that swell,
The storms that thunder, winds that sweep;
Always our captain holds the rudder well,
He does not sleep.

Many poets have imagined life as a journey but the object of most of them in showing the flux or march of life is primarily to point out the transitoriness and evanescent nature of worldly life; and "if they have given significance to this foaming sea as a progression towards a goal, they have envisaged that goal as something afar from this world. The representation of this movement primarily as a process of evolution, which will ultimately lead to the establishment of that true home upon earth has been beyond their range of vision," opines Agarwal (194). Sri Aurobindo has a different idea of that goal, as he writes in his commentary on *Isha Upanishad* (34):

> The idea of purpose, of a goal is born of the progressive self-unfolding by the world of its own true nature to the individual. Souls inhabiting its forms; for the being is gradually self revealed within its own becomings, real unity emerges out of Multiplicity and changes entirely the values of the latter to our consciousness.

Wordsworth speaks of this true home: 'Trailing clouds of glory do we come from God who is our home,' but to him life is a process of retardation, a forgetting, a turning further and further away from that true infinite light. The earthly life with its pleasures instead of serving to take man nearer to his goal and of evolving the concealed Godhead in him, his divine potentialities, serves only to make him forget the glories he has known. Sri Aurobindo on the other hand, points out the movement of life not as a process of fall but that of progression towards the true home, i.e. the vastness (*Brihat*). All human beings have an inherent urge, an aspiration consciously or subconsciously to move towards it.

> Amid the hundreds thronging Ocean's floor
> A wave upon the crowded sea
> With regular rhythm pushing towards the shore
> Our life must be.
> The power that moves it is the ocean's force
> Invincible, eternal, free,
> And by that it pursues its course
> Inevitably. ("To R—on her birthday")

A mightier force, *Shakti* produces and supports human upward aspiration. And such a higher state is to be attained not after death in some remote heaven away from this world, but, on this very earth. "Moreover in other poets the nature of that movement has not been fully analysed. They have only broadly and vaguely figured the entire life as a movement but have not analysed the complexity of the self-unfolding of consciousness in its cosmic action" opines Agarwal and adds that "Sri Aurobindo has visualized seven forms or grades of conscious activity descending from pure Being to physical being, the seven powers of *chit*" (194). The seven powers of *chit* are imaged by these *Vedic Rishis* as the seven rivers or "Currents flowing into or rising out of the general sea of consciousness in the human being, *Hrdaya Samudra*, Ocean of the heart." (*Rig Veda* IV 58.5 qtd. Harshananda. 2000: 3). Satprem (Bernard Enginger), an ardent disciple of Sri Aurobindo and the Mother, explains that "Poetry is the most convenient means of conveying what these higher planes of consciousness are: in a poem's rhythm we can easily perceive their vibrations" (204). Of the three movements of the lower hemisphere of which the human beings are habitually aware, Mind, Life and Body, have been imaged in Sri Aurobindo's poetry not only as movement of body and life but also mind. For example in his poem "Moon of the Two Hemispheres" mind is imaged as a moonship sailing in the ocean of our spirit's skies:

> A gold moon-ship sails or drifts ever
> In our spirit's skies and halts never, blue-keeled,
>
> ("Moon of the Two Hemispheres")

which will one day reach the day-break port, the Dawn. A similar image with only a substitution of a car for a ship is used in the *Rig Veda* where the *Rishi* prays to the dawn to "shine out immortal in thy car of happy light" for the word used for the car of happy light is *Chandra Rath*. The word *Chandra* which means the moon suggests that the moon is a chariot. Moreover like the word 'golden' in Sri Aurobindo's poem used in description of the moon-ship, in the *Vedic* verse also the colour of the horses, the figures of nervous forces, is golden, a symbol of luminous knowledge.

"May steeds well-guided bear thee here who are golden-brilliant of hue and wide their might." This horse and car occur again in "The hymn to the *Acwins*, Lord of Bliss" (IV. 45) "Full of honey upward rise-the delights; upward horses and cars in the wide-shinings of the Dawn and they shall roll aside the veil of darkness that encompassed on every side and they extend the lower world into a shining form like that of the luminous heaven (qtd. Agarwal 188-196).

The mind of which Sri Aurobindo speaks here is not the sense-mind but the intuitive mind for, mind or the *manas* has four grades: sense, sensational, emotional and aesthetic; pure intellect and Divine intelligence or intuitive reason which in the Veda are called the *tri-rochas*.

The flight of the bird represents the ascent in evolution. The swiftness of evolutionary movement depends upon the chariot. The body cannot be as swift as the mind. Similarly the spirit has a greater velocity than the mind, though the driver of all the means of conveyance is the same Divine Shakti. Just as labouring gallop of the Life-energy is expressed by the symbol of a horse, similarly the swift flight of the spirit liberated is symbolized by the wide-winged bird. As Sri Aurobindo writes in *The Secret of the Veda*:

> The bird in Veda is the symbol, very frequently of the soul liberated and upsoaring, at other times of energies so liberated and upsoaring, winging upwards towards the height of our being, winging widely with a free flight, no longer involved in the ordinary limited movement or the labouring gallop of the life-energy, the Horse, *Acwa* (560).

The human soul is in itself silent and free as he addresses the bird of fire,

> Angel, here unto me
> Bringest thou for travailing earth a spirit silent. ("The Bird of Fire")

But at the present stage of evolution, the soul being imprisoned in the cage of body, life and mind it is not able to fly. Though a monarch without whom nothing can be done, yet it is only a secret witness which allows the ministers—the body and life and mind to rule and does not itself control our being and life. As the poet writes in *The Life Divine*, "The true central being is the soul, but this being stands back and in most human natures is only the secret witness or, one might say, a constitutional ruler who allows his ministers to rule for him, delegates to them his empire, silently assents to their decisions and only now and then puts in a word which they can at any moment override and act otherwise" (1: 741).

> Who art thou in the heart comrade of man who sitst
> August, watching his works, watching his joys and griefs,
> Unmoved, careless of pain, careless of death and fate?
> Witness, what hast thou seen watching this great blind world,
> Moving helpless in Time, whirled on the wheel in Space,
> That yet thou with thy vast Will biddest toil our hearts,
> Mystic,—for without thee nothing can last in Time?
>
> ("The Witness and the Wheel")

Human life and mind can be lifted up into glory only when this true monarch, the soul comes forward and takes up the reins of government. For this reason the poet asks the soul to wake up from its darkness and recover its luster:

> Soul in the Ignorance, wake from its stupor.
> Flake of the world-fire, spark of Divinity,
> Lift up thy mind and thy heart into glory.
> Sun in the darkness, recover thy lustre. ("Soul in the Ignorance")

The poet calls this the "psychic transformation." Originally the soul came from the timeless. It is a spark or nucleus of the world-fire-consciousness, thrown into matter. Its growth or evolves behind the veil through the movements of body, life and mind; this is figured as the flight of a bird. The bird in its evolutionary flight has not yet reached its last term—the Supermind, which will evolve of the mind.

> One strange leap of thy mystic stress breaking the barriers of mind
> And life, arrives at its luminous term thy flight;
> Invading the secret clasp of the Silence and crimson Fire
> Thou frontest eyes in a Timeless Face. ("The Bird of Fire")

The word 'fire' used in association with the bird suggests its symbolic meaning. It is the flake of the world-fire, the Divine consciousness, fire being a symbol of the Divine will force. The Divine birthplace of that fire from which these sparks have been thrown is the *Mahat*—the unobstructed vastness where the Truth is born, the showless infinite. 'The sun face infinite,' is the home in which *Agni* takes his natural seat, and therefore the luminous term of the bird's flight. The first four lines of the poem "The Bird of Fire" describe the descent of the soul from its home.

> Gold-white wings athrob in the vastness, the bird of flame went
> Glimmering over a sunfire curve to the haze of the west,
> Skimming, a messenger sail, the sapphire-summer waste of a
> Soundless wayless burning sea.

Being involved in the darkness of the west, the inert soundless matter, the original lustre of the eastern sun is set and therefore on descent it is 'a sun in darkness' but as it begins to grow in matter and then in life, its original lustre, the colour and splendor of eternity begin to return. The next four lines describe this ascent from matter:

> Now in the eve of the waning world the colour and splendor returning drift
> Through a blue-flicker air back to my breast,
> Flame and shimmer staining the rapture-white
> Foam-west of the waters of Eternity.

The soul's complete lustre will be recovered when it arrives at the last term of its flight, i.e. the Supermind. The home being the sun of the supramental truth, its true nature is not ignorance but infinite wisdom. Nothing is hidden from its eyes. As the poet says,

> O marvel bird with burning wings of
> Light and the unbarred lids that look beyond all space.

Or again in another poem "The Blue Bird,"

> Nothing is hid from my burning heart;
> My mind is shoreless and still.

The Spirit has descended into the lowest particle of matter; therefore matter seeks to evolve into something higher than itself i.e. the mind. Similarly there is a descent of the Spirit into the mind, and consequently the mind must ascend into something higher than itself, namely, the Supermind. The highest principle so far evolved is the mind. But according to Sri Aurobindo's philosophy, evolution cannot stop with the mind for the mind is not its last destination. It must move further up and come to the next stage, namely, the Supermind. But when it does so, there will be a radical change in the nature of the world, for with the emergence of the Supermind, the process of evolution becomes a process through knowledge, the previous process being through ignorance. Such, in brief, is Sri Aurobindo's "optimistic scheme of evolution" hails V. Madhusudhan Reddy (21).

Here is a brief survey of the scriptural background of Evolution or Ascent and Involution or Descent (Involution of Spirit into Matter resulting in creation), especially in the Veda and the Upanishads. In the *Rig Veda*, the idea of evolution plays a very important part. In the tenth *Mandala* of this Veda the theory of evolution takes a definite shape, and what is of even greater significance, evolution is connected with involution. Thus, in the Purusha Sukta, it is stated, "The thousand-headed, thousand-eyed and thousand-footed *Purusha* covered the earth on all sides, and stretched ten fingers length beyond it. The *Purusha* was all that is and all that will be, ruling over immortality he was all that grows by food. Such was his greatness; and the *Purusha* was greater still; this whole world is a fourth of him, three-fourths are immortal in the sky." These verses make two things clear: first, that the *Purusha* or the Supreme Being involved himself in the world, resulting in the creation of the world, secondly, that this involution did not cover the whole of his Being but that ten fingers length of his remained uninvolved, that even with regard to the portion which has been involved, only one-fourth has appeared in the world, the rest remaining in the region of the sky. That is to say, three-fourths of him are yet to evolve. This view of involution and evolution has much in common with Sri Aurobindo's view of them. The monistic view in the theory of evolution is elaborately propounded in the Nasadiya Sukta of the *Rig Veda*. By way of illustration two parts of the *Suktas* are given below in English translation:

> There was then neither what is nor what is not, there was no sky, nor the heaven which is beyond. What covered? Where was it, and in whose shelter? Was the water the deep abyss (in which it lay)?
>
> There was no death, hence was there nothing immortal. There was no light (distinction) between night and day. That One breathed by itself without breath, other than it there has been nothing (qtd. Srivastava16).

We find in these and other hymns a most advanced representation of the theory of creation. The *Nasadiya* hymns are the highest intuitive vision of the Vedic sages. The steps of creation in the hymns have been stated in modern terms by S. Radhakrishnan in his treatise *Indian Philosophy*, as (i) the Highest Absolute, (ii) the bare self-consciousness and (iii) the self-projection of self-consciousness out of sheer delight (*Ananda*) as a pure *lila* without any logical necessity, thereby giving rise to a world of multiplicity (1: 103).

The Vedas believe in the real creation of the cosmos by the transformation of some parts of the Absolute by Its force of *Tapas*. They do not support the view that the world is illusory and unreal. For the sages the world is real, the evolution is real and all the created things of the universe are the real creations of the Absolute. The word "*maya*," wherever has it been used, signifies the dynamic creative force of the Absolute. As S. Radhakrishnan says, "We see clearly that there is no basis for any conception of the unreality of the world in the hymns of the *Rig Veda*. The world is not a purposeless phantasm, but it is just the evolution of God. Wherever the word *maya* occurs, it is used only to signify the might or the power, e.g., "Indra takes many shapes quickly by his *maya*" (*Rig Veda* V: 47,18 qtd. Radhakrishnan 103). Two essential and notable features can be observed in the Vedic hymns. Firstly, it is the Absolute which creates the cosmos out of Its own being. The cosmos represents only Its lower nature. As stated in the *Purusha Sukta*, only Its one-fourth evolution is a process of the self-revelation of the unmanifested nature of the Absolute. Secondly, the cosmos is a real creation of the Absolute by Its force of Tapas, *Maya* being conceived as the creative power of the Absolute. The universe is real and its evolution manifests Its Divine nature.

Now the conception of Evolution in the Upanishads. *Brahman* is the material as well as the efficient cause of the world. The *Taittiriya Upanishad* says, 'He desired, 'May I Procreate myself' The *Chandogya Upanishad* also declares, "It thought: 'Would that I were many. Let me procreate myself,' and then describes the emergence of fire, water and food in succession" (Trans. Harshananda. 1998: 39, 67). The dynamic Absolute creates the world out of Itself and reveals Its nature successively in various forms of existence. The Upanishads speak of the gradual revelation of the true nature of the Real to us. The Absolute is identified first with the lowest form of matter, then with the hierarchy of principles and finally with the supremely real *Brahman* in Its complete manifestation.

In the *Taittiriya Upanishad*, Bhrigu realizes the Absolute gradually as matter, life, mind, *Vijnana* and *Ananda*. The highest form of the Absolute is *Ananda* whereas matter, life, mind and *Vijnana* are his lower forms. The Absolute is implicit in Its lower forms and gradually becomes more and more explicit in Its higher forms. In *Ananda* It has Its perfect manifestation. Swami Harshananda, who has translated the above mentioned Upanishads into English, explains that "the material elements, the vegetative kingdom and the human society are all the parts of the Absolute and are looked upon as possessing different degrees of reality" (1998: 39). As life develops, consciousness emerges. But the principle of mind can express the nature of the Absolute only partially since it is limited, ignorant and weak. The Absolute manifests in a higher principle than mind, viz., *Vijnana* or the Supermind or Supraconscious reality. But It has Its full expression in the *Ananda* or Absolute Delight. All the successive grades of realities spring up or evolve in an emergent way. The emergent view of evolution is explicit in the Upanishadic cosmogony.

The Upanishads do not suggest the illusory nature of the world. They clearly state that *Brahman* manifests successively in different principles of being. We find real growth and creative evolution within the Absolute. Different types of lower and higher beings of the finite universe are the real forms of the Absolute. It is the Absolute which is the ground of all evolution and developments in the world. We find a real development in the world, an order and gradual ascent. The ways of nature are not to dwell in haphazard movements or create chaos and confusion but raise itself towards the Divine. Radhakrishnan remarks, "All that the Upanishads urge is that the process of time finds its basis and significance in an absolute which is essentially timeless. For real progress this conception of the absolute is necessary. Without this all-comprehending absolute we cannot be certain that the flux of the universe is an evolution, that change is progress, and that the end of the world is the triumph of the good. The absolute guarantees that the process of the world is not chaotic but ordered, that the development is not haphazard or the result of chance variations" (qtd. Srivastava16).

The Upanishads never say that *Brahman* excludes the finites, a point well emphasized in the philosophy of Sri Aurobindo. When it is emphasized in the Upanishads, that *Brahman* is the sole reality, it is always added that the world is in *Brahman* and is derived from It, and hence it has the reality of *Brahman*. As the *Chandogya Upanishad* says, "The finite is in the Infinite. This Atman is the entire universe" (Harshananda. 1998: 60).

4.4 Poems on Transformation

Sri Aurobindo's philosophy starts with a review of what Man has achieved so far in the course of evolution of the spiritual being. According to Sri Aurobindo, the supramental consciousness and Force reveal to the mind, life and body, their secret divinity or the spiritual truth that is involved in them, gift to them the perfect power and knowledge of Supramental Existence. Thus the descent of the Gnostic or Supramental Light brings about a complete or radical transformation of the ignorance in any part of being which is "completely surfaced with the Light of the Supermind," explains S.S. Antarkar in his article: "Sri Aurobindo and Spiritual Evolution: Man to Superman" (44). Thus the evolution process reaches the highest point when the new race of Gnostic beings is established on earth. The poems which envision supramental transformation have been studied in this section in the following three parts for better understanding: Nature in waiting, Transformation of the body, and The refusal of the ascetic.

Nature is yet to receive the supernal light. The present Man gets flashes of intuitive knowledge "transmitted from the sun of supramental truth-consciousness on the summits" writes Jagdish Saran Agarwal and explains that this knowledge is experienced by the seers and sages whose eyes are awakened and whose spirit listens or who have the supramental faculties of direct truth-vision and truth-audition called in Veda as *drishti* and *sruti*. The moments are so intense that they are "with all eternity packed." But such gleams are fleeting. That 'glimmer from Eternity's face' does not settle permanently in our earthly consciousness (290-316). It waits only for a moment and then wanders and passes away, as Sri Aurobindo points out in his poem, "In Horis Aeternum" which is written in new metre. About the poem, Sri Aurobindo writes in a letter, "'In Horis Aeternum' was meant as a first essay in this kind, a very simple and elementary model. The line here is cast into three parts, the first containing two stresses, the second and third each admitting three, four such lines rhymed constituting the stanza" (*Collected Poems* 581).

> Something that waits, something that wanders and settles not, a
> Nothing that was all and is found. "In Horis Aeternum"

A constant living in that supramental consciousness is possible only when one has reached the sun-peaks, says the poet. Nature at present is waiting for the descent of the supreme light:

> All waits hushed for the fiat to come and the tread of the Eternal;
> Passion of a bliss yet to be sweeps form Infinity's sea.
> ("Trance of Waiting")

for the concealed splendor of the earth behind her inconscient darkness will be wakened only "when God's stillness / Heavens the ocean of moveless Nature" ("Jivanmukta") "Space is a stillness of God building his earthly abode" ("Trance of Waiting"). The aim of all her (the nature's) labour and sorrow on the surface is to give birth to the child of 'bliss yet to be that is in her womb.' The voice of the Divine affirms, "I have laboured and suffered in Matter's night—To bring the fire to man" ("A God's Labour"). Several of his poems celebrate the bright future for the earth evolution which Sri Aurobindo foresees. For example, in "Trance of Waiting," he envisions the earth thus:

> Earth is now girdled with trance and Heaven is put round her for
> vesture.
> Wings that are brilliant with fate sleep at Eternity's gate.

The poet in his *Yogic* vision has seen that the time is now approaching when that Divine Grace will descend upon earth. A short poem, "Journey's End," written in new metre, reflects such a vision. As the footnote of the poem indicates, lines: 1, 2, 4 are epitrite, third paeon, trochee. In line 3, two double trochees occur (*Collected Poems* 570).

> The day ends lost in a stretch of even,
> A long road trod—and the little farther.
> Now the waste land, now the silence;
> A blank dark wall, and behind it heaven. ("Journey's End")

Sri Aurobindo does not suppose that the kingdom of heaven can be established upon the earth by an individual's own effort, by religious emotion and moral purification. This can only be possible by the supramental descent, as he writes in a letter written to one of his disciples:

> Unless there is a descent of a new Power of consciousness, not subject to the dualities but still dynamic which will provide a new foundation and a lifting of the centre of consciousness, above the mind, the kingdom of God on earth can only be an ideal, not a fact realized in the general earth-consciousness and earth-life." (*Future Poetry: Letters* 39).

What is required of man is only to open himself to that Light to make the necessary preparation for Its advent, so that when It chooses to descend It may find a suitable soil for Its working, a proper recipient of Its light and may not be denied entry when It comes. And the human preparation is to aspire for the Divine descent. Hence, Sri Aurobindo exhorts:

> Make thy knowledge too high for thought, thy joy too deep for emotion;
> At rest in the unchanging Light, mute with the wordless self-vision.
> ("Ascent: The Silence")

The poem, "Ascent" written in new metre, is presented in two sections: 1. "Ascent: The Silence" and 2. "Ascent: Beyond the Silence." While the first section like the conventional scriptures, exhorts the soul to seek its liberation by escaping "from the clutch of Nature," the second section is typically Aurobindonean in its message which urges the seeker to "Rise with the world in thy bosom." As pointed out in the footnote of the poem, "Ascent" is a free quantitative verse with a predominant dactylic movement (*Collected Poems* 567).

Man has to become conscious of the divinity that is in him and act and live only for the growth of the soul. Although Its advent is sure, It is destined to arrive only "when a mightier soul is created." The psychic and spiritual transformation must precede the supramental descent, as the poet writes:

> But before the supramental change can begin, the veil between the subliminal and the surface parts must have been already broken down; the influx, the descent will be in the entire consciousness as a whole, it will not take place partly behind a veil; the process will be no longer a concealed, obscure and ambiguous procedure but an open outflowering consciously felt and followed by the whole being in its transmutation. (*The Life Divine* 823)

It may be argued that if the individual cannot by his own effort cause the Divine Grace to descend then why should there be individual effort? Such a view seems to be unsound because the individual's effort to rise to a higher level of existence in order to make himself fit for the reception of the Divine Light, is itself due to the Divine Grace. And also the individual ascent is a part and parcel of the collective ascent. The two phenomena cannot be dissociated from each other as two opposites antithetical to each other.

> Outclimbing the summits of Nature
> Transcending and uplifting the soul of the finite,
> Rise with the world in thy bosom,
> O word gathered into the heart of the Ineffable.
>
> ("Ascent: Beyond the Silence")

The poet's answer to the question as regards our readiness to the Divine Descent is that we are not yet prepared for it. We cannot tolerate His luminous flame in our present state. We can bear His Light only when we have sacrificed our longings:

> I have sacrificed longing and parted from grief,
> I can bear thy delight. ("Bride of the Fire")

Our heart's fire would be ready to receive Him only if

> Soul escape from the clutch of Nature.
> All thou hast seen cast from thee, O Witness.
> Turn to the Alone and the Absolute, turn to the Eternal;
> ("Ascent: The Silence")

The same idea is conveyed in another poem, "The Dream Boat." The gold god 'with his flame brow and his sun-gold body' comes to the poet in a 'boat made of dream-fire' to take him to the other shore, the eternal land of supramental felicity but 'the boat passed and the gold god vanished' as his heart's fire at that time was not ready to receive the sun-god's intolerant flame. The protagonist cherished the egoistic pleasures of the earth, and was not prepared to give them up for the sake of the Divine, he feared and therefore denied to take the 'sea-plunge':

> Hidden in the recesses of the heart something shuddered,
> It recalled all that the life's joy cherished,
> Imaged the felicity it must leave lost for ever,
> And the boat passed and the gold god vanished. ("The Dream Boat")

The magical circle of birth and rebirth has to be broken in order to ascend to Unity and immortality:

> Arise, O Spirit immortal,
> Away from the turning wheel, breaking the magical circle.
> Ascend, single and deathless. ("Ascent: The Silence")

These lines echo Swami Vivekananda's popular poem "To the Awakened India" where the poet advocates desireless action as a means to attain liberation:

> Awake, arise, and dream no more! . . .
> Be bold, and face
> The Truth! Be one with it! Let visions cease,
> Or, if you cannot, dream but truer dreams,
> Which are Eternal Love and Service Free.
> ("To the Awakened India" by Swami Vivekananda)

Sri Aurobindo indicates in several of his writings, the necessary inward changes for seeking an outward or integral transformation, which is much beyond individual salvation. Man's surrender to the

Divine must be genuine and entire, he asserts and adds that Man should ask for nothing but the Supramental Truth. Man must act and live only for the divine presence on the earth like a *jivan-mukta*, described by the poet in the following lines:

> Only to bring God's forces to waiting Nature,
> To help with wide-winged Peace her tormented labour
> And heal with joy her ancient sorrow,
> Casting down light on the inconscient darkness,
> He acts and lives. ("Jivanmukta")

The poet's vision of the future is stated explicitly in the poems like those discussed above and others like, "The Miracle of Birth," "The Lost Boat," "The Inner Fields," "One Day" "The Mother of God," "The Blue Bird," "The Rishi," "The Life Heavens," etc. . Sri Aurobindo realizes the imperfection of human existence, as he observes in *The Life Divine*:

> Man is made in God's image but there is this difference between the divine Reality and its human representative that, every thing which in the one is unlimited, spontaneous, absolute, harmonious, self-possessed becomes in the other limited, relative, laboured, discordant, deformed, possessed by struggle, kept by subservience to one's possession lost by the transience and insecurity which come from wrong holding. (822)

But this recognition of man's present imperfection on the part of the poet, instead of giving rise to a poetry of despair and resentment against God, becomes in the poet's vision the cause of his liberation and aspiration. It is in this constant imperfection that there is a craving and an aspiration towards perfection. There is something in the poet which refuses to accept the semi-obscurity of his existing life as final. Therefore there is in him an innate aspiration towards a perfectibility ever beyond itself towards the concealed harmony of the Absolute which is his ideal. As he writes:

> Let the realms of thy flight
> Be eternity. ("Life")

To the poet, what man aspires to, is the sign of what he may be. The divine discontent in Man is the surest guarantee of his higher destiny

> He rises to the good with Titan wings:
> And this the reason of his high unease
> Because he came from the infinities
> To build immortally with mortal things. ("In the Moonlight")

Sri Aurobindo's poetry is pulsating throughout with a hope of the future supermanhood brought about by the future Messiah or *Avatar* who is nothing but the divine Seer-Will of the Supermind descending upon the human consciousness to reveal to it the divine meaning behind Man's half blind action. Sri Aurobindo gives to his prophecy of the future a scientific inevitability of the evolutionary movement of nature. To quote *The Life Divine* once again:

> As there has been established on earth a mental consciousness and power which shakes a race of mental beings and takes up into itself all of earthly nature that is ready for the change, so now there will be established on earth a gnostic consciousness and power which will shape a race of gnostic spiritual beings and take up into itself all of earth-nature that is ready for this new transformation (822).

His poems are songs of rapture in a luminous vision of the golden age. Each verse glows with a prophetic fire. Consider these lines from "Kuthumi" for instance:

> For the golden age
> In Kali comes, the iron lined with gold,
> The *yoga* shall be given back to men,
> The sects shall cease, the grim debates die out
>
> And atheism perish from the earth,
> Blasted with knowledge, love and brotherhood
> And wisdom repossess Sri Krishna's world. ("Kuthumi")

Or again consider these lines from "In the Moonlight":

> The old shall perish; it shall pass away
> Expunged, annihilated, blotted out:
> *And all the iron bands that ring about*
> Man's wide expansion shall at last give way.

Freedom, God, Immortality; the three
Are one and shall be realized at length,
Love, Wisdom, Justice, Joy and utter Strength
Gather into a pure felicity.
It comes at last, the day foreseen of old
That John in Patmos saw, what Shelley dreamed,
Vision and vain imagination deemed,
The City of Delight, the Age of Gold. ("In the Moonlight")

The famous British poet of the Romantic age, Shelly records the tragedy of an idealist who meets with frustration in his "Alastor." Keats longed for an immortal world, a refuge from the world of sorrow: "Where youth grows pale and spectre thin and dies," and where?

Where Beauty cannot keep her lustrous eyes,
Nor new Love pine at them beyond to-morrow.
("Ode to a Nightingale" by Keats)

The vision of the dynamic power of love on the Supramental level is an important contribution of Sri Aurobindo to the love poetry in English literature, points out J.S. Agarwal (300).

According to Sri Aurobindo, the spiritual reforms which have been taking place since the World War-II and the great upheaval in the world today are all indications that this period of crisis is a turning point in nature's evolutionary march which will give birth to a new age. Several centers of spirituality have come up throughout India and rest of the world in recent times. Brahmakumaries' Iswariya Viswa Vidyalaya (spiritual university), Art of Living Foundation, *Ashram* institutes of *Mata* Amritanandamayee, Barsanadham, etc., besides Ramakrishna Math and Sri Aurobindo *Ashram* are spreading the light of Spiritual knowledge in the present era. In view of the current trends, the following vision of Sri Aurobindo sounds very convincing:

The Iron age is ended. Only now
The last fierce spasm of the dying past
Shall shape the nations, and when that has passed,
Earth washed of ills shall raise a fairer brow. ("In the Moonlight")

As the poet envisages, the present ignorance and chaos is likely to shatter one's faith in a bright future. To those whose view is limited to human values, 'the passion to divine manhood' staking the old and the sure 'for a prize that was never yet laid on the table' may appear to be a vain ideal, a chimera. They can never imagine man to exceed himself, as depicted in the poem, "A God's Labour," which is written in dialogue form. One voice is that of a doubting and hesitating human mind while the other is the benevolent and uplifting voice of the Divine.

> How they mock and sneer, both devils and men!
> "Thy hope is chimera's head
> painting the sky with its fiery stain;
> Thou shalt fall and thy work lie dead." ("A God's Labour")

The poet is all optimistic as he holds that the world is ever progressing "to give form to the formless" to achieve her goal of bliss. This transformation is termed as a God's labour and the long toil and the suffering of the One who labours is described thus:

> My gaping wounds are a thousand and one
> And the Titan Kings assail,
> But I cannot rest till my task is done
> And wrought the eternal will. ("A God's Labour")

It reminds one of Prometheus who brings fire to human race after a great sacrifice. In spite of the suffering and the sacrifice the work continues inspired by a voice:

> Go where none have gone!
> Dig deeper, deeper yet
> Till thou reach the grim foundation stone
> And knock at the keyless gate. ("A God's Labour")

The poet sees through falsehood, conquers the surface Gods, plunges through body's blind alleys, pierces the void and walks in the bottomless pit. Then he hears His voice, the gulf between heaven and earth is bridged and the Golden waters pour down:

> Like flames to the Kingdoms of Truth and Bliss:
> Down a gold-red stair-way wend
> The radiant children of Paradise

Clarioning darkness's end. ("A God's Labour")

The present darkness is only a pointer to new birth. As the Mother (Spiritual collaborator of Sri Aurobindo who established and ran his *Ashram*) puts it, as the dawn approaches nearer, the night becomes more and more dark. She further points out, "It matters not if there are hundreds of beings plunged in the densest ignorance. He whom we saw yesterday is on earth; his presence is enough to prove that a day will come when darkness will be transformed into light, when Thy reign shall be established in effect upon earth" (*Prayers and Meditations* 30).

The poet gives a very inspiring vision of the transformed human life, of the coming supermanhood; and he believes this to be the highest function of poetry. As he observes in *The Future Poetry*, "To embellish life with beauty is only the most outward function of art and poetry, to make life more intimately beautiful and noble and great and full of meaning is its higher office, but its highest comes when the poet becomes the seer and reveals to man his eternal self and the godheads of its manifestation" (qtd. Agarwal 302). He holds that the future poetry will largely occupy itself more and more with a prophecy of the future, the song of the growing godhead. On the descent of the Supermind all the conflict and discord of the world would change into harmony and beauty. There will be complete extinction of all pain and suffering which exists at present on account of the triple bondage of mind, life and body, as the Supramental Golden Light illumines these realms:

Thy golden light came down into my brain
And the grey rooms of mind sun-touched became
A bright reply to wisdom's occult plane,
A calm illumination and a flame. . . .
My earth is now Thy Playfield and Thy seat. ("The Golden Light")

"In the emergence of the Gnostic being," says the poet, "would lie the hope of a more harmonious evolutionary order in terrestrial Nature" (*The Life Divine* 826). The resistance of the earth's inconscience explains the failure of all the saints and, seers to establish God's light permanently upon the earth. This is due to the inert inconscient make of the bodies. Our inconscient base strongly rejects all such 'sun-thoughts.' In "A God's Labour," the poet calls this inconscient base 'the grisly Elf' which shudders from all pure things.

> For man's mind is the dupe of his animal self,
> Hoping its lusts to win,
> He harbours within him a grisly Elf
> Enamoured of sorrow and sin
> The grey Elf shudders from heaven's flame
> And from all things glad and pure,
> Only by pleasure and passion and pain
> His drama can endure.

All the efforts of man at his moral purification and the rooting out of all evil fail, because in spite of his pure and holy life, there is always some kinship with the inconscient. That is why in Sri Aurobindo's *yoga*, stress is laid not so much on the realization of God which is comparatively a very easy thing as on the transformation of our nature which according to the poet is a very difficult task and takes a long time. The poet observes thus in *The Life Divine*, "This rule of the Inconscient will disappear: for the Inconscience will be changed by the outburst of the greater secret consciousness within it, the hidden Light, into what it always was in reality, a sea of the secret superconscience. A first formation of a Gnostic consciousness and nature will be the consequence" (823). This change which is not a mere possibility but something decreed and inevitable is experienced and celebrated by the poet thus:

> I passed into a lucent still abode
> And saw as in a mirror crystalline
> An ancient Force ascending serpentine
> The unhasting spirals of the aeonic road.
> Earth was a cradle for the arriving god. . . .
> Mind liberated swam Light's ocean vast,
> And life escaped from its grey tortured line;
> I saw Matter illumining its parent Night. ("Evolution")

"The supramental change" says the poet is a thing decreed and inevitable in the evolution of the earth-consciousness, for its upward ascent is not ended and "mind is not the last summit" (*The Mother* 84).

On the supramental plane the transformation will be not only of the mind and life but also of the body. To achieve the Life Divine one need not relinquish this body. It can be found on this earth by perfecting the human might and the human race. This is the message Sri Aurobindo gives to the world. *Jnana* or knowledge can be a path to the Divine. This Divine life can be established on earth by the self-knowledge "Thou art He." Man, the lover, should be raised to God, the Goal. "Transformation" is another deeply philosophical poem in which Sri Aurobindo describes the transformation of the earth nature into Divine Nature. He feels a change coming over his body and spirit.

> Now are my illumined cells joy's flaming scheme
> And changed my thrilled and branching nerves to fine
> Channels of rapture opal and hyaline
> For the influx of the Unknown and the Supreme. ("Transformation")

The poet feels that he is no longer a vessel of flesh and that he has won over the earthly nature and sensual desires. His soul's vision widens and his body is now the living instrument of God's will. His spirit is a "vast sun of deathless light." It is the light of the Divine knowledge pervading the entire spirit.

> All my cells thrill swept by a surge of splendour
> Rigid, stone-like, fixed like a hill or statue
> Vast my body feels and upbears the world's weight.
> Dire the large descent of the Godhead enters
> Limbs that are mortal. ("Descent")

Sri Aurobindo envisages the vision of supramental transformation for the first time not only as a great possibility but an inevitable end towards which nature is constantly marching in her evolutionary course. He holds out this hope to the children of time that on the descent of the Supermind they will become deathless. He prays to 'Rose of God' to transform the body. "Transform the body of the mortal, like a sweet and magical rhyme." It does not imply a change in the external features of man but a transformation of cells. As he writes in *The Life Divine*, the gnostic individual "would feel the presence of the Divine in every centre of his consciousness, in every vibration of his life-force, in every cell of his body" (827).

> My illumined cells are joy's flaming scheme ("Transformation")

That such a 'transformation' is not an idle dream but an actuality of the perfectly organized superconscient reality is evident from these autobiographical poems of Sri Aurobindo. The poet does not like the ascetic look down upon the body as inherently evil, a bar to spiritual progress holding that God's glory is forbidden upon earth and can be achieved only when we depart from this body. The questions by men in disbelief in "A God's Labour" reflect the orthodox view:

> Who art thou that babblest of heavenly ease
> And joy and golden room
>
> To us who are waifs on inconscient seas
> And bound to life's iron doom?
> This earth is ours, a field of Night
> For our petty flickering fires.
> How shall it brook the sacred Light
> Or suffer a god's desires?

Denouncing such a refusal of the body he writes in *The Synthesis of Yoga*, "It can be, therefore, no integral *yoga* which ignores the body or makes its rejection indispensable to a perfect spirituality. Rather, the perfecting of the body also should be the last triumph of the spirit and to make the bodily life also divine must be God's final seal upon his work in the universe" (Ch. "The three steps of nature" qtd. Agarwal 313). The poet no doubt recognizes the bondage of man's soul in the meshes of the flesh as he writes in the same poem,

> Man lights his little torches of hope
> That lead to a failing edge;
> A fragment of Truth is his widest scope,
> An inn his pilgrimage. ("A God's Labour")

For this reason the poet wants that the human soul should escape from the clutches of Nature:

> When from the urge ceaseless of Nature turn
> Our souls, far from the breast casting her tool, desire.
> ("The Witness and the Wheel")

But the fact that the physical 'clouds the spirit-fire' does not point to the necessity of its annulment (a phrase used in "Builders" by Arjava, a poet among Sri Aurobindo school of poets). "The obstacle which the physical presents to the spiritual," says Sri Aurobindo in "The three steps of nature" and adds, "is no argument for the rejection of the physical for in the unseen providence of things our greatest difficulties are our best opportunities. A supreme difficulty is Nature's indication to us of a supreme conquest to be won and an ultimate problem to be solved; it is not a warning of an inextricable snare to be shunned or of an enemy too strong for us from whom we must flee." He says that in the gnostic consciousness, life and body would be no obstacles but a means for the expression of the spirit. "Life and the body would be not longer tyrannous masters demanding nine tenths of existence for their satisfaction, but means and powers for the expression of the spirit" (*The Life Divine* 941). Therefore what is required is not a rejection of matter and the body but the transformation of the inconscient into the conscient.

> The gulf twixt the depths and the heights is bridged
> And the golden waters pour
> Down the sapphire mountains rainbow-midged
> And glimmer from shore to shore. ("A God's Labour")

As against the *Sunyam* or nothingness of the nihilistic Buddhists, the unknowable, the *Turiya* or 'featureless' and 'relationless absolute' of the monistic Vedanta, attained by the negation of all this existence, the poet writes that such is not the goal of life. Beyond this is the richness of the Supermind. A little more and the doors of new life will open to a bare and bright world. That is a state of "Seer deep-hearted." He is a 'Divine king of Secrecies.' He receives the fountain of love, springing from the heart of God. He is rich with knowledge hitherto unknown to man. Words of wisdom leaped out like flame-billows. The tide of his soul washes the coasts of heaven. Thoughts from him break out burning the dark ignorance of human night and

> White star-scripts of the gods born from the presses of Light
> Page by page to the dim children of earth were given.
> ("Seer deep-hearted")

The autobiographical tones of the poem are quite obvious. The transformation and resultant seer-hood naturally fetch *Nirvana*, a state of perfect Bliss.

> All is abolished but the mute Alone.
> The mind from thought released, the heart from grief
> Grow inexistent now beyond belief. ("Nirvana")

The 'I' ness of the poet vanishes as he sings:

> Only the illimitable Permanent
> Is here. A peace stupendous, featureless, still,
> Replaces all,—what once was I, in it
> A silent unnamed emptiness content
> Either to fade in the unknowable
> Or thrill with the luminous seas of the Infinite. ("Nirvana")

The thrill that the poet experiences as this *Nirvana* sets in is stupendous and unique. Thus Sri Aurobindo's preoccupation with the intellectual application of his spiritual visions is revealed and suggested in a series of poems by such words as mind, thought, soul and spirit. They are the instruments for the attainment of God-knowledge. These poems are the stepping stones for the poet in his journey towards Superconscient realms.

Coming to the scriptural background, the Concept of Transformation is present in its seed form in the treatise of the *Bhagavad Gita*. Since Sri Aurobindo has greatly developed the concept of Transformation, several scholars and disciples of the master hold that it is his original contribution to the science of spirituality. The *Bhagavad Gita* speaks of the spiritual origin and creation of the universe and the gradual evolution and manifestation of the supreme. Creation of the universe is due to the involution of the Consciousness-Force, the *Para prakrti* into the *Apara Prakrti*. It is the *Purusottama* who creates the universe and manifests Himself in it. Evolution is a reverse process: it is the transformation of the lower nature (*Apara prakrti*) into the higher nature (*Para prakrti*). Thus in the *Gita*, the whole phenomenal universe is transformed into the higher spiritual supernature. The cosmic evolution continues incessantly till it is completely transformed into the Divine Supernature.

The *Gita* does not believe in a stagnant world. Its watchword is progress. And that is why it brings in the *Avatara* to cut the Gordian knot, when owing to the slackness of the process of evolution and the consequent decline of *Dharma*, a hitch occurs in its progress. The *Avatara* then comes with his Messianic message that the world is not to remain where it is, but that its destiny is to move forward. Not only that, but the *Avatara* also shows that there is no limit to the world's progress, for his main purpose in descending in human form is to give man an ocular demonstration that he is divine, and that until he attains divinity his destiny is not fulfilled. He gives man the assurance that He will descend from age to age (*yuge-yuge)* until man's destiny is completely fulfilled. The *Bhagavad Gita* reaffirms in its statement of *madbhavam agatah*, Sri Aurobindo's conception which holds that the descent of God into humanity, the manifestation of Godhead in human form and nature reveals the possibility of the birth of man into the Godhead and that man has the possibility of rising into the divine nature and consciousness (*Essays on the Gita* 216).

The *Avatara* helps man to ascend to such a new and divine birth. As Lord Krishna says in The *Gita*, "Delivered from liking and fear and wrath, full of me, taking refuge in me, many purified by austerity of knowledge have arrived at my nature of being" (*madbhavam*--the divine nature of the *purushottama*) (IV: 10 trans. Subba Rao167). By taking birth in human form Lord Krishna practically teaches that man is essentially Divine. The progress of the divine evolution cannot be attained by merely the preservation of *dharma* for it requires elevation and transformation of man to the Divine. Even the maintenance of *dharma* is not possible in a society that is not divine, opines R.S. Srivastava as he points out that this also needs complete divinisation of man and society (20-22).

Chapter 5

Devotional Poetry of Swami Vivekananda and Sri Aurobindo

There are many poems written by Swami Vivekananda and Sri Aurobindo, which record their religious experiences rather than their philosophical thought. Poems addressed to Shiva, Kali and Krishna of both the poets overflow with ardent adoration and devout self-surrender. The fervent longing of the devotee to reach the Divine or the yearning of the self to discover the Self mark the tone of these poems. Swami Vivekananda's "My Play is Done," "Kali the Mother," "Dance of Shiva," etc., and Sri Aurobindo's poems like "Krishna," "Shiva," "The Cosmic Dance—Dance of Krishna, Dance of Kali" are some of the fine examples of this genre. It is important to understand at the very outset that the two authors adore the Supreme Being through these forms and are therefore outside the cult perceptions and schools of devotional literature associated with these Deities.

The attributes and mythological account of these personal deities have drawn from primary and authentic scriptures—besides the established streams of devotion concerned, namely, Shaivism, Shaktism and Vaishnavism. The two poets see the omnipotent power operating in the creation, preservation and dissolution of the universe sometimes as Kali and sometimes as Shiva or as Krishna. As Vijayasree points out, even when they identify this power by name of a personal god, they only refer to the Absolute, the Formless and the Nameless *Brahma* (170). These forms only provide a concrete object for devotion allowing the emotive component of worship to thrive. Another important feature to be noted here is that even these poems which are addressed to personal deities of the poets, are not only emotive, but are under girded with the concepts of *Brahma*, the Divine essence from which all creation emanates. The themes of Involution of God, Evolution of man and Divinisation of the world radiate from Divine grace. The poetry of the two sages provides not verse for an hour, but concepts for all times. The combination of intellect and emotion, distinguished by their appropriate styles, results in powerful devotional verse. Referring to the poetic power of his disciple, Sri Ramakrishna is reported to have said:

> As the snake remains spellbound with its hood up on hearing the sweet music of the flute, so does He who is in the heart, the '*Antaryami*' when Naren (Vivekananda) sings! (*LSVEWD* 163).

5.1 The Nature of *Bhakti*

It would be interesting here to briefly analyze the nature and ontological commitments of '*bhakti*' for a better comprehension of the poems being studied. '*Bhakti*' as a means to '*mukti*' or liberation has already been discussed in the second chapter as a part of the philosophy of the *Bhagavad Gita* (refer: 2.4). '*Bhakti*,' often translated as 'devotion' includes faith, love, surrender and devotional attachment. *Bhakti* is religious orientation which is common in association with theism. "The philosophers who wrote on *bhakti* defined it as extreme love for God. Why a man should love God is the question to be solved;" wrote Swami Vivekananda in his essay, "The first steps to *Bhakti*." He arrives at an answer later in the essay:

> God Himself is the highest goal of man; see Him, enjoy Him. We can never conceive anything higher, because God is perfection (*Selections from C.W.* 37-39).

It is a dispositional state, a state which is complex in nature having different components like cognitive, emotive etc. The notion that it is purely emotive or affective is not correct. The cognitive element of the complex state is evident from the intentionality of the emotive component. That is the devotee can direct his love towards God when he has an apprehension of what God is. The resulting emotive state is also complex which evinces states of reverence, awe, dependence etc. The principal determining characteristics of *bhakti* in the light of this definition are:

- Firstly, the awe-centric character manifesting itself in the attitudes of adoration or reverence, attitudes which are correlated to the nature of the object thereof;
- Secondly, the compelling or the over whelming character as expressed in its intensity and totality;
- Thirdly, its dialectic nature, and
- Finally, the unmotivated and disinterested character.

The nature of *bhakti* is that the attachment involves awe. Attachment and awe, as it may be pointed out, interpenetrate. Awe is the sense of the majesty or the greatness of the object that is longed for. The source of the awe is the nature of the object. The object in this case is the Infinite or the Perfect being. The *bhakta* or the devotee has the sense of attachment to the Supreme Being—to the exceeding or the unsurpassable character of the object of seeking. As Santosh Chandra Sengupta elaborates, "the Perfect being can be characterized as *Brahma*: the determinate forms of *Brahma, purushottama* and *Bhagavan* being richer than the indeterminate Ultimate. It is the sense of the infinitude of the Supreme Person which is the Ultimate object of devotion, that is, the principal source of the longing or the attachment thereto." It is the same being which causes and fascinates or attracts. It follows that *bhakti* in view of this Infinite-centeredness, is Spiritual in nature. It is the divine attachment or Love (80-81).

The thesis that *bhakti* is the way of liberation connects itself with the Ontology of *bhakti*. In its fully developed form, *bhakti* is a highly articulate system which can be used to justify the tendency of many to express ultimacy in terms of intense love or devotion to a personal god. In India the doctrine of *bhakti* can be traced to the ancient scriptures, the Vedas, the Upanishads, the *Mahabharata* and the *Bhagavad Gita*. It had a development on the conditions which were natural to the growth of religious life in India and attained systematization and impact in the middle ages. Besides the *Bhagavata Puranas* and the schools of Bengal Vaishnavism, perhaps the most concise and systematic accounts of *bhakti* theology are to be found in the *Narada Bhakti Sutras* and the *Shandilya Sutras* while these are not much older than the twelfth century A.D. As Baird and Bloom observe, they articulate a religious orientation which is approximated in various degrees by other movements in India (48).

It is significant to note that the decline of Advaitavada and Buddhism in the middle ages led to a vacuum which the spiritual life in India abhorred, and was filled up in the form of revival in a systematic expression of the doctrine of *bhakti.* While followers of Shiva have had a greater tendency toward *advaitin* views than the bhaktas previously considered, there have still been those whose message was devotional and emotional rather than meditative. Shaivism agrees closely with the *Sankhya* in its dogmatics, and with the *yoga* school in its practical discipline, which are discussed in the succeeding section 5.2. The Advaita philosophy of Shankara gave a new turn to Shaivism.

The Indian poetry of the middle ages was full of the devotional fervor, brought in by these movements, like the Hindi poetry of the *Bhakti-kaala* (the era of devotional poetry). The poetry of those times with its disparate streams, adoring the forms of Sri Rama, Sri Krishna, etc., is still very popular throughout India in the form of *Bhajans* and prayers. In the poetry of Swami Vivekananda and Sri Aurobindo, Shiva, Shakti (Kali) and Krishna remain the most adored forms of the Divine.

5.2 Shiva *Bhakti* and Shiva Poems of Swami Vivekananda and Sri Aurobindo

Some significant streams and aspects of Shaivism may briefly be considered before embarking on a detailed study of Shiva poems written by the two sage-poets. Shiva, meaning "auspicious," is conceived as the lord of the *yogis*, who seek union with the world-soul by intense '*tapas*' (meditation and penance). As the great ascetic, Shiva is considered as destroyer, creator and preserver of the universe. Known as Shambhu, Shankara and Mahadeva, Shiva is also depicted as Rudra—who wears a garland of skulls and venomous serpents. On the high slopes of the Himalayan Mount Kailasa, Shiva, the great yogi, sits on a tiger skin, deep in meditation and through his meditation the world is maintained. He is depicted thus as wearing his long matted hair (*jata*) in a top-knot, in which the crescent moon is fixed, and from which also flows the sacred river Ganga. In the middle of his forehead is a third eye, emblem of his superior wisdom and insight. His neck is blue scarred by a deadly poison which was one of the objects churned out from the cosmic ocean, and which he drank to save the entire universe from destruction. Snakes, of which he is the lord, encircle his neck and arms. His body is covered with ashes, a favorite ascetic practice. A. L. Basham sums up the disposition of Shiva thus "beside him is his weapon, the trident, while near him are his beautiful consort Parvati (also known as Shakti) and his vehicle, the bull Nandi" (307). Shiva is also the lord of animals and the lord of dance. As Nataraja, his dance supports the rhythm of the universe. Powerful and creative, he is worshiped most commonly in the form of the *linga* (the phallic symbol). In the innermost heart of the Shaiva temple is the *linga*. Nandi the bull stands outside the inner sanctum, his eyes fixed on this most sacred symbol, the *linga*, which is even more commonly used than anthropomorphic representations of the deity.

Shaivism agrees closely with the *Sankhya* in its dogmatics, and with the *yoga* school in its practical discipline. The *Advaita* philosophy of Shankara gave a new turn to Shaivism. In the *Shvetashvatara* Upanishad, *bhakti* or devotion to Shiva is enjoined. The final verse of this Upanishad states that the truths contained therein are to be told to a "high-minded man who feels the highest devotion (*bhakti*) for God and for his guru as for God." As early as the second century B.C., the grammarian Patanjali makes the mention of a Shiva-bhagavata sect. In the instance of Vishnu, the *Avataras*, particularly Krishna and Rama, were more prominent than Vishnu himself. Such is not the case for Shiva although a few attempts were made to popularize different *Avataras* of Rudra.

While followers of Shiva have had a greater tendency toward *advaitin* views than the *bhaktas* previously considered, there have still been those whose message was devotional and emotional rather than meditative. The Vaishnava Alvars have their counterparts in the Shaiva Nayanars. Some sixty-three of the Shaiva Nayanars wrote hymns of a devotional nature. Some of these hymns form the Devaram, the first of twelve canonical books called *Tirumurai* which are considered by some Shaivites (Shaiva Siddhanta) as *shruti* which may thus be considered as equivalent to the Vedas. These hymns are not an attempt at a systematic theology but an account of a vivid experience. Optimism reigns as God's mercy and grace are proclaimed. Devotion to Shiva is helpful for all. Shiva exists universally and appears even to the illiterate if, as a true *bhakta*, his mind is intent on Shiva's love and service. The prominence given to grace cannot be ignored. When man realizes his condition, the freely given grace of God seems even more wonderful as expressed in a Shaiva hymn.

> Thou gav'st thyself, thou gainest me;
> Which did the better bargain derive?
> Bliss found in infinity;
>
> *But what didst thou from me derive?*
>
> (A devotional hymn popular among Shaivites, qtd. Baird & Bloom 63)

A theological tradition called Shaiva Siddhanta developed in South India. The first systematic attempt to discuss Tamil Shaivism is the Shiva-*jnana-bodham* of Meykandar in the first half of the thirteenth century. Meykandar's position is realistic and theistic, opine Baird and Bloom (64). Shiva is the *guru* par excellence whose grace illuminates the intellect when one submits to the teachings of the human *gurus.* Shiva, the soul of man, and the bonds of ignorance are all considered real. *Karma* and *maya* are not evils, but agencies used by Shiva for the liberation of the soul from ignorance and its purification. The three paths of service, worship, and meditation are proposed, but all are to be animated by *bhakti.* This makes the soul open to Shiva's grace, by which union with him is possible. Shiva imparts divine knowledge (*pati jnana*) by way of intuition to highly advanced souls. To the less advanced, He works through a human *guru*. This explains the need for the *bhakta* to meet a *guru* through whom Shiva can give divine knowledge. Liberation is union with Shiva, but not a complete cessation of separateness. Shiva is bliss itself, while the soul can only enjoy bliss. Hence in this emphatically *bhakti* system, theism is maintained.

The Kashmir sect of Shaivism is quite different. It developed in the late eighth century. Here Shiva is merely a form for presenting *Advaita* philosophy. Shiva is the underlying reality of the universe, the world being an emanation from him. While the world is quite real inasmuch as it has the reality it appears to possess, it is illusory in the sense that Shiva, the prime reality, remains unaffected by change in the sensible world. In its true nature the soul is identified with Shiva, but by reason of its ignorance it considers itself finite and imperfect. "The awakened soul," assert Baird and Bloom, "realizes its true nature as Shiva through *bhakti* in the form of worship and devotion" (61-64).

Finally the integration of Shiva and Shakti is also very significant. The manifestation of the universe is affected through the power of Shiva known as Shakti, His consort. The cult of Shakti, attained predominance, upon the *Sankhya* philosophy, according to which 'Spirit' or *Purusha* (identified with Shiva) is inactive while *prakriti* (identified with Shakti) is productive and the material cause of the universe. Hence, some sects of Shaivism, hold Shakti, in a sense, superior to Shiva. A.R. Mohapatra, in his treatise on Philosophy of Religion, enlightens, "Shakti is distinguishable from Shiva only in theoretical and conventional analysis, but in realization She is identical with Shiva; hence if Shiva is *Sat* Shakti is *Sati*; if Shiva is *Chit-* (pure and perfect consciousness), Shakti is *Chiti-* (consciousness as power)" (23-24).

The Para stream of Kashmir Shaivism consists exclusively of Shiva, Shakti and their union. The other two streams of "Trika" or Kashmir Shaivism being 'Apara' and 'Nara.' The Shaivism of Kashmir deeply influenced Swami Vivekananda, who spent some time in the mystical valley of Kashmir. A pilgrim had once seen him suddenly stopping at the turn of a mountainous path—standing awed with the words "Shiva, Shiva." "In this abode of Shiva, he indeed became Shiva himself," writes swami Jitatmananda, who also recounts Swami Vivekananda's visit to Mayavati on 3 January, 1901 along with his fellow disciple, Swami Sivananada. Despite his ill health, Swami Vivekananda enjoyed the sixteen day stay at this home of *Advaita*. "One day while looking at the snow capped Himalayas and describing the eternally white Shiva dreamt of by Indians on these peaks, he went into a deep meditation" (176, 181). Swami Vivekananda's "Hymn to Shiva" celebrates the manifold glories of Shiva in sweet, mystical devotion. Shiva is but a name of the Absolute, the Supreme lord and a personification of love—who contains duality in Him:

> In which the dual consciousness of "I" and "Thou" plays on
> ("Hymn to Shiva")

Because of ignorance, the individual has never looked upon himself as the Lord, though in reality he is the Lord himself. L.N. Sharma in his treatise, *Kashmir Shaivism* observes that the Shaiva Absolutist is careful to avoid the pitfalls of dualism and attempts at harmonizing the duality into an integral unity (*Samarasya*) (47). This leads to the formulation of an integral Advaitism in the Shaiva tradition, which Swami Vivekananda swiftly sums up in the Hymn,

> Where the ideas of parent and produced, purified thoughts and
> endless varied forms, merge in the Real one. ("Hymn to Shiva")

Shiva is the unity which contains 'endlessly varied forms,' He is the 'parent and the produced,' in whom, the 'tempest of past blows,' who annihilates delusion and is the Lord of all who 'transcends Himself.' The Hymn not only sings of the unity underlying the apparent duality of *Atma* and *Paramatma* but also focuses upon unity of several forms—representing the Absolute in Its various aspects. The meaning of the noun 'Shiva' as given in the fourth verse of *Sri Vishnu Sahasranam* may be considered here. It occurs along with other names like 'Sarvah,' 'Sthanuh' and 'Bhutadih.' *Shivah* itself means "The Pure' who is free from the three *gunas*. Shankara quotes the Shruti text: *sa Brahma sa Shivah*, etc. Hari (i.e. Vishnu) is praised by "Shiva" and other names as there is no difference between these deities who represent the creating, preserving and destroying aspects of God. As Swami Vivekananda writes in the opening stanza of the Hymn which corresponds to Shankara's interpretation of the name 'Sarvah' (the All) which runs thus "He is everything. All things seen and unseen came from Him and go back into Him. He always knows everything. He is therefore called 'Sarvah,' the all" (Trans. Parthasarathy 77).

> to whom are attributed
> The Phenomena of all creation,
> The preservation and dissolution
> Of the universe! ("Hymn to Shiva")

The poet discovers with awe that there is nothing apart from Shiva who is luminous with knowledge and is Trinity in Himself. Then Swami Vivekananda fervently sings that one owes all one's devotion to Shiva alone—the master of sacrifice who removes all evil, Himself accepting or swallowing the 'poison' of the world. His kind gaze is evenly fixed upon the humble and His love is unsurpassed by any other. The love contained in the human heart is but a fraction of the Love of Mahadeva—the great god. He is the benevolent father—easy to propitiate, who is ever ready "To part with life for others' good" ("Hymn to Shiva").

Another poem of Swami Vivekananda, "A Song I Sing to Thee," is addressed to *Purusha* and *prakriti*—the static and kinetic aspects of the Absolute. And it celebrates the glory of *prapatti* or total surrender to the Divine. The poet declares,

> Servant am I, true servant of Thee Both [*Purusha* and *Prakriti*]
> Low at thy feet, with Shakti, I salute. ("A Song I Sing to Thee")

The poet voices an ardent desire to seek union with the Divine and wipe away all distinction between the individual self and the cosmic Self. In a moment of supreme spiritual discovery the devotee cries out: "Aye! I am Thee—and Thou my Lord art me!" In this poem, as Vijayasree points out, Swami Vivekananda "deliberately uses both feminine and masculine appellations to address the Supreme power." Swami Vivekananda's God is both *para* and *Apara*, Shiva and Shakti, Mother and Master at the same time (171).

"The Dance of Shiva" and "Shiva in Ecstasy" are short poems which adore Shiva in His dynamic aspect. Filled with powerful images of *tandava* of Lord Shiva and energizing symbols these lyrical poems mirror the central image of dancing Shiva which "is the clearest image of the activity of God" describes Ananda Coomaraswamy saying that "Its significance is felt when it is realized that it takes place within the heart and the self" (67). That Shiva is simultaneously identical with emanation and absorption is beautifully summed up in "The Dance of Shiva":

> Lo, the God is dancing
> —Shiva the all-destroyer and Lord of Creation,
> The Master of *Yoga* and the wielder of Pinaka.
>
> ("The Dance of Shiva")

The Lord assumes the creative function and appears in the state of emanation with reference to those manifestations, which are about to come into being. The same power appears as constituting the state of absorption, when He assumes the function of destroyer of the previously manifested objects. *Isvara Pratyabhijna vimarshini* (II. IV, 10) states that, "in reality He alone, who essentially is nothing more than the five powers of creation, destruction etc., shines" (qtd. Sharma 225). *Pinaka* or the Trident, the symbol used in the poem, signifies the three aspects, viz. the creative, the sustaining and the destructive aspects of the Divine. The frightening dance and flaming locks of Shiva symbolize dissolution which aims at merging the universe with Himself during the *Pralaya* (i.e. the Dooms Day). The seven worlds and revering earth abide in his cosmic dance of doom. Swami Vivekananda actually invokes the Divine dance into the recesses of his heart and makes a pyre of his earthly bonds and attachments. For this purpose the ascetic-poet worships the destructive aspect of the Divine represented by Shiva and Kali. Another Bengali song, translated into English, "Shiva in Ecstasy" focuses entirely upon this aspect:

> His tabor is playing and the garland of skulls is swinging in rhythm.
>
> ("Shiva in Ecstasy")

The roaring Ganga stands for *Pralaya* or an all submerging flood and the 'garland of skulls' depicts a Cosmic devastation. As against the usual lunar image, even the moon is fiercely flaming and the Trident vomits fire.

> The waters of the Ganga are roaring among his matted locks.
> The great trident is vomiting fire, and the moon on his
> forehead is fiercely flaming. ("Shiva in Ecstasy")

There seems to be a natural tendency in the poet to hail the destructive aspect of the Divine. Swami Vivekananda was fully aware of the fact that *bhakti* or religious devotion can be a mask for weakness, hypocrisy and so on. He had no sympathy for any weak sentimental *bhakti*, and asserted that "God cannot be reached by the weak either physically, mentally, morally or spiritually." Genuine *bhakti*, according to Swami Vivekananda, implies the singleness of attachment (*nishta*) to the object of love, namely, God or *Iswara*. In this connection he elucidates the concepts of *Iswara* and *Brahma*. Asking "Who is *Iswara*?" he answers: "It is He from Whom is the origination, continuation and dissolution of the universe" (*C.W.* 3: 37; reference to the "*janmady—asya yatah*" of *Brahmasutra*, 1.1.2).

"The God of *bhaktiyoga* is the one generalized abstract person, in loving whom one loves the whole universe and all created beings," writes Swami Nikhilananda of Sri Ramakrishna Math (117). The path of *bhakti* is the easiest and most natural of all the means to reach God, because it does not demand any tough intellectual exercise from the spiritual aspirant. "Even from the non-dualistic viewpoint, the personal God is as real as the universe and living beings. When the universe and living beings ultimately merge in *Brahma*, God too becomes one with it" explains Swami Nikhilananda and adds:

> Spiritual love, or *bhakti*, is directed only to God, whose effulgence puts to shame 'a million suns, a million moons and a million gods of beauty.' He is the personal God, or the spirit in the form of a person (108).

Swami Vivekananda's "Hymn to Shiva" suggests that a channelized mind and a controlled heart lead to such a devotion.

who, by undivided meditation,
Is realized in the self-controlled heart:
May that lordly swan of the limpid lake
of my mind, guard me, prostate before Him! ("Hymn to Shiva")

Sri Krishna outlines the procedure for this 'self-control' in the sixth chapter of the *Gita* thus:

> A yogi should first control his senses and withdraw them from all their several objects of enjoyment. He should next purify the intellect by eliminating or purging his desires, born of past tendencies or '*Vasanas*' with a determined effort of will, he should detach the intellect by slow degrees from *Vasanas* and fix it on the self. He should not think of anything else but steadfastly meditate on the self alone (Verses: 24, 25. Trans. Subba Rao 227).

Swami Vivekananda celebrates the power of mind as follows, because mind is the tool which alone can ever take the soul to the Lord:

I salute that mind unstable,
centered in Shiva, the abode of calm! ("Hymn to Shiva")

The *Gita* explores into the nature of the mind and indicates the process of its subjugation:

> O Partha, the mind is doubtless fickle and difficult to control, but it is not impossible to steady it. By the practice of meditation and by dispassion it is subdued (II: 35).

This verse is explained by S. Subba Rao thus: "Dispassion prevents the acquisition of fresh *vasanas* or tendencies, while meditation does not allow the past tendencies to sprout up. When the mind is thus brought into a state of tranquility and equanimity the self reveals itself" (233). Thus the *Gita* seems to suggest that diligence and intelligence should be coupled with self-control to achieve perfection in *yoga*. Devotion too is a great tool to bring mind into one pointedness and Swami Vivekananda expresses this *yogic* view in his fervent aspiration:

May the devotion,
The burning devotion of this my life
Attach itself to Him, to Shiva, who

While being Lord of all, transcends Himself. ("Hymn to Shiva")

Apart from this, the pure white colour of Shiva has been mentioned in two instances by the poet to describe the beauty of Lord Shiva:

From whom all gloom and darkness have dispersed;
That radiant Light, white, beautiful
As bloom of lotus white is beautiful;
Whose laughter loud sheds knowledge luminous; . . .
who, like the charming water-lily white,
Is beautiful. ("Hymn to Shiva")

The 'White' colour has twofold significance in the Hymn. Firstly, the white light containing all the seven colours of the spectrum is a metaphor of Shiva who contains everything in Himself. Secondly, white symbolizes radiance or bliss, and qualities like purity and sanctity—all of which are personified in Shiva. The poem ponders over some glorious names of Shiva like 'Mahadeva,' 'Hara' and 'Neelakanth.' Name-worship is a potent way to remember God.

Bhakti can be developed by constant remembrance of the Lord, association with devotees and by incessant study of scriptures and lives of saints. In "The Song of the Free" (which is published in Vol. 8 with the title: "An Interesting Correspondence"), the poet says that the soul, freed from ignorance, realizes the Eternal and feels complete identification with Him:

Nor angel I, nor man nor brute,
Nor body, mind, nor he, nor she;
The books do stop in wonder mute
To tell my nature—I am He
Before the sun, the moon, the earth,
Before the stars or comets free,
Before e'en Time has had its birth—
I was, I am, and I will.

The deluded world, enveloped in the illusion of *maya*, does not know Him as the Unborn and Imperishable. So Swami Vivekananda exhorts the ignorant masses to give up false delusions and to realize the Supreme. The poem does not refer to the Lord by any particular name or image.

From dreams awake, from bonds be free;
Be not afraid. This mystery,
My shadow cannot frighten me,
Know once for all that I am He! ("An Interesting Correspondence")

In the concluding stanza of the lyric, he again says:

That God is true, all else is nothing!

This world's a dream
Though true it seem.
And only Truth is He the living!
The real me is none but He
And never never matter changing.

The Christian mystics too share such an idea and idiom: "In the deepest, most inner and most secret depth of the soul, God essentially, really and substantially exists"; God is said to be the 'rock bottom of the soul' (*der allerborgenste, innerste, tiefe Grund der Seele*) (qtd. Rolland 244).

As indicated earlier, while discussing Advaita in the second chapter (2.7), Swami Vivekananda tries to show through reasoning also that *Brahma* and the world, the infinite and the finite, should not be looked upon as two entirely different and distinct realities. As Jacob Kattackal explains, "for if *Brahma* is all comprehensive, infinite and omnipresent and if everything is ultimately derived in *toto* from *Brahma* and *Brahma* pervades and sustains it all, it is meaningless to view '*Brahma* and the world' as two totally distinct, different and independent entities" (237). For Swami Vivekananda, the strongest proof of his argument is the *Brahma*-experience corroborated by the Upanishadic pronouncements.

Like Swami Vivekananda, Sri Aurobindo too perceives Shiva as not only loving but also terrible. Shiva is not only the God of deep unutterable love, "sweet fulfiller of desire," the "tender Flame," but also 'Rudra,' "fierce, august and dire," "the God of wrath," as described in "Epiphany."

The vision that changed and in His place there stood
A Terror red as lightning or as blood;
His fierce right hand a javelin advanced
And, as He shook it, earthquake reeling danced

Across the hemisphere, ruin and plague
Rained out of heaven, disasters swift and vague
Threatened, a marching multitude of ills.
His foot strode forward to oppress the hills,
And at the vision of His burning eyes
The hearts of men grew faint with dread surmise
Of sin and punishment. ("Epiphany")

The idea of universal destruction symbolized by Lord Shiva "is closely associated with the notion of all dark elements that stand in the path of progress" explains J.S. Agarwal while discussing Sri Aurobindo's conception of Shiva (226). Lord Shiva's weapon is the light by which He pierces the darkness as imaged in Sri Aurobindo's poem "Shiva the Inconscient Creator."

A moon-ray on the forehead, blue and pale,
Stretched afar its finger of still light
Illumining emptiness. Stern and male
Mask of peace indifferent in might!
("Shiva the Inconscient Creator")

In this poem, the white radiance of eternity, the blueness of Shiva's face, and the vibrance of crimson flame and the burning gold—all indicate the qualities of the Divine. Consider these lines:

A face on the cold dire mountain peaks
Grand and still; its lines white and austere
Match with the unmeasured snowy streaks.
("Shiva the Inconscient Creator")

Sri Aurobindo employs different colours to suggest different shades of thought and meaning. The various levels of concentration in his *yoga*, when conveyed through his poetry, are suggested by the use of different colours. The Mother (Mirra Alfazza—The spiritual collaborator of Sri Aurobindo) explains the meaning of the twelve colours as follows: (i) Sincerity is represented by blue; (ii) Humility by blue-green; (iii) Gratitude by Green; (iv) Perseverance—Greenish-yellow; (v) Aspiration—yellow; (vi) Receptivity—light orange; (vii) Progress—dark orange; (viii) Courage—red; (ix) Health—magenta; (x) Generosity—light mauve; (xi) Equality—violet and (xii) Peace—dark blue. Some of these colours when seen in Sri Aurobindo's poetry suggest the same qualities (Pearson *Life Positive Plus* 53). But in addition to these, it might be said that Sri Aurobindo uses colours in a more distinctive and suggestive way.

In "Shiva the Inconscient Creator," white signifies grandeur, austerity and infinity of Shiva. The rest of the poem discovers in wonder that the apparently inconscient is the source of conscience of beings created by Itself. As the poet sings, the still light of moon upon the blue and pale forehead of Shiva, the 'white and austere' lines upon His awesome face with aeon-coiled hair portray His superconscient trance.

> But out from some infinite born now came
> Over giant snows and the still face
> A quiver and colour of Crimson flame. . . .
> In that diamond heart the fires undrape,
> Living core, a brazier of gold. ("Shiva the Inconscient Creator")

The crimson and golden flames symbolize Life, vibrance and vitality of creation. The cold mountain peaks, the lifeless air and the vast emptiness depict the inconscience of matter. This inconscient and the superconscient trance 'veil' Shiva-the Supreme consciousness from both sides, and this veil is torn apart by the dynamics of creation. In the process of creation this Supreme consciousness raps inconscience around Itself for involving into matter. Life springs from this lower 'veil' and Love sprouts forth from His superconscient trance—the upper 'veil.' Thus for the poet, God's dynamic nature is revealed through His glorious Manifestations:

> This was the closed mute and burning source
> Whence were formed the worlds and their star-dance;
> ("Shiva the Inconscient Creator")

"The Inconscient as the source and author of all material creation is one of the main discoveries of modern psychology, but it agrees with the idea of a famous Vedic hymn." writes Sri Aurobindo in his note on this poem, and adds:

> In the Upanishads, Prajna, the Master of Sushupti, is the Ishwara and therefore the original creator out of a superconscient sleep. The idea

> of the poem is that this creative Inconscient also is Shiva creating here life in matter out of an apparently inconscient material trance as from above he creates all the worlds (not the material only) from a superconscient trance (*Collected Poems* 579).

This Spiritual hypothesis seems to have taken roots from Kashmir Shaivism, which was also influenced by Buddhist thought. It is the Buddhist concept of *Sunyata* which provided the metaphysical foundation for the growth of integral Advaitism within the Shaiva tradition. The influence of *Sunyavada* upon Tantricism is widely recognized. With its phenomenalising aspect of *Karuna*, which in many respects resembles the Shaiva concept of Shakti, the *Sunya* (i.e. nothingness) manifests itself as the concrete world. As TRV Murti explains in his treatise, *The Central Philosophy of Buddhism*, "the forms neither exhaust, nor modify the Absolute in any way. Further, it is through these forms that the individual ascends to the level of the Absolute" (109). It is through the process of manifestation, the self knows itself in various ways. Quoting from *Siva Dristi*, LN Sharma asserts that the only valid explanation of creation is that, knowing himself though the multiplicity of objects, Shiva alone shines (210).

The free will of the Lord always manifests itself in the form of the five-fold function of universal creation, maintenance, destruction, self-concealment and self-revelation. Thus, the Lord always performs these five-old functions, and there is no break in his Shining as the universe in various phenomena, such as creation, destruction etc. As *Isvara Pratyabhijma Vimarshini Bhaskari* enlightens, "He always diverts Himself in creation ever rests in pleasure of maintenance, and is ever satisfied with the food of the three worlds" (Vol I. qtd. Sharma 239).

While the functions of creation, destruction and maintenance operate on the phenomenal plane, the functions of self-concealment and self-revelation, *nigraha* and *anugraha,* operate at the transcendental level. Sri Aurobindo's hypothesis attempts to explain these functions of self-concealment and self-revelation thus:

> The reality is a supreme consciousness—but that is veiled by the appearance on one side of the superconscient sleep, on the other of the material Inconscience." In the poem "Shiva—the inconscient Creator, the emphasis is on the latter; the superconscient is only hinted at, not indicated, it is the Infinity out of which comes the revealing flame" Sri Aurobindo (*Collected Poems* 579)

To consider a few lines of the poem which contain the same idea,

> Light-spear tips revealed the mighty shape,
> Tore the secret veil of the heart's hold;
> In that diamond heart the fires undrape,
> Living core, a brazier of gold. ("Shiva the Inconscient Creator")

Shiva's creation is His method of self-revelation. Sri Aurobindo further elaborates that "Creation is the manifestation of separation (*Sristi*); keeping the manifest as separate, is maintenance (*Sthiti*); the manifestation is of unity or integrality is destruction" (*Samhara* or *laya*) (*Collected Poems* 223). All these functions are manifest simultaneously in the Absolute. Mythology might well bifurcate or trifurcate these various functions into separate figures for better comprehension, but the reality is that the one Supreme being always performs the five functions—"not only in the case of cosmic creation, destruction etc., but also in practical life" says *Isvara Pratyabhijna Vimarshini* (Vol. I. VI: 7 qtd. Sharma 239). Sri Aurobindo highlights the multifarious faces of Shiva as he writes about Rudra in his commentary on the "Hymn to Vishnu":

But this violent and mighty Rudra who breaks down all defective formations and groupings of outward and inward life, has also a benigner aspect. He is the supreme healer. Opposed He destroys; called on for aid and propitiated He heals all wounds and all evil and all sufferings. The force that battles is His gift, but also the final peace and joy (*Thoughts and Glimpses* qtd. Agarwal 235).

In the poem "Shiva," Sri Aurobindo presents a picture of serenity and an implicit celebration of the celestial union of Shiva and Shakti leading to the glorious creation. The white colour represents Divinity and peace in the poem. And Shiva, who represents pure light of consciousness (*bodha*), is seated on the celestial, white summit of Kailash with His overflowing ecstasy, guarded by "a fire-screen of peace." Shakti stands for the power of freedom (*Svatantrya*) of consciousness, the infinite form without light, or the principle of becoming. Devoid of Shakti, Shiva would be inconscient (*Jada*) and, consequently, as good as 'dead' (*Shava*). Shiva knows Himself only through His Shakti. Consider the poet's vision of this phenomenon:

> A single soul of bare infinities,
> Guarded he keeps by a fire-screen of peace
> His mystic loneliness of nude ecstasy.
> But, Touched by an immense delight to be,
> He looks across unending depths and sees
> Musing amid the inconscient silences
> The Mighty Mother's dumb felicity. ("Shiva")

Sri Aurobindo personifies 'Shakti' as 'Mighty Mother" in the poem and picturizes her mystical union with Shiva in the serene summits of Himalayas which is summarized in a reading of the first and final lines of the poem:

> On the white summit of eternity . . .
> The Spirit leaps into the Spirit's embrace. ("Shiva")

As regards the question of the relationship between Shiva and Shakti, the Shaivite holds that *'Samarasya,'* the equilibrium of Shiva and Shakti, is the very nature (*Svarupa*) of the Absolute. L.N. Sharma in his treatise, *Kashmir Shaivism* clarifies that, "*Parama* Shiva is not a juxtaposition of the two; it is an essential unity, of which these two are eternal manifestations" (281-82). Shakti also depends upon Shiva for Her functioning. Traditionally described as chit-Shakti, she is the conscious power of the Supreme Being. This is centered in 'chit' or pure consciousness—(Shiva). Sri Aurobindo explains this fact through the beautiful metaphor of planets revolving around the Sun. Rising to His glance, as she goes in a circular fashion—dancing around Shiva,

> Half now awake she rises to his glance;
> Then, moved to circling by her heart-beats' will,
> The rhythmic worlds describe that passion-dance.
> Life springs in her and Mind is born; her face

> She lifts to Him who is Herself, until
> The Spirit leaps into the Spirit's embrace. ("Shiva")

As the innumerable rays are nothing but a manifestation of the Sun, so is Shakti who is nothing but a self-manifestation of Shiva Himself. They are united with each other in the relation of *Tadatmya* or *Samarasya,* which means that they are inseparable and yet distinguishable in thought. The unqualified pure substance, which is the support of the entire universe, has been called '*Chit*' in the masculine gender, and '*Chiti*,' in the feminine. These are merely two names of one and the same entity which in its female aspect is worshipped as Isvari, Durga, Kali or Bhagavati, and as Isvara, Shiva or Bhagavat, in its male aspect. The relationship between them, viz. *Tadatmya,* is of the nature of unity in diversity. It might be described as "non-duality tolerant of duality—*bheda Sahisnu abheda*" (Sharma 283-84).

As Shiva is hailed not only the Destroyer, but the friend of creatures, so also Mahakali is represented as not only the terrible goddess but also the loving and beneficent Mother. The poems of Swami Vivekananda and Sri Aurobindo, discussed in the subsequent section: 5.3 vindicate that the Mother's love is as intense as Her wrath.

5.3 Shakti *Bhakti*: Kali Poems of Swami Vivekananda

Shakti worship is the worship of the deity's power in the form of his consort. This has taken various forms, from simply representing the deity with his consort to singling her out as the chief object of worship. The texts which describe the elaborate rites and theories connected with Shaktism are called *Tantras*. Although extensive research is being carried on the *Tantric* texts, Robert. D. Baird and Alfred Bloom observe that the "rites and rituals of a sacramental and magical nature accompanied with diagrams and gestures comprise a wide-ranging practice, which has not been sufficiently studied for us to get an overview or a very penetrating understanding" (64).

While the Mother Goddess seems to have been venerated in the Indus valley civilization, little place is given to goddesses in the Vedic literature. Female deities were probably worshipped to some extent on the popular level from the earliest times, but in the fourth century they came to be worshipped in special temples, and the from the sixth to the tenth centuries the cult association with Shakti worship became elaborately developed. Worship of the Mother Goddess grew in importance until early in the Muslim period. Even as devotion of a kind was directed to Sarasvati, the goddess of learning, and to Lakshmi, the goddess of wealth, Shakti is most commonly worshipped as the consort of Shiva. Since the name Shakti has been used to identify various aspects of the Mother, she is referred by different names like Durga, Kali, Parvati and Uma. The concept underlying worship of Shakti is that since the eternal Shiva is inactive while his consort is Shakti or pure activity, the creation of the world and the work of grace and liberation are Her functions. Hence Shakti becomes more significant than Shiva Himself who is static and ineffective without Her.

The Shaktas (devotees of Shakti) made use of adoration *mantras*, which were brief expressions of reverence for the Goddess. The Shaktas also made use of diagrams of mystic import (*mandalas*), ritual gestures with fingers (*mudras*), and ritual movements of the hands (*nyasa*) for bringing the Goddess into the body. The worship of Shakti became more prevalent from AD 550—900, when an elaborate cult developed. Some of it was closer to *Bhakti* principles than were other parts. It was the view of the Shaktas that in the *Kaliyuga* (black age) in which we now exist, their methods were the only appropriate ways to liberation. One of the means was the public worship of the Goddess in temples. A second method was circle worship (*chakra puja*), sometimes called left-handed Tantra. A third method was meditative exercise or discipline (*sadhana*), intended to bring the participant to perfection. Finally some psychic practices were taken up as a mode of worship. As with other sects, the Shaktas advised serious spiritual aspirants to select a *guru* and undertake initiation.

Perhaps the most adored form of the Mother in India today is Kali, the Shakti of Shiva, who is worshipped in Her own right. In Bengal particularly in the Kalighat temple in Calcutta, devotees prostrate before Her image and sacrifices are offered in Her courtyard. The image of Kali is similar to the description in the *Kali Tantra*:

Most fearful, Her laughter shows Her dreadful teeth. She stands upon a corpse. She has four arms. Her hands hold a sword and a head and show the gestures of removing fear and granting boons. She is the auspicious divinity of sleep, the consort of Shiva.

Naked, clad only in space, the Goddess is resplendent. Her tongue hangs out. She wears a garland of heads. Such is the form worthy of meditation of the Power of Time, Kali, who dwells near the funeral pyres (qtd. Kumar 85-86).

Thus portrayed, Kali manifests both the powers of destruction and grace. All the pleasures of the world are transient, while only Kali is permanent and can grant happiness. Why is She black? She is the ultimate energy. Colours are distinctions, while in Kali all colours dissolve into shapelessness and darkness.

According to Sri Ramakrishna, both personal and impersonal forms of God are true from two different standpoints. "There is no distinction between Impersonal God (*Brahma*) on the one hand and Personal God (Shakti) on the other. When the Supreme being is thought of as inactive, He is styled God the Absolute (*Suddha Brahma*); and when He is thought of as active—creating, sustaining and destroying—He is styled Shakti or Personal God" (qtd. Singh 49). Coming to the mode of worship of Swami Vivekananda, one finds that though he believed in both the personal and impersonal forms of God, he worshiped Mother Goddess in Her personal form throughout his life. Following the tradition of his master Sri Ramakrishna, the sustaining or governing aspect and destroying aspect of the Mother are adored most in his poems dedicated to the Mother. Poems like "Who Knows How Mother Plays," "A Hymn to the Divine Mother," etc., hail the Mother as the Empress of the universe while other poems like, "Kali the Mother," "And Let Shyama Dance There" sing of Her glory as the 'dark—one' who absorbs all created beings back into Herself—a process known as dissolution or destruction. A full comprehension of the Divine Mother and unconditional self-surrender, liberates the soul from the 'great illusion' as Sri Ramakrishna himself explains to Mahendranath Gupta, a householder disciple of the Master in one of his interactions at Dakshineshwar—recorded on 24 August 1882:

The Master: One must propitiate the Divine Mother, the Primal Energy, in order to obtain God's grace. God Himself is *Mahamaya*, who deludes the world with Her illusion and conjures up the magic of creation, preservation and destruction. She has spread this veil of ignorance before our eyes. We can go into the inner chamber only when She lets us pass through the door. Living outside, we see only outer objects, but not the Eternal Being, Existence—Knowledge—Bliss Absolute. Therefore it is stated in the *purana* that deities like *Brahma* praised *Mahamaya* for the destruction of demons Madhu and Kaitabha (*The Gospel of Sri Ramakrishna* 116).

The demons Madhu and Kaitabha symbolize the inner foes like anger, lust etc., whom the Divine Mother alone can cut asunder with Her sword of dispassion. She adorns the terrific form of Kali to dispel the illusion of Her devotees. Swami Vivekananda adores the glory of Elokeshi (She with untied hair—a name of Kali) in a stirring poem "And Let Shyama Dance There"—which is rendered from Bengali:

> Thou dreaded Kali, the All-destroyer,
> Thou alone art true; Thy shadow's shadow
> Is indeed the pleasant Vanamali.*
> O Terrible Mother, cut quick the core,
> Illusion dispel—the dream of happiness,
> Rend asunder the fondness for the flesh.
> (*Literally, he who is garlanded with wild flowers. The Shepherd Krishna in His aspect of youthful sport: footnote of the poem)

The poet exhorts his readers to rise above the futile run after happiness and beauty so-as-to love the terrific—the all-engulfing death and destruction symbolized by the dreaded form of Kali. When the mind frees itself from the fear of misery and death, as also from all weakness for worldly pleasures, it attains equanimity—which is essential for God-realization. The poem is suffused with the spirituality of the *Gita*—which was also taught to a soldier on the battlefield of Kurukshetra. The poet here, symbolizes the soldier for fearlessness, detachment and duty-mindedness and inspires the readers to be as bold in the battle of life. The wise man who has transcended the fright of death and leads a pure, detached and desireless existence, becomes eligible to be intoxicated with the Love for the Divine in its true form. So the poet unveils the terrific form of the Mother and sings:

> True, they garland Thee with skulls, but shrink back
> In fright and call Thee, "O All-merciful!"
> At Thy thunder peal of awful laughter,
> At Thy nudeness—for space is Thy garment—
> Their hearts sink down with terror, but they say,
> "It is the demons that the Mother kills!"
> They only pretend they wish to see Thee,
> But when the time comes, at Thy sight they flee.
> Thou art Death! To each and all in the world
> Thou distributest the plague and disease
> —Vessels of venom filled by Thine own hands.
>
> ("And Let Shyama Dance There")

In the Tantras, She—the Mother, is the goddess who leads to the other shore. She has a dual aspect, the one pacified and luminous and the other fierce. It is to initiate the readers into this feared other side and to inspire love for the *Kalika* aspect of the Mother that the poet apparently denounces the weak hearted humanity which clings to the pleasant form of the Mother. This terrific form of the Mother, from which the ignorant devotees "flee" from has great spiritual significance. The *svarupa* (real form) of this *Mahashakti* has been revealed in *Tantric* texts. The *Mahanirvana Tantra* says that She is the great progenitor of the minutest as well as the grossest manifestations of the universe—both animate and inanimate beings. This universe is begotten of Her free will, who is the beginning of all. The *Vidyas* (the powers of the Divine Mother) and the Trinity, all owe their existence to Her. The *Mahanirvana Tantra* further states that She is cognizant of the entire universe but none in the universe knows Her (4.10-13). The scripture describes Her as all the ten *Maha-vidyas* (these are called *Maha-*

vidya, as sources of all that is to be known), like Kali, Tara, Shodasi, Bhuvaneswari, Dhumavati, Bagala, Bhairavi, Chinnamasta, Matangi and Kamala, which correspond to the ten chief incarnations of Vishnu. She is described as surrounded on all sides by the gods and goddesses. Grossest and subtlest at the same time, She is devoid of all dimensions and yet takes various forms. For the fulfillment of the desires of the *sadhaka*, She assumes various forms (4.16-18). The *Jnanarnava Tantra* explicates that She appears at times to destroy the *asuras* and assumes "four hands and occasionally two, six, eight, ten or thousand hands." She wears various weapons for the maintenance of Her world (qtd. Kumar 3). Swami Vivekananda hails the Mother in the above mentioned glories in his *Ambastotram* or "A Hymn to the Divine Mother" (originally written in Sanskrit). More than any other weapon adorning the hands of the Mother, the poet is awe struck at the rope which She holds in Her hands, the rein that controls all created beings:

> O Thou most beautiful! Whose holy hands
> Hold pleasure and hold pain! Doer of good!
> Who art Thou? The water of existence
> By Thee is whirled and tossed in mighty waves.
> Is it, O Mother, to restore again
> This universe's broken harmony
> That Thou, without cessation, art at work?
>
> Oh! May the Mother of the universe—
> In whose activity no respite rests,
> Incessantly distributing the fruits
> Of action done, guiding unceasingly
> All action yet to come—bestow Her boon
> Of blessing on me, Her child, for evermore.
> I realize, I know, that it is Thou
> Who holdest in Thy hands dread *karma*'s rope.

That the law of *Karma* is the foundation of the Mother's government has already been discussed in the third chapter (3.2). As regards content and the style of adoration, Swami Vivekananda's Hymn synchronizes closely with the adoration of the Mother by the *devas* after She destroys two invincible *asuras*, Shumbha and Nishumbha, which reads thus:

> Thou art the Ruler of the Universe; Thou dost keep up the Universe. Thou art the Universe and Thou holdest it up. . . .
>
> O Goddess, benignly look on us! . . . Favour us O Goddess. The people of the three worlds worship Thee. Be a giver of boons to them. (qtd. Kumar 85-86)

There are four main features of the *Tantra*, particularly in respect of *Shakta Tantra*. First, this *Tantra* presents the Supreme Reality as Mother. Secondly it urges the devotees to make their bodies the temple of the Mother through a process of psycho-physiological practices. Thirdly, it stresses the importance of images and symbols in worship. Fourthly, it accepts the world as the ground of our transcendental ideal. Swami Vivekananda "found a firm basis of all these four aspects of *Tantra* in Vedantic and Sankhyan philosophy and in Patanjali's *Yoga*-Darshana," writes R.K. Dasgupta in his article on Swami Vivekananda and the Tantric Tradition (241). Recent researchers, like M. Gopinath Kaviraj's *Tantric Sadhana* (in Bengali) or S.C. Banerjee's works in English have created a new interest in Tantra. But a study of the works of Swami Vivekananda and the life of Sri Ramakrishna reveal that neither of them went too far in stressing the importance of an intricate psycho-physiological exercise in spiritual life. Nevertheless, Sri Ramakrishna and his disciples, including Swami Vivekananda, reveled in singing and listening to the Shakta songs during their congregations. For example, one evening, at the temple garden of Dakshineshwar on October 16, 1882 recounts Mahendranath Gupta in his treatise, *The Gospel of Sri Ramakrishna*,

After supper the devotees rested on the mat spread on the floor of the Master's room. They began to talk with him. It was indeed a mart of joy. The Master asked Narendra to sing the song beginning with the line: "In Wisdom's firmament the moon of Love is rising full." Narendra sang, and other devotees played the drums and cymbals:

> In Wisdom's firmament the moon of Love is rising full,
> And Love's flood-tide, in surging waves, is flowing everywhere.

O Lord, how full of bliss Thou art! Victory unto Thee! . . .
Upon the sea of the world unfolds the lotus of the New Day,
And there the Mother sits enshrined in blissful majesty.
See how the bees are mad with joy, sipping the nectar there!

Behold the Mother's radiant face, which so enchants the heart
And captivates the universe! About Her Lotus Feet
Bands of ecstatic holy men are dancing in delight.

What matchless loveliness is Hers! What infinite content
Pervades the heart when She appears! O brothers, says *Premdas
I humbly beg you, one and all, to sing the Mother's praise!

(*The poet who composed this song.")

Sri Ramakrishna sang and danced, and the devotees danced around him. (122)

The songs written in adoration of the Mother in the lore of *Bhakti*, by famous Shakta poets like Premdas (whose song has been quoted above), Ramprasad, etc., find an ardent reflection in the Kali poems of Swami Vivekananda. The poems, "Who Knows How Mother Plays" and "Kali the Mother" sing the Mother's praise in Her mystic and dissolving aspects. In these poems, one does not find the typical philosophical musings and mythological imaginations except a few images and symbols. Even these images are presented through a fresh and subjective imagination.

In "Who Knows How Mother Plays," the poet reverently ponders over the governing aspect of the Mother. She is the nameless and formless Absolute, inscrutable and awe-inspiring are Her ways:

Perchance the child had glimpse
Of shades, behind the scenes,
With eager eyes and strained,
Quivering forms ready
To jump in front and be
Events, resistless, strong.
Who knows but Mother, how,
And where, and when, they come?

She, the Supreme being inhabits all objects and scenes, but remains unseen for the ordinary eye. The prophet with clear intellect or the innocent child, occasionally perceive Her presence "behind the scenes." The Mother unfolds various forms and events on the universal stage. It is not for the rational mind to fathom Her as Sri Ramakrishna once sang to Pundit, a Brahmin from Sinthi (Brahmo Samaj), who occasionally visited Sri Ramakrishna:

> How are you trying, O my mind, to know the nature of God?
> You are groping like a madman locked in a dark room.
> He is grasped through ecstatic love; how can you fathom Him without it? . . .
> And, for that love, the mighty *yogis* practice *yoga* from age to age;
> When love awakes, the Lord, like a magnet, draws to Him the soul.

Continuing, the Master said: "You may speak of the scriptures, of philosophy, of Vedanta; but you will not find God in any of these. You will never succeed in realizing God unless your soul becomes restless for Him."

> Only through affirmation, never negation, can you know Him,
> Neither through Veda nor through Tantra nor the six *darshanas*.
> It is in love's elixir only that He delights, O mind;
> He dwells in the body's inmost depths, in Everlasting joy.
>
> (Gupta 607)

Besides these songs and sources from the Tantra, the other sources which influence his poetry are the devotional hymns attributed by tradition to the philosopher Shankaracharya, a few from the *Mahabharata* and the *puranas*. Most are well known *stotras* addressed to the various forms and names of the female Energy, Mother of the worlds, "whose worship" in the words of Sri Aurobindo "is an important part of that many sided and synthetic whole which we call Hinduism" (*Views and Reviews* 25).

The destructive force, *Mahakala* is also one of Her aspects—as "She destroys at the time of *pralaya*, and She is called Kali (*Saktisangama Tantra*—Tara Khanda, 36.19-12). She is black in colour which means that all "contradictions like black and white, cold and heat, possible and impossible, birth and death, merge at Her feet, and all distinctions disappear" (Bose and Halder—*The Tantras*: 202. and Alain Danielou—*Hindu Polytheism*: 273 qtd. Kumar 4). The Tantras portray the Mother's terrific form and also drive home to the readers its true significance. She is sitting on a corpse which means that She exists in all inanimate objects. She has got terrible teeth yet She is conferring boons to all. She is open mouthed and yet is most affectionate to Her children, (*Kali Tantra* 71, *Mahanirvana Tantra* 2.4) bearing as in Her bosom all their belongings, physical, mental, and spiritual. She has a laughing attitude, yet engrossed in wielding the terrible Spirit of Time (qtd. Kumar 3-4). Swami Vivekananda's "Kali the Mother" adores such a dissolving aspect of the loving Mother and the poet exhorts the readers to love Her in this aspect and be qualified for liberation:

> Dancing mad with joy,
> Come, Mother, come!
> For Terror is Thy name,
> Death is in Thy breath,
> And every shaking step
> Destroys a world for e'er.
> Thou "Time," the All—Destroyer!
> Come, O Mother, come!
> Who dares misery love,
> And hug the form of Death,
> Dance in destruction's dance,
> To him the Mother comes.

The poet's fervent longing to remain Her devotee for all time to come, is recorded in many of his poems, to quote a few:

> To friend and foe Thy lotus—eyes are even;
> Ever Thine animating touch bring fruit
> To fortunate and unfortunate alike;
> The shade of death and immortality—
> Both these, O Mother, are Thy grace Supreme!
> Mother Supreme! Oh, may Thy gracious face
> Never be turned away from me, Thy child!
>
> ("A Hymn to the Divine Mother")

> Let never more delusive dreams veil off Thy face from me
> My play is done; O Mother, break my chains and make me free!
>
> ("My Play is Done")

The Mother in Her glorious forms, pervades the poetry of Swami Vivekananda. In the poem "To the Awakened India," She figures as the gentle and resplendent Uma—who bestows the vision of Truth and also the strength needed for reaching there upon Her children:

And all above,
Himalaya's daughter Uma, gentle, pure,
The Mother that resides in all as power
And Life, who works all works and
Makes of One the world, whose mercy
Opens the gate to Truth and shows
The One in All, give thee untiring
Strength, which is Infinite Love.

She as the fourth *Mahavidya*, is considered to be the consort of Shiva. She takes care of the three worlds and feeds them—which is why She is called Bhuvanesvari. Her marvelous radiance illumines the universe. Ambika—the Mother, is also called Gauri, or the White, to distinguish Her from Kalika, or Kali, the Black. She is also called Chandika or the Furious, in Her fight with the *Asuras*.

The word Kalika has also reference to Kala or periodicity as Pushpendra Kumar points out in his chapter entitled "Kalika and Ambika.' He explains that the evolutionary process has intimate connection with the law of periodicity, which brings in moulds and ends all differences and further writes, "By Her independent will she begets universe with all its diversifications, and again sucks them to Her breast in the twinkling of an eye. Unobstructed is Her motion and modification is Her disport" (55, 4).

The Mother is worshipped as *Adya*, being the beginning of all. After *Mahapralaya* She alone remains as *Tamas* or *Avyakta prakriti* in a state, inconceivable by words or mind. The Tantras are unanimous in describing Her, as in a state of eternal bliss and playing in the bosom of Shiva (*Mahanirvana Tantra*, 4.34). Her feet do not rest on anything except the breast of Shiva (*Yoginihrdaya* 11: 128). She resides in the cremation ground, where all the worldly objects are being reduced to ashes i.e. their seed stage.

She is also described as in a destructive mood standing on the bosom of Shiva with a garland of several heads around Her girdle, in the cremation ground resounding with the howling of jackals (*Shakta Pramoda* 27 qtd. Kumar 3-5). According to Swami Vivekananda, when the little self, hope, name and fame are all transcended at the heights of spiritual exaltation, the *Antha-hakaran* or the heart turns into such a *Smashana* where Shyama dances endlessly. This idea is presented in an invigorating poem "And Let Shyama Dance There":

> Awake, O hero! Shake off thy vain dreams,
> Death stands at thy head—does fear become thee?
> A load of misery, true though it is—
> This Becoming*—know this to be thy God!
> His temple the Shmashan** among corpses
> And funeral pyres; unending battle—
> That verily is His sacred worship;
> Constant defeat—let that not unnerve thee;
> Shattered be little self, hope, name and fame;
> Set up pyre of them and make thy heart
> A burning-ground.
> And let Shyama dance there.
> (*The wheel of constant birth and death, hence the world.
> ** The cremation ground—As given in the footnote of the poem.)

The poem "Kali the Mother" also presents scenes of devastation with the aim of knocking out the primal fear of death from the reader's mind. The powerful imagery of the poem brings out the awe and glory of the destroying and bond-breaking Kali:

> The sea has joined the fray,
> And swirls up mountain—waves,
> To reach the pitchy sky.
> The flash of lurid light
> Reveals on every side
> A thousand, thousand shades
> Of Death begrimed and black—
> Scattering plagues and sorrows. ("Kali the Mother")

Kali, the Mother, represents death in its various forms—which in turn are brought home to the reader's mind through known images of annihilation, like the raging tempest or the tumultuous sea. The visual images of "the stars blotted out," "the roaring whirlwind," "the pitchy sky," etc., create the dramatic effect and set the tone of the poem. It is said that the poem itself was composed after the poet had a mesmeric vision of the Mother, Kali. "One evening, after an intense meditation, he had a vision of Kali, the Terrible, and he jotted down his experience in the form of a poem "Kali the Mother." As he finished the poem, he dropped to the floor unconscious, his soul soaring into the highest form of *Bhava Samadhi*" (*The Apostles of Sri Ramakrishna*. qtd. Rajendra Prasad 79). Swami Vivekananda's poetry thus abounds with the touches of "the cosmic consciousness, revelations of a greater spiritual life and suggestions of the Infinite" points out C. Vijayasree in her note on Swami Vivekananda's Poetry and aptly says that "His rhapsodies reflect the vision of his soul and of his people" (173). Briefly, it is the realization of Sri Aurobindo's conception of future poetry:

> The poetic vision of life is not a critical or intellectual or philosophic view of it, but a soul-view, a seizing by the inner sense; and the *mantra* is not in its substance or form poetic enunciation of a philosophic truth, but the rhythmic revelation or intuition arising out of the soul's sight of God and nature and the world and the inner Truth—occult to the outward eye—of all that peoples it the secrets of their life and their being (*The Future Poetry* 46).

Swami Vivekananda also composed a poem in Hindi "To Sri Krishna" which is in sharp contrast with his Kali poems. The *gopi* going to fetch water is being detained by the truant boy Krishna. The complaint of the *gopi* "why play tricks with one who is already thy slave" is a fine exposition of *Madhur Bhava* like that of the Vaishnava poet Jaideva.

> O Krishna, my friend, let me go to the water,
> O let me go today.
> Why play tricks with one who is already thy slave?
> O friend, let me go today, let me go.
> I have to fill my pitcher in the waters of the *Jumna.
> I pray with folded hands, friend, let me go.

(*river Yamuna of Northern India)

In the *Bhagavata Purana* and all the vernacular literature, it is the legend of Krishna-Gopala and its erotic side, describing the god's amorous encounters with the *gopis* (milk-maids) of 'Vrindavan,' which becomes the favorite theme of all *Bhakti* literature. It is He who gives the Vaishnavaite synthesis its ultimate form and who becomes for modern India *Bhagavat*, the 'Adorable,' the 'god of gods.' As Akhouri Rajendra Prasad underlines in his note on the poem, the sexual difference gets eliminated only in *Madhur Bhava* (81). One finds brilliant expositions of the significance of the ecstatic love of the *gopis* in quite a few conversations of Sri Ramakrishna. Once, on 2nd of June 1883, when Sri Ramakrishna visited the house of a devotee known as Ram, he listened to the story of Krishna-Gopala, in which the *gopis* say: "we do not understand big words like 'liberation.' We want to see the Krishna of our hearts." The Master said: "Yes, the *gopis* were right." And continued after singing a song, "the *gopis* had ecstatic love, unswerving and single-minded devotion to one ideal. Do you know the meaning of devotion that is not loyal to one ideal? It is devotion tinged with intellectual knowledge. It makes one feel: 'Krishna has become all these. He alone is the Supreme *Brahma*. He is Rama, Shiva, Shakti.' But this element of knowledge is not present in ecstatic love of God" (Gupta 228).

In his London lecture Swami Vivekananda affirmed: "The ignorant man, by prayer and devotion, can reach beyond the philosopher (*jnani*). To know God, no philosophy is necessary." Further in America, he stated on 9th July, 1894: "the *bhakti* is indirectly helped by good works. . . . Work, but give up the result to the Lord. He who follows the God of Truth with devotion—to him the God of Truth reveals Himself" (*Inspired Talks* 92).

5.4 Krishna *Bhakti*

Krishna and Shakti Poems of Sri Aurobindo

The boy with the flute is Sri Krishna, the Lord descended into the world-play from the divine *Ananda*; his flute is the music of the call which seeks to transform the lower ignorant play of mortal life and

> bring into it and establish in its place the *lila* of his divine *Ananda.* (Sri Krishna: Words of Sri Aurobindo and the Mother 2)

Sri Krishna, who is believed to be the ninth incarnation of Vishnu, is mentioned in the Vedic and Upanishadic texts even before the *Mahabharata*. The Bhagavata elaborates the life and the *lila* of Sri Krishna, who is known to the world as the author of the *Bhagavad Gita*. In the Harivamsha, a detailed account of the circumstances in which Vishnu and Adisesha incarnate themselves in the two brothers Sri Krishna and Balarama has been narrated. In the 45th chapter, *Brahma* suggests to Vishnu to incarnate Himself in order to save *Dharma* or righteousness and the saints of the God recounts Charlotte Vaudeville in her treatise *Myths, Saints and Legends in Medieval India* (147). She further explains the form in which the *Adyashakti* or the Divine Mother accompanies this particular incarnation of Vishnu:

> It was in *Brindavan*, in the heart of the 'Braj' country, that the *gopi* Radha, Krishna's sweetheart in popular tradition and the very embodiment of pure love (*mahabhava*) for Krishna, came to be established as the latter's Shakti and his consort in the theological and the cultic sphere. The treatises of the Gaudiya sect, written by the Gosvami of *Brindavan*, disciples of Chaitanya, conceived her as the supreme Lord's *ahladini—shakti*, his 'energy of bliss' and elevated her to the rank of *Adyashakti*, cosmic energy, the primeval mother of the world (155).

India has produced innumerable theologians, admirers, poets and devotees in the Vaishnavaite stream of Krishna—*Bhakti* from the past four to five millennia, following the incarnation of Sri Krishna. From the sixth to the ninth centuries there was a series of twelve poet-saints who significantly influenced South Indian religious life. They were called the *Alvars*, or those who are immersed in God. More devotional than theological, they sang about the lives of Krishna and Rama throughout South India. *Bhakti* lauds various types of love toward the deity, such as that between father and child, mutual friendship, and that between the lover and the beloved. The *Alvars* were followed by a series of *Acharyas* or theologians who provided philosophical basis for *Bhakti* and theism. Ramanuja was one in this succession.

In South India, sometime during the twelfth or fourteenth centuries, Nimbarka identified Krishna with *Brahma*, the essence of the Universe. Other *Bhakti* philosophers in the South (Ramanuja and Madhva) had been devoted to Krishna, but had placed little emphasis on the cowherd element and had ignored Radha. For Nimbarka, Radha was the eternal consort of Krishna and was incarnate like Him at Vrindavan. Nimbarka was emphatic in his worship of Krishna and His consort Radha, even to the exclusion of other gods. His Sect became popular in the North as well, and the success of the *Bhakti* movement there is dependent on him to a large degree. The worship of Krishna has been strong in Bengal, appearing in literary form as early as the twelfth century with the *Gita*govinda of Jayadeva. A movement which stems from Chaitanya (1486-1533) places considerable emphasis on the cowherd manifestation of Krishna and on the *gopi* Radha. Whatever was said by Rupa Gosvami and other Gaudiya theologians about the *Bhakti rasa* had only one purpose writes Krishna Sharma in his note: '*Bhakti* as a *rasa*' and continues, "It was to strengthen the Gaudiya Vaishnava cult of intense love for the personal deity Krishna" (292). Emotionalism was the most dominant characteristic of the Chaitanyaite cult of Krishna worship. One can still walk along the Yamuna river in the northern India and visit the temples in Brindavan and Mathura which are dedicated to Krishna and Radha. The images here may be plain or elaborate. Sometimes they are placed in a swing so that devotees can rock them. Special festivals are held in their honour.

Countless saints and poets throughout India, like Soordas, Meerabai, Raheem, Andal, etc., have sung of the glories and beauty of Sri Krishna in distinct tones or *rasas*. In the modern age even the Indo-English like Sarojini Naidu, Rabindranath Tagore, Swami Rama Tirtha, etc., have continued to write in the tradition of Krishna-*Bhakti*.

Krishna and Shakti poems of Sri Aurobindo like "The Cosmic Dance—Dance of Krishna, Dance of Kali," "The Stone Goddess,"

"Who," "Krishna," "Krishna Cretics," etc., are mostly spiritual in nature. In each of these poems Sri Aurobindo has expressed his spiritual experiences of the Overmental plane through earthly symbols and images. One doesn't find much of a conscious literary or metaphysical exercise on the part of the poet. In his correspondence with the disciples, Sri Aurobindo has once in a while written about his own poetry. These letters help the readers to some extent in fathoming his poems, writes Aniruddha Sircar in his article "Introducing Sri Aurobindo's Poetry" and quotes the following letter. "On 3rd June, 1934 Sri Aurobindo writes about "Jivanmukta":

> This "Jivanmukta" is not merely a poem, but a transcript of a spiritual condition, one of the highest in the inner Overmind experience. . . . Silence, Light, Power, Ananda, these are the four pillars of the "Jivanmukta" consciousness.

And again, the lines:

> Revealed it wakens when God's stillness
> Heavens the ocean of moveless Nature

express an exact spiritual experience with a visible symbol which is not a mere ornamental metaphor but corresponds to exact and concrete spiritual experience, an immense oceanic expanse of Nature-consciousness (not the world) in oneself covered with the heavens of the Divine Stillness and itself rendered calm and motionless by that over-vaulting influence" (219).

Sri Aurobindo has revealed to some extent, in some of his writings and the famous Uttarapara speech, about his direct experiences, glorious visions and mystic union with Sri Krishna. Sri Aurobindo was initiated into the *Bhagavad Gita*, as he claims, through its archetypal author, Sri Krishna himself. The following are a few excerpts from Sri Aurobindo's speech delivered at Uttarapara on 30th May, 1909, under the auspices of the *Dharma Rakshini Sabha*, soon after his acquittal in the Alipore bomb case. These have been collected from the section entitled 'Sri Krishna Reveals Himself to Sri Aurobindo' which forms a part of the booklet, *Sri Krishna: Words of Sri Aurobindo and the Mother*. Its original source is SABCL, Vol.2: 1-7.

During his active participation in freedom struggle, the British government sent Sri Aurobindo to prison under a conspiracy. As the mission he had taken up for his country remained yet incomplete, Sri Aurobindo poured out his sorrow and frustration to Lord, Sri Krishna. In the complete seclusion of Alipore jail, emerged the figure of Sri Krishna telling him as it were, "The bonds you had not the strength to break, I have broken for you because it is not my will nor was it ever my intention that that should continue. I have had another thing for you to do and it is for that I have brought you here, to teach you what you could not learn for yourself and to train you for my work." "Then" observes Sri Aurobindo, "He placed the *Gita* in my hands. His strength entered into me and I was able to do the Sadhana of the *Gita*" (37). Later on he believes that it was due to some inspiration from Sri Krishna that he was permitted to take a walk outside his cell for half an hour in the morning and in the evening. In course of such a walk the strength of Sri Krishna entered into him once again. Consequently, he says,

> I looked at the jail that secluded me from men and it was no longer by its high walls that I was imprisoned; no, it was Vasudeva who surrounded me. I walked under the branches of the tree in front of my cell but it was not the tree, I know it was Vasudeva, it was Sri Krishna whom I saw standing there and holding over me his shade. I looked at the bars of my cell, the very grating that did duty for a door and again I saw Vasudeva. It was Narayana who was guarding and standing sentry over me. Or I lay on the coarse blankets that were given me for a couch and felt the arms of Sri Krishna around me, the arms of my Friend and Lover. (38)

Sri Aurobindo characterizes this as the "first use of the deeper vision" Sri Krishna gave him. Later on he was placed for some time among those who were accused along with him. In contrast to the nobility and steadfastness of some of these co-prisoners what he felt about himself he says, "I knew then that I the man was a mass of weakness, a faulty and imperfect instrument, strong only when a higher strength entered into me." Then again the figure of Sri Krishna emerged from within him and said to him, "What have you to fear? If you stood aside or slept, the work would still be done . . . you have only got some strength from me to this nation which will help to raise it." Immediately after the above instruction what occurred has been put by Sri Aurobindo as follows:

> Then a thing happened suddenly and in a moment I was hurried away to the seclusion of a solitary cell. What happened to me during that period I am not impelled to say, but only this that day after day He showed me his wonders. (42)

What he abstained from disclosing in public, finds a beautiful expression in the following sonnet:

> At last I find a meaning of soul's birth
> Into this universe terrible and sweet,
> I who have felt the hungry heart of earth
> Aspiring beyond heaven to Krishna's feet.
>
> I have seen the beauty of immortal eyes,
> And heard the passion of the Lover's flute,
> And known a deathless ecstasy's surprise
> And sorrow in my heart for ever mute.
>
> Nearer and nearer now the music draws,
> Life shudders with a strange felicity;
> All nature is a wide enamoured pause
> Hoping her lord to touch, to clasp, to be.
>
> For this one moment lived the ages past;
> The world now throbs fulfilled in me at last. ("Krishna")

Beginning from the time of his imprisonment until that time the world had become entirely irrational and life meaningless to Sri Aurobindo. Everything had assumed the look of vacuity, terrible for sight. He was put in some such a state of utter bewilderment in which *Dirghatamas*, a Rig Vedic seer seems to have felt himself observes Shubhada Joshi in her article "RgVeda and Sri Aurobindo," and quotes Sri Aurobindo saying "I do not know what I am like; in utter deprivation do I move associated with mind." Joshi continues further, "it was on account of this bewilderment perhaps that the seer was nicknamed as above, meaning 'one steeped in long darkness.' The darkness, however, got eventually transformed for him into eternal light characterized as *ekam sat*, 'sole existence,' bearing within it the supreme footstep of Vishnu with its fountain of bliss as well as the manifest world of dolorous look" (61). Some such transformation takes place in the life of Sri Aurobindo following the vision of Sri Krishna. As a result of the vision the otherwise empty world begins to throb fulfilled within the visionary as its epicenter for whom one moment of this experience becomes more than ages. Inspired by this beatific experience, Sri Aurobindo eventually exclaims:

> O immense Light and thou, O spirit, wide, boundless space,
> Whom have you clasped and hid, deathless limb, gloried face?
> Vainly lie Space and Time, "Void are we, there is none."
> Vainly strive Self and World crying, "I, I alone."
> One is there, Self of self, Soul of Space, Fount of Time,
> Heart of hearts, Mind of minds, He alone sits, sublime.
> Oh, no void Absolute self-absorbed, splendid, mute,
> Hands that clasp hold and red lips that kiss blow the flute.
> All He loves, all He moves, all are His, all are He!
> Many limbs sate His whims, bear His sweet ecstasy.
> Two in One, Two who know difference rich in sense,
> Two to clasp, One to be, this His strange mystery.
>
> ("Krishna Cretics")

Thus the vision ultimately settles down as a constant realization. Hence onward Sri Aurobindo began to experience his oneness with Sri Krishna not as a matter of momentary flash of vision but as an eternal verity. This is why the Mother addressed him on her very first sight of him in Pondicherry in 1912 as Sri Krishna. It was Krishna-consciousness which he claims to have brought down on his *Siddhi* day on Nov. 24, 1926 from the region of the Overmind. But not satiated with this much, he continued his *Sadhana* until his leaving the mortal coil on Dec. 5, 1950 for bringing down a still higher locus of consciousness called by him as Supermind. On account of his identification of the Overmind with the Krishna-consciousness and further effort for bringing down Supramental consciousness that he happened to create doubt in certain minds that he was going to prove himself as higher than Sri Krishna even. In answer to this sort of doubt expressed in a letter to him, he writes as under on 25th February 1945:

> You can't expect me to argue about my own spiritual greatness in comparison with Krishna's. The question itself would be relevant only if there were two sectarian religions in opposition, Aurobindoism and Vaishnavism, each insisting on its own God's greatness. That is not the case. And then what Krishna must I challenge—the Krishna of the *Gita* who is the transcendent Godhead, *Paramatma, Parabrahma, Purushottama*, the cosmic Deity, Master of the universe, Vasudeva who is all, the immanent in the heart of all creatures, or the Godhead who was incarnate at Brindavan and Dwaraka and Kurukshetra and who was the guide of my *yoga* and with whom I realized identity? All that is not to me something philosophical or mental but a matter of daily and hourly realization and intimate to the stuff of my consciousness. Then from what position can I adjudicate this dispute. (Sri Krishna: Words of Sri Aurobindo and the Mother 43).

This position of Sri Aurobindo with regard to Sri Krishna is quite explicable in terms of cognate examples found in the Vedas and the Upanishads. In the *Rig Veda*, writes Shubhada Joshi, there is a female seer, daughter of one Ambhrni, who comes to realize her identity with *Vak*, speech as such (61). Another well known seer Vamadeva elucidates how he realized his identity with a number of gods explains Kamalakar Mishra in his article, "Facets of the Tantric Wisdom" (94). The whole thing is summarily explained by the famous Upanishadic observation: *Brahmavid Brahmaiva bhavati,* "The knower of *Brahma* becomes *Brahma* Itself." This is further testified by Sri Krishna Himself in the *Bhagavad Gita* when He asks Arjuna to contemplate Him all the time, to devote himself wholly to Him, to sacrifice everything of his to Him, to pay his obeisance to Him and promises that thereby he would infallibly reach Him (XVIII: 65. Trans. Subba Rao 458). Thus what was set as the goal for Arjuna, was attained by Sri Aurobindo before taking to write anything on the *Gita* or giving exposition to his philosophy as such which was started in right earnest in 1914 with the publication of *Arya*.

Again the poet says in *The Ideal of the Karmayogin*, "The dance of Brindaban is not complete without the death—dance of Kurukshetra; for each is a part of that great harmonic movement of the world which progresses from discord to accord, from hatred and strife to love and brotherhood, from evil to the fulfillment of the evolution by the transformation of suffering and sin into beauty, bliss and good, *Shivam, Shantam, Suddham, Anandam*" (111 qtd. Agarwal 237). The same idea is beautifully summed up in the poem, "The Cosmic Dance—Dance of Krishna, Dance of Kali":

> Two measures are there of the cosmic dance.
> Always we hear the tread of Kali's feet
> Measuring in rhythms of pain and grief and chance
> Life's game of hazard terrible and sweet.
>
> The ordeal of the veiled Initiate,
> The hero soul at play with Death's embrace,
> Wrestler in the dread gymnasium of Fate
> And sacrifice a lonely path to Grace,
>
> Man's sorrows made a key to the Mysteries,
> Truth's narrow road out of Time's wastes of dream,
> The soul's seven doors from Matter's tomb to rise,
> Are the common motives of her tragic theme.

Till the present age, the ways of life which lead us to *Sadhana* have been challenging and painful—which the poet symbolizes as Kali's dance. But towards the end the sonnet is given a new turn with an aspiration for transformation. The poet wonders as to when these harsh ways would turn sweet and delightful—symbolized as Krishna's dance:

> But when shall Krishna's dance through Nature move,
> His mask of sweetness, laughter, rapture, love?

The images of Kali and Krishna play an important role in the metaphysical poems of Sri Aurobindo, like—"Who," "The Mahatmas: Kuthumi," etc. After singing the glories of these contrasting forms, the poet finally hails them as one. The two forms seem to be interconnected as complimentary halves.

> We have love for a boy who is dark and resplendent,
> A woman is lord of us, naked and fierce. ("Who")

One of the earlier poems of Sri Aurobindo, "Who" is "an experiment in the galloping anapaestic measure" notes K.R. Srinivasa Iyengar (150). Casting the poem in the form of question and answer, the poet tries to grasp the Divine principle in the glories of nature and then tries to comprehend It through some known forms of the Divine like Krishna, Kali or Shiva. In "The Mahatmas: Kuthumi," the *Kshatriya yogin*—Kuthumi, rises steadily in consciousness from birth to birth and gathers the folds of knowledge incommensurable, comes to Vyasa—the great sage. As directed by Vyasa, Kuthumi does *Hatha Yoga* and *Raja Yoga* in the ancient, luminous mode. Directed now by Vyasa to seek out Krishna, make total surrender to Him and then manifest the Divine Truth on earth, "an easy task enough till the Iron Age of Kali when the fight against Darkness must prove more and more difficult—Kuthumi finds the Lord concealed in a 'hermit mad' and loses himself in Him" explains K.R. Srinivasa Iyengar in his article "Musa Spiritus" (160). Consider the following lines from the poem:

> Then full of light and strength and bliss I soared
> Beyond the spheres, above the mighty Gods . . .
> In Kali comes, the iron lined with gold,
> The *Yoga* shall be given back to men,
> The sects shall cease, the grim debates die out
> And atheism perish from the Earth,
> Blasted with knowledge; love and brotherhood
> And wisdom repossess Sri Krishna's world.

It is clearly the *Mahatma*'s destiny—as seen by Kuthumi, one of them—to preserve and activise the Truth, age after age, till the Truth can possess and transform humanity altogether and make earth an extension of heaven. And for any of these transformations, the key is the Mother, as Sri Aurobindo has clarified himself to his followers in a letter written on 18th of June 1943:

> This struggle in you (between *Bhakti* for Sri Krishna and the sense of the divinity of the Mother) is quite unnecessary; for the two things are one and go perfectly together. It is he (Sri Krishna) who has

> brought you to the Mother and it is by adoration of her that you will realize him. He is here in the *Ashram* and it is his work that is being done here (*Sri Krishna: Words of Sri Aurobindo and the Mother* 45).

The poet of the *mantra* instantly perceives the presence and purpose of the "great World-Mother" and V.K. Gokak sums up the situation as "the Spirit of all seems to be there speaking out sovereignly its own secrets" (qtd. Prasad 222). The following sonnet was written on 13th September, 1939, after Sri Aurobindo visited the Mother's shrine situated in Kashmir. The stone idol in the shrine during those days was without any features or details, which has now been placed at the backside of the temple and is replaced by a modern idol with features, recounts Ananda Reddy of SACAR, in a personal interview (SACAR: Sri Aurobindo Centre for Advanced Research). It may be noted that the poet doesn't denote the Mother by any name.

> In a town of gods, housed in a little shrine,
> From sculpted limbs the Godhead looked at me,
> A living presence deathless and divine,
> A Form that harboured all infinity.
>
> The great World-Mother and her mighty will
> Inhabited the earth's abysmal sleep,
> Voiceless, omnipotent, inscrutable,
> Mute in the desert and the sky and deep.
>
> Now veiled with mind she dwells and speaks no word,
> Voiceless, inscrutable, omniscient,
> Hiding until our soul has seen, has heard
> The secret of her strange embodiment,
>
> One in the worshipper and the immobile shape,
> A beauty and mystery flesh or stone can drape.
>
> ("The Stone Goddess")

The Mother lives concealed in the stone idol at a mystical shrine, silently pouring out Her message of transformation and Sri Aurobindo recognizes the unity of his own spirit with that of the Mother at once.

Ontologically, Sri Aurobindo's position is *Tantric* through out. Self or Consciousness (*Chit*), according to Sri Aurobindo, is not a static entity but a dynamic reality—Consciousness or Consciousness-force (*Chit-Shakti*). "The activity of higher Consciousness (higher Self) is free and spontaneous activity, what is technically called *Spanda* in Tantra" explains Kamalakar Mishra in the above mentioned article. Unlike the ordinary *Karma* which is effortful action and which arises out of some lack or want in ordinary consciousness, *Spanda* is effortless and free activity emanating out of the fullness of *ananda* (joy) of the Self, he points out (108). Only a thin veil separates us from that state of the Mother, stops our actions from reaching the plane of *Spanda*. In spite of the spiritual unity between man and God, man remains an incognitive incarnate of God due to this veil of ignorance, as Sri Aurobindo points out in a sonnet, "The Universal Incarnation":

> A Witness dwells within our secrecies,
> The incarnate Godhead in the body of man. . . .
> Only on the heart's veiled door the word of flame
> Is written, the secret and tremendous Name.

Just the removal of the veil by inner purification, would render man a cognitive God. And the poet claims to have set the ground for such transformation before praying to the Divine Mother. "Bride of the Fire" is a poem of four stanzas and in each stanza the poet has manifested one special aspect of the Divine Mother and has asked for the corresponding boon, having first made himself worthy of receiving it. The Goddess is the Bride of the Fire, she is the Beauty of the Light, she is the Image of Ecstasy and she is the Voice of Infinity. In order to receive Her Grace, the poet has slain desire, sacrificed longing and parted from grief. "He is capable of bearing the Ganges flow of Her Delight" writes Aniruddha Sircar and adds that "The Blue Bird directly refers to the Spiritual World" (219). To quote a few lines of the poem:

> I am the bird of God in His blue . . .
> My pinions soar beyond Time and Space
> Into unfading Light. . . .
> I have perched on Wisdom's tree

> Thronged with the blossoms of Paradise
> By the streams of Eternity.

The poet clearly identifies himself with the Blue Bird with its ruby eyes, burning heart and the shoreless and still mind, as he declares:

> My song is rapture's mystic art,
> My flight immortal will.

These lines do not merely form part of "The Blue Bird," they are a recondite indication of the true nature of Sri Aurobindo's poetry. In this context Swami Vivekananda aptly points out that there is a natural desire or innate tendency in man to be united with God, the supreme object of human love. "There is a power behind, impelling us forward; we do not know where to seek for the real object, but this love is sending us forward in search of it" (qtd. Rolland 210). And this unseen Power which goads mankind towards transformation is personified in the poetry of Swami Vivekananda and Sri Aurobindo sometimes as the bond-breaking Kali or the Divine Mother and sometimes as the enchanting and guiding Sri Krishna. And the poetry itself is a means for invigorating the urge for human regeneration as Swami Vivekananda sums it up in his comments on the *Gita*:

> The teachings of Krishna as taught by the *Gita* are the grandest the world has ever known. He who wrote that wonderful poem was one of those rare souls whose lives send a wave of regeneration through the world. The human race will never again see such a brain as his who wrote the *Gita* (*C.W.* 7: 22).

This great poem is held to be the crown jewel of all Indian literature. . . . It shows us that our battle for spirituality must be fought out in this life; so we must not flee from it, but rather compel it to give us all that it holds. As the *Gita* typifies this struggle for higher things, it is highly poetical to lay the scene in a battlefield. . .through chapter after chapter, Krishna teaches the higher truths of philosophy and religion to Arjuna. It is these teachings which make this poem so wonderful; practically the whole of the Vedanta philosophy is included in them (*Teachings of Swami Vivekananda* 87).

Chapter 6

A Comparative Assessment of the Two Poet-Philosophers

The poetry of Swami Vivekananda and Sri Aurobindo is the apex of their religious and spiritual experiences. It is redolent of the mystical and transcendental poetry of the *Gita* and the Upanishads. Their poetry is the consecration of the common place and is remarkable for the sincere expressiveness of the self. They felt oneness with all animate and inanimate objects of the world. The One alone is the Ultimate Reality which ever is the same. The two sages present before the world a spiritual vision of life, which clears our blurred sights and raises our minds to a very high plane and infuses us with lofty aspirations. Their poetry gives us a glimpse of the inner joy of one who has cut asunder the bondage of *Maya* and has attained to "liberation in life," which has been elucidated in the *Gita*. The sublime poems of Swami Vivekananda and Sri Aurobindo present a lofty message: the message of detached and desire less action for man, caught in the toils of political, social, moral and spiritual crisis.

The poetry of Swami Vivekananda and Sri Aurobindo is full of the scriptural light and authenticity of personal realization. Hence their poetry can be referred to as Spiritual-Philosophical poetry. Though deeply rooted in Indian spiritual ethos, their poetry is wide in its sweep and far transcends all geographical boundaries in its aspiration. The two poets have pioneered *mantric* poetry in English language and defined the contours of Indo-English poetry which was to come in the following decades. Apart from the incantatory effect, the scope and content of their poems is also '*mantric*.' It seeks a spiritual awakening and transformation of the entire mankind as well as its collective liberation. Sri Aurobindo's own elucidation of the *mantric* poetry is as follows:

> What the Vedic poets meant by the *mantra* was an inspired and revealed seeing and visioned thinking, attended by a realization, to use the ponderous but necessary modern word, of some in most truth of God and self and man and Nature and cosmos and life and thing and thought and experience and deed. It was a thinking that came on the wings of a great soul rhythm (*The Future Poetry* 280).

Swami Vivekananda, a poet of cosmic consciousness, possessed an all-embracing vision, which enabled him to see "a world in a grain of sand." His constant preoccupation was with the doctrine of the self as "*Atman-Brahman*" (self-Divine Self), or, "I am He, I am He, *Shivoham*, *Shivoham*." Swami Vivekananda's apocalyptic vision had its roots in the prayer from the Katha Upanishad, "from the unreal lead me to the real, from darkness lead me to light, from death lead me to immortality" (qtd. Cooper. 1984: 61). Hence in his poem "The Living God," Swami Vivekananda was able to write with confidence, "Him worship, the only visible! / Break all the other idols!." Swami Vivekananda's search for *Amritatvamichhan* (immortality) led him to look within himself and beneath the many ego-phantoms, to find the "*Paramatma*," or real existence.

Swami Vivekananda was the master of many poetic styles, among them the ballad form with its haunting refrain akin to a *mantra*, "I am He, I am He, *Shivoham*, *Shivoham*." His metrical technique resembles an important form of the music of India, the *Raga*. This is a melodic framework from which the virtuoso projects his most profound sentiments, through improvisations. Like a ballad it repeats the same motifs, with variations on the predominant melody. This technique of repetition and variation characterizes Swami Vivekananda's verse and is clearly seen in the poem "The Cup." The predominant theme (melody) is "Life," while symbols and metaphors (variations) intensify the experience of living. Variants of the main theme are portrayed in the first four words of each of the three stanzas: "This is your cup . . . ," a metaphor for life—and is explicated in the first verse, "dark drink . . .

of fault and passion," introducing a colourful timbre. The second verse employs a variant of the main theme: "This is your road" which, the devotee "must travel" despite it being painful and dreary. Verse three has yet another variant of the theme of life—"This is your task." The poet urges the devotee to accept that particular life for only by total acceptance can he be assured of Divine grace. Swami Vivekananda's love and knowledge of music is subtly revealed in this *Raga*-like poem, which could easily be termed "Life or the Autobiography of the soul."

During 1938-40 and later, Sri Aurobindo wrote a number of sonnets (around sixty), most of them appear to be snaps of spiritual autobiography. Sri Aurobindo was of the firm conviction that the function of *mantric* poetry is more than anything else, to arrive at the highest Reality. He has given very elaborate and substantial definitions of the *mantric* poetry in his critical treatise, *The Future Poetry*. And here is a poetically vivid, precise and revealing description of the way in which it operates upon the recipient of the *mantra*:

> As when the *mantra* sinks in *Yoga*'s ear,
> Its message enters stirring the blind brain
> And keeps in the dim ignorant cells its sound;
> The hearer understands a form of words
> And, musing on the index thought it holds;
> He strives to read it with the labouring mind,
> But finds bright hints, not the embodied truth;
> Then, falling silent in himself to know
> He meets the deeper listening of his soul:
> The word repeats itself in rhythmic strains:
> Thought, vision, feeling, sense, the body's self
> Are seized unalterably and he endures
> An ecstasy and an immortal change;
> He feels a Wideness and becomes a Power
> All knowledge rushes on him like a sea:
> Transmuted by the white spiritual ray
> He walks in naked heavens of joy and calm,
> Sees the God—face and hears transcendent speech.
>
> (Savitri, Book IV Canto III: 426)

Mantra in poetry is obviously a dual movement linking the human with the ultimate Reality. This is what exactly Sri Aurobindo himself has achieved in some of his short poems and in the epic poem, Savitri. "In poem after poem," notes K.R. Srinivasa Iyengar, "the surge of aspiration rises to the Timeless—to coax it to consort with what is implicated in Time or in "travailing earth." It is a double movement, the aspiration from below and the response from above, and either movement implies the other too" (1972: 612). "Thought the Paraclete" has been described by the poet as "a vision or revelation of an ascent through spiritual planes," but the ascent of consciousness is suggested by the imagery and the music rather than closely argued out in terms of logical reason:

> Past the long green crests of the seas of life,
> Past the orange skies of the mystic mind
> Flew my thought self—lost in the vasts of God. . . .
> Crossing power-swept silences rapture-stunned,
> Climbing high far ethers eternal-sunned,
> Thought the great-winged wanderer-paraclete
> Disappeared slow-singing a flame-word rune.
> Self was left, lone, limitless, nude, immune.
>
> ("Thought the Paraclete")

It may be noted here that Sri Aurobindo uses poetry to elevate the reader's consciousness to higher planes. The reader, in turn, has to practice some mental silence in order to participate in his 'overmental' poetry. The Mother of Sri Aurobindo *Ashram* had indicated this in her advice on how to read Sri Aurobindo:

> the best thing would be to obtain perfect silence—and achieve a state of immobility of the brain, I might say, so that the attention becomes as still and immobile as a mirror, like the surface of absolutely still water. Then what one has read passes through the surface and penetrates deep into the being where it is received with a minimum of distortion. Afterwards—sometimes long afterwards—it wells up again from the depths and manifests in the brain with its full power of comprehension, not as knowledge acquired from outside, but as a light one carried within. (qtd. *Complete Descriptive Catalogue* 11)

On the other hand, Swami Vivekananda's being a moral teacher is established by his poems as well. As he would often spell out, his objective of bringing intricate philosophical truths to everyday life, was to be accomplished through the lively medium of poetry. Hence the preacher—poet Swami Vivekananda reaches out to the common man or the ordinary intellect, ensnared in the usual cares of life, without demanding any special effort from the reader for comprehending his poems. C.L. Khatri explains the poet's compassion thus:

> There is complete identification of his personality with the poverty, sufferings and sorrows of his countrymen, nay of the whole world. He could partake of the griefs of millions because he was himself one with them
>
> Not two or many, 'tis but one.
>
> ("An Interesting Correspondence," 117)

In devotional verse, Swami Vivekananda is "inside" his poem, and we are with him in our reading. For example, in the poem "My Play is Done," we identify with his emotions and passionate craving to never let "delusive dreams veil off Thy face from me." Swami Vivekananda's poetry springs from a profound personal emotion experienced during periods of struggle for the vision of God and during his joyous union with the Divine. Swami Vivekananda is highly intense and personal as he relates to his Deity. Consider some more lines from the poem, "My Play is Done":

> Rescue me, merciful Mother, from floating with desire!
> Turn not to me Thy awful face, 'tis more than I can bear,
> Be merciful and kind to me, to chide my faults forbear.
> Take me, O Mother, to those shores where strifes for ever cease;
> . . .
> My play is done; O Mother, break my chains and make me free!

Swami Vivekananda's verses like those of the Transcendentalists, have a healing power, a soothing tone not entirely sad or entirely joyous. It is an inner happiness that remembers sorrow, that is familiar with a resilience, which will not allow it to be cast down. A vignette of the pleasure-seeker in "Angels Unaware" reveals the tone of this special bitter-sweet healing.

One drunk with wine of wealth and power
And health to enjoy, them both, whirled on
His maddening course, till the earth, he thought,
Was made for him, his pleasure garden. . . .
Then sorrow came—and Wealth and Power went—
And made him kinship find with all human race
In groans and tears, and though his friends would laugh,
His lips would speak in grateful accents. ("O Blessed Misery")

Swami Vivekananda is primarily a lyric poet. He perfected his own method of infusing intensity and complexity into his verse by various means, the most favorite technique being the repetition of symbols with varying meaning:

. . .stones and trees ne'er break the law,
But stones and trees remain; that man alone
Is blest with power to fight and conquer fate
Transcending bounds and laws. ("Angels Unaware")

Like Keats' sensuous power, Swami Vivekananda's gift of visualization arouses a sensory impression associated with feeling, hearing, smelling, seeing, which illuminates the meaning of the poem. We see and hear the agony in "The Song of the Free."

The wounded snake its hood unfurls,
The flame stirred up doth blaze,
The desert air resounds the calls
Of heart-struck lion's rage.

We smell the fragrance of the
. . . violet, sweet and pure,
(That) ever pours (it's) sweet perfume
Unasked, unstinted, sure! ("To an Early Violet")

Sri Aurobindo's early poems, especially from his first collection of verse, *"Songs to Myrtilla" and Other Poems* (1895) are examples of his lyricism. Consider the following lines from "Songs to Myrtilla"

In the soft springtide comes the bird
Of heaven whose speech is one sweet word,
One word of sweet and magic power to bring
Green branches back and ruddy lights of spring.

Summer has pleasant comrades, happy meetings
Of lily and rose and from the trees divinest greetings.

Back in India inevitably Sri Aurobindo had been led to Indian themes, and it was obvious that henceforth he would be drawing upon the native consciousness nurtured in the Vedic-Upanishadic-*itihasa* tradition.

Mine is not Byron's lightning spear,
Nor Wordsworth's lucid strain
Nor Shelly's lyric pain,
Nor Keats,' the poet without peer.
I by the Indian waters vast
Did glimpse the magic of the past,
And on the oaten-pipe I play
Warped echoes of an earlier day. ("To a Hero-Worshipper")

To the final phase of Sri Aurobindo's poetic career belong the symbolistic and visionary poems like "A God's Labour," "Bride of the Fire" and "Surrealist." In the poem, "Thought the Paraclete" which has been quoted above, the flight of the thought is described in terms of the flight of the bird. It suggests the upward flight of the human mind towards the vasts of God. In the early stages the bird in Sri Aurobindo's poetry is just a vague idea suggesting the soaring spirit of man. "The Blue Bird" is a short poem in which the bird, the questioning human soul sings in high and ecstatic delight, of its Divine traits:

I am the bird of God in His blue;
Divinely high and clear
I sing the notes of the sweet and the true
For the god's and the seraph's ear.

I rise like a fire from the mortal's earth
Into a griefless sky

Apart from the symbols connected with the forces of nature like seas, rivers, fire and *ushas*, Sri Aurobindo has made an extensive use of characters from the Indian mythology to interpret his spiritual visions. His spiritual interpretation of many of the characters of Indian mythology is unique in the sense that no other Indo-

Anglican poet has attempted it before. The stories of Indian mythology were translated into English by poets like Michael Madhusudhan Dutt, Toru Dutt, Romesh Chander Dutt and Manmohan Ghose. Sri Aurobindo, unlike them, sought to interpret and explain these stories in a symbolic sense. The significance and luminosity of these symbolic interpretations are also profound and gather in strength as the poet progresses in his journey towards seerhood.

The poet of the cosmos, Swami Vivekananda had gained his release from delusion by a withdrawal from "*Samsara*" (panorama of the world), for as he stated in "The Song of the Sannyasin," "fetters though of gold, are no less strong to bind." His knowledge of the world convinced him of the limiting range of all earthly achievements with its frustration of "ever running, never reaching" the goal. His credo as a *sannyasin* was to renounce the unstable for the eternal truth, namely, the self, and his constant prophetic refrain was "He conquers all who conquers self."

Sri Aurobindo, on the other hand, is no ascetic poet, for he discerns that in the past "the seeker of the spirit tended to become the cloistered monk, the ascetic, and the mystic and thus caused to set the spiritual apart from and against the material life" (qtd. Narasimhaiah 30). Sri Aurobindo holds that the original Indian drive was towards a many-sided harmony, towards an accord of the Here and the Beyond. A firm believer in the descent of the Supermind into the earth consciousness, he claims that poetry dealing with this new area of experience 'need not make our earthly life less, but more real.' To bring God into life is to help to divinise our actual being, he asserts. The future poetry of the Spirit wouldn't need to go away from the world, but be in it as a harbinger of Gnostic consciousness. Integral in its approach, Sri Aurobindo's literary output is sumptuous. "His subject matter is one giant arc subsuming the traditions of the East and the West" explicates Prema Nandakumar in her book *Sri Aurobindo: A Critical Introduction*, and further adds that "he approaches the problems besetting man from within in his poetry and philosophy, and from without in his writings on politics and sociology" (107). Moreover, Sri Aurobindo is a force whose literary works are part of a *sadhana* for the advent of a new consciousness to free earth of all evil and usher in the life divine.

Compared to Swami Vivekananda's invisible work—the training of monks, the arousing of man's awareness of his *atma*, his visible work—publications, speeches, poems—appears small. The ordinary intellect sometimes fails to realize the depth and breadth of his works, neither see the subtle forces activated, nor understands their ultimate effect upon the visible world. Towards the end of his life, Swami Vivekananda was often heard to say "If there were another Vivekananda, he would have understood what Vivekananda has done!" (qtd. Burke 706)

It was Swami Vivekananda's mission to bring out 'the most wonderful truths' from our Upanishads and *Puranas*, from the monasteries and the possession of selected bodies of people and broadcast them to the world so that 'the truths may run like fire all over the country.' The expressions 'noblest truths' and 'run like fire' at once provide a clue to "his profound spiritual concerns, his sense of urgency and the transmuting artistic cast of his mind," writes C.D. Narasimhaiah and adds that "'Run like fire' is a vivid image, and Swami Vivekananda thought in images; his expression was strewn with analogies, anecdotes and parables which became the very medium of his thinking" (42); Swami Vivekananda explains his mission in the following lines thus:

> To put Hindu ideas into English and then make out of dry philosophy and intricate mythology and queer startling psychology, a religion which shall be easy, simple, popular, and at the same time meet the requirements of the highest minds—is a task only those can understand who have attempted it. The abstract *Advaita* must become living—poetic—in everyday life; out of hopelessly intricate mythology must come concrete moral forms; and out of bewildering *Yogi*—ism must come the most scientific and practical psychology—and all this must be put in a form so that a child may grasp it. That is my life's work (*C.W.* 5: 104-5).

His speech as well as his writing, even when it was religious and philosophical, was almost always that of an artist because they both fell into the category the 'literature of power,' as against the mere 'literature of knowledge' asserts C.D. Narasimhaiah in his article "A Tongue of Flame" and places Swami Vivekananda in the tradition of the poet-teachers of the Vedas and the Upanishads (43). The description 'tongue of flame' was used by Romain Rolland in his treatise *The Life of Vivekananda and the Universal Gospel*. But Swami Vivekananda's intensity was never like the vicious rhetoric of a political *Gita* or—he treated politics as trash—or a social reformer, but a rhetoric which was as C.D. Narasimhaiah describes, "alive with truth, reason and imagination" (43).

Towards the end of his life, Swami Vivekananda's style became more gentle and serene—a radical change from the fervent intensity of his earlier diction. He renounced his body in an attitude of communion and mystical identification. In June 1900, two years before his passing away (July 4, 1902) and in a reflective vein, Swami Vivekananda wrote to Sister Nivedita and other disciples, "I am more calm and quiet now than I ever was. . . . My boat is nearing the calm harbor from which it is never more to be driven out" (qtd. Burke 701). While Swami Vivekananda has always been respected in India, his laudative acceptance on a global scale resulted from his writings, both by himself (*Raja Yoga*, poems and voluminous correspondence), and the writings of his amanuensis (The three *Yogas*: *Karma*, *Bhakti*, *Jnana*, and transcribed speeches). Perhaps therefore, Swami Vivekananda may survive longer in the memory of man, not as an orator or *Acharya* (religious teacher), but as an author whose writings have relevance for our generation.

Raja *Yoga*, an esoteric development of the later Upanishads, places concentration and controlled canalization of the consciousness by which a *yogi* is said to arrive at the higher levels of spiritual awareness and fulfillment. Sri Aurobindo the accomplished *yogi* has rightly given consciousness a central place in his metaphysic of human-divine emergence. This upsoaring of consciousness to the Supramental regions and beyond is given a poetic recordation in short poems of Sri Aurobindo, which are also illustrative of the "overhead" aesthesis enunciated by him.

Sri Aurobindo was a seer in the tradition of the Indian seers, and is counted among the great visionary philosophers of the recent times. He was a poet too, and combined in himself the literary traditions of the Indian classics and the western modernism. As a *Yogi*, he had, by his own admission, attained to and experienced the higher realms of consciousness. All his later works are a recordation of his own spiritual experiences. In his prose treatises, notably *The Synthesis of Yoga* and *The Life Divine*, he was expounding his specific system of metaphysics. Much of this was being poetized in his later poems, and reached its highest expression in his magnum opus, *Savitri*.

Unlike the poems of the Western metaphysicals, Sri Aurobindo's poems are hard to analyze. They are built up through a recondite symbolism and result in a certain obscurity in expression. As the poems are a record of his own inner spiritual vision and experience—"an experience which is not of the common kind and often very far from what the general human mind sees and experiences"—they defy analysis, highlights S. Krishna Sarma and asserts that "A reader who has the right equipment of mind and spirit and a knowledge of the ancient Indian metaphysics, and who brings a humble, persistent mind to the task, alone can reap some reward from a study of Sri Aurobindo's poems" (1).

There is little of deliberate obscurity, obscurity for its own sake, in the poems. This obscurity belongs, first and foremost, to the central theme itself, the esoteric experiences, which the poet is seeking to transmit through the poems. It is a kind of experience "which is not of the common kind," and hence requires an amount of stepping down to a lower key. In the process, the poet has to use a number of symbols and images, which themselves cannot be of common kind. The symbols and images are perhaps related to, and result from, the central vision itself. In addition, most of them are rich with Vedic and Upanishadic connotations, and most of the symbols have specific significance in *yogic* practices. So a reader is understandably mystified at this hieratic obscurity and profundity. For the poet himself, the entire process of transmission is achieved in a flash, as Sri Aurobindo recurrently points out in his treatise *The Future Poetry*. Unless the reader too can respond similarly, the central significance and even the outer meaning of the poems elude him altogether.

There is, perhaps, a certain deliberateness in this obscurity, for the poems result from an "overhead aesthesis." Sri Aurobindo maintained that poetry in future would divest itself of the outward trappings like meter, rhyme, and even the emotional connotations of the words. The poetic essence or the essences of poetry would leap like a spark from the poem to the reader. In this, the sounds of the words, would assume a special importance: they would be incantatory, *mantric*, as in the Vedic *mantra*s. The poet declared, "the more directly the word reaches and sinks deep into the soul, the greater the poetry." This kind of poetry was termed "overhead poetry" by Sri Aurobindo (qtd. Sarma 2).

A Vyasa of the inner life, Sri Aurobindo is likely to be one of the influences towards a change of consciousness and a new life, which every crisis in world history brings a little nearer. He stands for a renewal of the cognitive and delight self, the *Vijnana* and *ananda purusha*, the ecstasy of the 'brooding bliss of the Infinite,' remarks Sisir Kumar Ghose, an Aurobindonian scholar (61). The poet's prayer in "Musa Spiritus" mirrors the function of future poetry:

> O Word concealed in the upper fire,
> Thou who hast lingered through centuries,
> Descend from thy rapt white desire,
> Plunge through gold eternities.
>
> Break the seals of Matter's sleep,
> Break the trance of unseen height . . .
> O Muse of the Silence, the wideness make
> In the unplumbered stillness that hears thy voice . . .
>
> All make tranquil, all make free,
> Let my heart-beats measure the footsteps of God . . .
> Weave from my life His poem of days,
> His calm pure dawns and His noons of force.

Having discussed the poetry of the two sages, let us now briefly study the background and response to the colonial encounter of the two authors and their basic philosophies, which inform their unique body of poetry. The present section elucidates modes of Humanism and approaches towards transformation advocated by the two sages. The similarities, like love for India, ancient scriptures—esp. the *Gita* and differences in their outlook have also been discussed besides attempting to assess the specific contribution and influence of the two sage-poets.

The longing for *Mukti* or liberation was originated for the two sages in their reaction against oppressive foreign rule and rampant poverty. The first reaction of the soul of India to the impact of Western materialism was a reaffirmation of her ancient spiritual legacy, which reached its epitome in the lives and works of Swami Vivekananda and Sri Aurobindo. In Sri Ramakrishna, Indian spirituality came to close grips with the materialistic culture of the West and the result of the combat were Swami Vivekananda and resurgent India, observes an Aurobindonian scholar, Rishabhchand in his treatise *The Integral Yoga of Sri Aurobindo* (40). Swami Vivekananda, the "cyclonic Hindu," as he was described in America, the preacher of the gospel of Vedanta, shook the whole world with his message of the unity of all life and the divinity of all men.

Swami Vivekananda and Sri Aurobindo lay stress on salvation for all as the ideal. The idea of universal salvation is the influence of the Upanishads and is the corollary to the doctrines of *Advaita* metaphysics. It is further asserted that the spiritually realized souls do not continue to be immersed in their own bliss. They seek to work out their ideal through service to humanity and spiritual transformation of the earth. The stress is on universal salvation and not on individual liberation. The oneness of the spiritual goal is emphasized. The sentiment is best expressed in the doctrine of *Sarva-Mukti*. A synthesis of *Yogas* means an integration of all the parts of the human being, including even the physical, which has as much claim to perfection and divine fulfillment as any other part, and their global turning to the Divine. The synthesis that Sri Ramakrishna foresaw, foreshadowed, and foretold, a synthesis like that of the *Gita*, seems to be the destined means of the integral perfection aspired after by the progressive mind of modern man. A totality in aspiration betokens a totality in realization. Sri Aurobindo stands for this entire turning, this complete synthesis and integral spiritual fulfillment of man. Having realized it in himself, he calls upon humanity to proceed towards the Divine by the way of this synthesis. As Rishabhchand rightly puts it, "His call is the call of the earth—soul, the call of the Time—Spirit, the call of the East and the West, and the call of the awakening soul of man himself." The world moves forward to a multi—dimensional synthesis (42).

During the late nineteenth century and early twentieth century, many religious organizations came forward to perform public service (*seva*) in times of famine, floods, epidemics or other natural calamities. The Sri Ramakrishna Mission may very well be called the pioneers in this respect. Swami Vivekananda was quite categorical when he said that he did not see any point in worshipping stone gods in a temple. He taught people that to offer service to humankind was really offering service to God. In his teachings, he advocated working for people in distress as the best form of worship. *Karma—Yoga*, selfless service, is the central thought of the teachings of Swami Vivekananda. But in the case of the Sri Aurobindo *Ashram*, one finds very little of public service in that sense. When he was asked whether offering service to the masses in distress was not part of his *Yoga*, Sri Aurobindo replied that he was engaged in the deeper work of bringing down the Divine consciousness to the world and when that was achieved, the necessity of service to man in distress would be eliminated. He did not forbid any followers to participate in public welfare works as a general instruction, but he always emphasized the fact that when the inner call came, one had to concentrate and devote all one's energy to it. This is the reason for an absence of philanthropic work in the philosophy of Sri Aurobindo. In a letter to one of his disciples Sri Aurobindo remarks thus on Swami Vivekananda's concept of *seva*; the following letters have been collected from the compilation, *Swami Vivekananda and Sri Ramakrishna in Sri Aurobindo's Writings*.

> His ideal of *seva* was a need of his nature and must have helped him—it does not follow that it must be accepted as a universal spiritual necessity or ideal. (31)

In another letter, Sri Aurobindo underlines a further difference in his perception of the divine in contrast with that of Swami Vivekananda's. This letter was a reply to a query of a *sadhaka*:

> As to the extract about Vivekananda, the point I make there does not seem to me humanitarian. You will see that I emphasize there the last sentences of the page quoted from Vivekananda, not the words about God the poor and sinner and criminal. The point is about the Divine in the world, the All, *sarva-bhutani* of the *Gita*. That is not merely humanity, still less, only the poor or the wicked; surely, even the rich or the good are the part of the All and those who are neither good nor bad nor rich nor poor. Nor is there any question (I mean in my own remarks) of philanthropic service; so neither *daridra seva* is the point. I had formerly not the humanitarian but the humanity view—and something of it may have stuck to my expressions in the Arya. But I had already altered my viewpoint from the "Our *Yoga* for the sake of humanity" to "Our *Yoga* for the sake of the Divine." The Divine includes not only the supracosmic but the cosmic and the individual—not only Nirvana or the Beyond but Life and the All. It is that I stress everywhere. (31)

The life-giving ideal, "*Atmano Mokshartham Jagaddhitaya ca*—for one's own liberation and welfare of the world" is the essence of *Advaita* Vedanta. This is the motto Swami Vivekananda placed before himself and all spiritual aspirants to dedicate their lives to carry the torch of freedom to every dark corner of the world, to inflame every soul, including the wretched and the poor to regain his manhood, and, acclaim his inherent divinity.

The works of Sri Aurobindo carry an unmistakable stamp of the poet's humanism and of his belief that the human race is destined to attain higher levels of existence. He asserted that Man could make the "Life Divine" on earth a distinct possibility. As a *yogi*, Sri Aurobindo was convinced that the establishment of the divine life on earth was neither a myth nor a utopian dream; one could, he had held, arrive at the supramental levels of Existence through *Yoga* and the path of *jnana*, and then live in Bliss through total self-surrender or *Bhakti*, and that, finally, one could return to the field of action and be a *karma-yogi*.

That Sri Aurobindo is a spiritual heir of Vivekananda-Ramakrishna Vedanta tradition has already been discussed in the second chapter. An interesting similarity in their philosophical thought and ideals, which lies beneath an apparent disparity may now be deliberated. Both Swami Vivekananda and Sri Aurobindo seek a spiritual transformation of the world, through differing pathways of selfless service and through descent of the Supermind, respectively.

The centre round which revolve the varied facets of Swami Vivekananda's spiritual world is the concept of "Divinity of Men" or deified humanity. It is not a mere intellectual Deity composed of bloodless categories, but the perennial spring from which flow love and compassion ceaselessly, to elevate, transform, and spiritualize all service rendered, either for the betterment or alleviating the sufferings, weal or woe of the humanity, as modes of worship. Sri Ramakrishna's realization of Divinity in the phenomenal world and spiritual realization of fundamental unity opened the eyes of his disciple, Swami Vivekananda to the fact that unity in variety was a law good not only so far as religious creeds were concerned but it also operated behind the entire panorama of nature and governed even the social customs of man. He realized the Divine Mother and this world of suffering humanity as phases of the same reality. He did not altogether reject the world as *maya* or cosmic illusion, rather towards all these manifold, varied appearances of *Vidya-maya* he maintained the same attitude of unbounded love. In this aspect he was widely different from the traditional *jnanins* or *Advaitin*s. Those who are followers of the *Advaitavada* cannot but remain totally indifferent to the world. To them, compassion for the agonized humanity or sympathy for a sufferer would also amount to an affirmation of reality of the illusory appearance. Sri Ramakrishna by his unique *Sadhana* imparted to the monistic Vedanta a practical shape by emphasizing its positive aspect that all is Brahman, that *jiva* is no other than *siva* (Shiva), and that every creature is God Himself in a particular garb of name and form.

Therefore service of man as form of God is divine worship. The ethics of love are here based upon monism of Vedanta. Swami Vivekananda followed the traditional endeavor of saints and seers of India to raise mankind as a whole to higher and still higher levels of existence by gradual spiritualization of the vital plane, sanctification of the empirical, deification of the material. This is how Swami Vivekananda made a bold attempt to convert the metaphysical abstraction of Vedanta to a live force, which would galvanize the world, generate a new kind of humanity and awaken the divinity dormant within us to manifest in full splendor. This is his bringing the Vedanta of the forests and caves to the din and bustle of the market place, the larger horizon of the world, the battlefield of life, the veritable *Kurukshetra.* Twofold missions, Swami Vivekananda carried in his short yet majestic life. First, he was primarily and deeply concerned with finding a practical and radical solution of the manifold problems facing the world. Second, being God-inspired he was equally zealous to propagate the ideals of his master and become a living commentary of Vedanta in its pristine and complete form.

According to Sri Aurobindo, Reality is Infinite. The logic of Sri Aurobindo's Infinite is not based on the principle of exclusion of the finite. It is as an all-inclusive, rich Infinite. Man has not merely to realize the life divine in a Transcendent Absolute and merge his individuality in It, but has to divinise earth. *Moksha* is not the flight into the Transcendent from the snares of the unreal manifestations, it is not the setting aside of all that is other than *Brahman* by negating it. It is not the partial affirmation of the Transcendent. *Moksha* according to Sri Aurobindo, is an 'integral, positive affirmation of all.' It is the mighty attempt to divinise all. It does not exclude any aspect of Reality. Its logic is the logic of comprehensive inclusion and not one of negation.

Sri Aurobindo affirms out of the strength of his mystic experience that the 'contraries' found in Reality are really complementaries. The different poises of the Absolute are complementary to one another and are not exclusive of one another. In a celebrated sentence in *The Life Divine*, Sri Aurobindo sets forth the ideal:

> To know, possess and be the divine being in an animal, egoistic consciousness, to convert our twilight or obscure physical mentality into the plenary supramental illumination, to build peace and a self existent Bliss where there is only a stress of transitory satisfactions besieged by physical and emotional suffering, to establish an infinite freedom in a world which presents itself as a group of mechanical necessities, to discover and realize the immortal life in a body subjected to death and constant mutation—this is offered to us as the manifestation of God in matter and the goal of Nature in her terrestrial evolution. (qtd. Rao 97)

The mind of man or his reason is a limited instrument. It is groping its way and so it cannot give us the knowledge of the Ultimate Truth. Consciously, man must surrender his will to the Supermind which Sri Aurobindo variously calls the Real idea. The Supermind is not the personal God of the theist. It is the Divine Will. Its descent alone can transform human existence into divine glory. Man has to stand aside and willingly make room for the descent of the Supermind. The self-emptying must be done before the Divine filling takes place. The Supermind is a divine level of consciousness. It alone can impose a complete and radical re-integration of human personality. It goes without saying that this attainment is not an easy task. There are conditions to be fulfilled for this transformation from the human to the Divine. It requires intense spiritual *Sadhana*. The concept of the Supermind is central to Sri Aurobindo's philosophy.

Although the methods of *Sadhana* followed by Swami Vivekananda and Sri Aurobindo are widely divergent at the practical level, one finds immense similarity at the intellectual plane. As nationalists and lovers of India they had few equals. They loved India and believed that it has a message for the world as Sri Aurobindo points out in one of his writings about Swami Vivekananda:

> But why should not India then be the first in the world? Who else has undisputed right to extend spiritual sway over the world? This was Swami Vivekananda's plan of campaign. India can once more be made conscious of her greatness by an overmastering sense of the greatness of her spirituality. This sense of greatness is the main

> feeder of all patriotism. This only can put an end to all self-depreciation and generate a burning desire to recover the lost ground. (*Swami Vivekananda and Sri Ramakrishna in Sri Aurobindo's Writings* 14)

And Swami Vivekananda asserts:

> India shall rise only through a renewal and restoration of that highest spiritual consciousness which has made India, at all times, the cradle of the nations and the cradle of faith. (*ibid.*, cover page)

Sri Aurobindo recalled that as soon as he set foot on Indian soil (6 February, 1893 at Bombay) he felt a great spiritual calm and it continued to stay within for the rest of his life. "It was as if Mother India had given loving shelter to her dear son to protect him from the chaos and outer consciousness" elaborates Parthapratim Ray in his article, "Prophet of Transformation" (32). In the same year, a few months later, Swami Vivekananda had left Bombay (on May 31, 1893) to reach Chicago, America in order to take India's message to the West and in return get material help for his Motherland. And this exchange, he believed, would result in mutual benefit and global uplift, as he says:

> Do you know what my idea is? By preaching the profound secrets of the Vedanta religion in the Western world, we shall attract the sympathy and regard of these mighty nations, maintaining forever the position of their teacher in spiritual matters, and they will remain our teachers in all material concerns. . . . I believe that by this cultivation of religion and the wider diffusion of the Vedanta, both this country and the West will gain enormously. (*C.W.* 6: 448-49)

Sri Aurobindo recalled later, that from the very beginning he felt an apathy for passivity. He was all for a life of action and believed that his *yogic* pursuit could greatly enhance his work of liberating his Motherland from foreign domination. During the years 1900-1908 he was in the thick of revolutionary activities and started a publication called *Bande Mataram* to propagate his ideas. In that context, he made a rousing call to the young India, which seems to be so poignantly relevant today:

> You cannot cherish these ideals, still less can you fulfill them if you subject your minds to European ideas or look at life from the material standpoint. Materially you are nothing, spiritually you are everything. It is only the Indian who can believe everything, dare everything, sacrifice everything. First, therefore, become Indians. Recover the patrimony of your forefathers. Recover the *Aryan* thought, the *Aryan* discipline, the *Aryan* character, the *Aryan* life. Recover the Vedanta, the *Gita*, the *Yoga*. Recover them not only in intellect or sentiment but in your lives. Live them and you will be great and strong, mighty, invincible and fearless. Neither life nor death will have any terrors for you. Difficulty and impossibility will vanish from your vocabularies. For it is in the spirit that strength is eternal and you must win back the kingdom of yourselves, the inner *Swaraj*, before you can win back your outer empire. There the Mother dwells and She waits for worship that She may give strength. Believe in Her, serve Her, lose your wills to Hers, your egoism is the greater ego of the country, your separate selfishness in the service of humanity. Recover the source of all strength in your selves and all else will be added to you, social soundness, intellectual pre-eminence, political freedom, the mastery of human thought, the hegemony of the world. (*Light for Students* qtd. Ray 35)

It is clear from his words quoted above, that he believed in spiritualizing the core of Indian culture and interpreted it in a way that suited the modern life and transcended the limits of our national ethos to bring in entire humanity in this project. In order to achieve this goal he wanted young Indians to reject the imitative acceptance of the material culture of the West and, at the same time, be open to new ideas from them for assimilation in our philosophy. Sri Aurobindo, like Swami Vivekananda, advocates reverence towards the scriptures and towards the Motherland for national regeneration.

The *Gita* is one text that both the seers constantly admire and preach. This is in spite of their inestimably wide range of study, beginning from the *Rig Veda* to the modern disciplines of knowledge, and all of them getting so skillfully synthesized in the philosophy so as to make it the most comprehensive system of thought envisaged by any modern philosopher so far. Swami

Vivekananda adored the *Gita* most for its harmonious blending of the three *margas* or pathways to God:

> Wherein lies the originality of the *Gita* which distinguishes it from all preceding Scriptures? It is this: Though before its advent, *Yoga*, *Jnana*, *Bhakti*, etc. had each its strong adherents, they all quarreled among themselves, each claiming superiority for his own chosen path; no one ever tried to seek for reconciliation among these different paths. It was the author of the *Gita* who for the first time tried to harmonize these. He took the best from what all the sects then existing had to offer, and threaded them in the *Gita*. (*C.W.* 4: 106-7)

Basing himself on this wider *Yoga* of the *Gita*, Sri Aurobindo does not only synthesize all the systems of the traditional *Yoga* together organically but also takes the whole of life as a *Yoga* meant for condensing the process of man's progression to the Divine and the latter's descent to the human world. In him *Yoga* has become a tool not only of developing the conscious but also of illuminating the unconscious; it lies not only in ascent but also in descent, integration and transformation culminating eventually in the prospect of divinising the world. This is not only theoretically explained in his philosophical works but is also artistically presented in his poems.

Describing the *Gita* as the best authority on Vedanta, Swami Vivekananda was explicitly impressed by the concept of *Advaita* and the theory of *Karma Yoga* taught by Sri Krishna in the scripture. To quote the prophet's own words:

> Aye, if there is anything in the *Gita* that I like, it is the two verses, coming out strong as the very gist, the very essence, of Sri Krishna's teaching: "He who sees the Supreme Lord dwelling alike in all beings, the Imperishable in the things that perish, he sees indeed. For seeing the Lord as the same, everywhere present, he does not destroy the Self by the self, and thus he goes to the highest goal." (*C.W.* 3: 193-94)

> The *Gita* teaches that all works should be done thus: He who is one with the Lord through *Yoga* performs all his works by becoming immersed in concentration, and does not seek any personal benefit. Such a performance of work brings only good to the world, no evil

> can come out of it. Those who work thus never do anything for themselves. (*C.W.* 5: 247-48)

Lastly, Sri Aurobindo's idea of Integral *Yoga* also has its foundation particularly in the *Gita*. As regards his doctrine of evolution, involving progression from Matter to Supermind and eventually return of the creation to *Satchidananda*, has its basic structure in the *Gita*'s doctrine of the final recovery of the cosmos to the highest *Purusha*. The present critical observations do not in any way question or minimize the contribution and influence of Swami Vivekananda and Sri Aurobindo to Indian philosophy and Indian English poetry.

Swami Vivekananda's contribution to Indian spirituality and thought has been the source of inspiration to all Renascent Indian thinkers. From Gandhi to Radhakrishnan, all have been influenced by him. Radhakrishnan writes,

> my pride as a Hindu was roused by his enterprise and eloquence. His philosophic mission to The World Congress of Faiths in Chicago, is an historical data. There he spoke not as a scribe or scholar but as the authentic sage of India. It made an abiding impression on all. The East was made known to all, in all its splendor. Swami*ji* paved the way for the East-West dialogue which is gaining momentum and is working towards a fruition, in every walk of life and in every field of human activity.

And in the words of Goethe, "No longer can the orient and the occident remain apart" (qtd. Rao 41).

It is difficult to describe fully the influence of Swami Vivekananda. His message is true to the soul of India and her spiritual genius. Swami Vivekananda's version of Hinduism is deeply rooted in the national and racial consciousness of India, and it is full of possibilities for becoming a universal religion. Swami Vivekananda's intuitive powers apprehend and reveal, in his literary works, the truths implicit in the universe, observes Carebanu Cooper. Consistent with this dynamism and fullness of being, Swami Vivekananda's contribution to the English poetry is unique. He broke away from the poetic trends of early Indo-English poets known as "Derozio men" (called so after the name of the poet, Henry Louis Vivian Derozio) to experiment, though unconsciously, with a new kind of his own in lyric form. C.L. Khatri, in his note on Swami Vivekananda's poetry draws attention to the fact that Swami Vivekananda's "spiritual and mystic creativity led to the development of *Mantric* poetry, which was later perfected by Sri Aurobindo" and adds that "He brought poetry close the Vedic *Mantra*" (114).

Considering the total poetic output, Swami Vivekananda may be regarded as a minor Indian-English poet, but he remains a significant and influential poet among his contemporaries when one studies his poetic sensibility and his exposition of spiritual and religious themes in poetry. One of the unique aspects of Swami Vivekananda's work (oratory or writing) lay in the fact that neither notes nor reference books were used, and above all, he never patently repeated himself. When he reduplicated himself, a special awareness would be revealed, a surprising angle explored and a novel meaning given to the original statement. He gave something of himself in his dynamic, arousing speeches, quick repartees, whimsically humorous anecdotes, and authoritative statements laden with quotations from the ancient Hindu scriptures. Like a golden thread, the autobiographical element of his transcendental self, holds Swami Vivekananda's moralism, humanism and globalism together. The themes and style of his works, in English and Bengali, gave vitality, variety and originality to these literatures. The major work *Raja-Yoga*, together with his poems and hymns, volumes of lectures and dialogues, letters and stories, essays and expositions, distinguish him as a modern man of letters from India, whose specialty lay in the portrayal of a non-dualistic conception of the universe, wherein "the self alone is to be meditated upon," for he "who sees with an equal eye . . . enjoys peace from within. . . . . has conquered his self and attained the calm of self-mastery" (*Gita* VI: 9 trans. Subba Rao 219).

Swami Vivekananda is still too contemporary for any final judgment to be made about his work or his place among inspirational world authors. Yet the impact Swami Vivekananda made, not only on modern India, but on the world-scene during his lifetime, as the messenger of mystical or transcendental realism, cannot be ignored. R. Ramakrishnan feels that Swami Vivekananda, the Master-teacher, holds pride of place among makers of modern India, and that Swami Vivekananda's presence reveals itself in the "aspirations and achievements of Awakened India. We . . . are heirs to the Vivekananda legacy" (109). In India, this "legacy" appears in organized *Maths* (monasteries), and Missions, relief centers, orphanages and schools, publication houses, and above all, in the exchange of disciple-workers between India and the West.

The impact of Sri Aurobindo on the contemporary Indian scene is indeed very great and profound. Many of his disciples have followed most arduously the path set by their Master and they even regarded him as an *avatar* and worshipped him as such—Nirodbaran, K.D. Sethna, Anil Baran Roy, Nolini Kanta Gupta, Dilip Kumar Roy, Amrita, Prithwi Singh Nahar, Suddhananda Bharathi, Panjalal, Nishikanto, Romen, Themis, Madhusudan Reddy and V.K. Gokak are some of the poets who had found their literary mentor in Sri Aurobindo and wrote in the same vein. The symbolistic expression is seen at times in the poems of these poets also and they could justifiably be called the neo-symbolists in Indo-English poetry.

But it must be admitted that, outside a small if growing circle, Sri Aurobindo is as yet not sufficiently known to the poetry reading public. Outside this group, the response to his poetry has been rather mixed, and his value as a poet is far from being fully understood. While many have seen its merits clearly, especially the great afflatus of the later poems, a few like A.K. Ramanujan, R. Parthasarathy, Keki Daruwalla, etc., have not hesitated to express their disapproval, points out K.R. Srinivasa Iyengar while quoting their viewpoints (1995: 710). The polarity among '*pundits*' is not surprising. To put it at its simplest, Sri Aurobindo's successive roles as a nationalist leader, a thinker and a *yogi* have tended to throw his work as a poet to the background. There are other reasons as well. In his maturer verse he seems to deal, almost exclusively, with ranges of experience, or states of the being, that are, by common consent, hard to grasp. There is also a section of his writings where he has used new or unfamiliar metres and rhythms. All in all, he seems to stand apart from what has imposed itself as the main stream of modern poetry. Sisir Kumar Ghose in his article "The Poetry of Sri Aurobindo," emphasizes this point:

> Sri Aurobindo's essential poetry is original in the strict philological sense of being derived from the origin. It is futuristic in the sense that it stands for a marriage of true minds, the mind of the East and the West, and is an earnest of the change in consciousness for which the age is ripe and waiting. Hence its value. (88)

Even as of today, quite a few poets and philosophers have followed the path set by Swami Vivekananda and Sri Aurobindo in theme and technique. Some of them have used the same symbols that they perfected. The number may not be large but their output is considerable. It clearly establishes that the neo-symbolist trend is one of the significant aspects of modern Indo-English poetry. This trend may not have the strength of numbers. But as Sri Aurobindo himself has prophesied, a day will come in the not too distant future when man will be tired of the poetry of the senses, the so called realistic poetry which deals with the contemporary situation, and crave for the poetry of the soul, poetry that is incantatory. Swami Vivekananda and Sri Aurobindo will then be the guiding stars and the leading light of the enlightened future era. The power and glory of their spiritual poetry will then be more fully realized by humanity. V.K. Gokak, one among the Aurobindo school of poets, while paying tributes to the Master, sings:

> "A kindler of new, luminous constellations
> On the verge of human sight;
> A builder of light-pillars in the Ocean
> Of Time, impouring light."
> "The Marvellous Master, the seeker's Rock of Ages,
> The Force of deathless laughter,
> The Wonder-Worker, the new world's great Law-Giver,
> Seer of Before and After" (Gokak 5)

One can only join the poet in his ardent vision and aspiration regarding the future poetry.

Bibliography

Primary Sources

Anand, K.C, ed. *Sri Krishna: Words of Sri Aurobindo and the Mother.* (Reprint from *All India Magazine*, September, 1993. A Monthly Magazine of Sri Aurobindo Society) Pondicherry: Sri Aurobindo Society, 1998.

———, ed. *Swami Vivekananda and Sri Ramakrishna in Sri Aurobindo's Writings.* (Reprint from *All India Magazine* September, 1993.—A Monthly Magazine of Sri Aurobindo Society) Pondicherry: Sri Aurobindo Society, 2nd ed. 2003.

Aurobindo, Sri. *Collected Poems.* Pondicherry: Sri Aurobindo Ashram, 1972.

_____. *The Complete Works of Sri Aurobindo.* 18 Vols. Pondicherry: Sri Aurobindo Ashram, 2003.

_____. *Essays on the Gita.* New York: The Sri Aurobindo Library, 1950.

_____. *The Future Poetry: Letters on Poetry, Literature and Art.* Pondicherry: Sri Aurobindo Ashram 1953.

_____. *The Life Divine.* Pondicherry: Sri Aurobindo Ashram, 1972.

_____. *The Mother.* Pondicherry: Sri Aurobindo Ashram, 1972.

_____. *On Himself.* 5th ed. Pondicherry: Sri Aurobindo Ashram, 1989.

_____. *The Riddle of This World.* Pondicherry: Sri Aurobindo Ashram, 1933, 8th ed. 1984.

_____. *SABCL: Sri Aurobindo Birth Centenary Library.* 30 Vols. Pondicherry: Sri Aurobindo Ashram, 1972.

_____. *Savitri, A Legend and a Symbol and Letters on Savitri.* Pondicherry: Sri Aurobindo Ashram, 1973.

_____. *Sonnets.* Pondicherry Sri Aurobindo Ashram, 1999.

_____. *The Synthesis of Yoga.* Pondicherry: Sri Aurobindo Ashram, 1972.

Teachings of Swami Vivekananda. Kolkata: Swami Mumukshananda, Advaita Ashrama, 2003.

Vivekananda, Swami. *The Complete Works of Swami Vivekananda.* 9 Vols. Calcutta: Advaita Ashrama, 1978.

_____. *In Search of God and Other Poems*. Kolkata: Advaita Ashrama, 2004.

_____. *Inspired Talks*. Madras: Sri Ramakrishna Math, 1969.

_____. *Selections from the Complete Works of Swami Vivekananda*. Calcutta: Advaita Ashram 1993.

Secondary Sources

Agarwal, Jagdish Saran. *The Splendour of Sri Aurobindo's Muse*. Bikaner: Ratna Smriti Prakashan, 1983.

Ahluwalia, B.K. and Shashi Ahluwalia. *Vivekananda and Indian Renaissance*. New Delhi: Associated, 1983.

Antarkar, S.S. "Sri Aurobindo and Spiritual Evolution: Man to Superman." *Sri Aurobindo and Vedic Interpretations*. Ed. Kala Acharya and Shubhada Joshi. Bombay: Somaiya, 1996. 29-48.

Arya. 2 Vols. Pondicherry: Sri Aurobindo Ashram, rep. 1990.

Audi, Robert. Gen. ed. *The Cambridge Dictionary of Philosophy*. New York: Cambridge U P, 1995.

Baird, Robert D. and Alfred Bloom. *Indian and Far Eastern Religious Traditions*. New York: Harper & Row, 1972.

Basham, A.L. *The Wonder that was India*, New York: Grove Press, 1959 (1st ed. 1954).

Brahma Sutras: Sri Bhasya. Trans. Swami Vireswarananda and Swami Adidevananda. Calcutta: Advaita Ashrama, 1995.

Burke, Marie Louise. *Swami Vivekananda in America, New Discoveries*. Calcutta: Advaita Ashrama, 1966.

Chanda, NDR and A.J. Sebastian. *Literary Terms in Poetry*. Delhi: Authorspress, 2001.

Chatterjee, Satish Chandra and D.M. Dutta. *An Introduction to Indian Philosophy*. Calcutta: University of Calcutta, 1968.

Chaudhuri, Haridas. *Sri Aurobindo: The Prophet of Life Divine*. Pondicherry: Sri Aurobindo Ashram, 1960.

Commentary to the Vedic Sutras (The Sacred Books of the East, Vol. XXXIV). Trans. George Thibant. London: Oxford UP, 1890.

Complete Descriptive Catalogue: February 2003. Pondicherry: SABDA Sri Aurobindo Ashram, 2003.

Complete Writings of Walt Whitman, Vol. VI, Part I. New York: G.A. Putnam's, 1902.

Coomaraswamy, Ananda. *The Dance of Shiva*. New York: The Noonday Press, 1957.

Cooper, Carebanu. *Swami Vivekananda—Literary Biography*. Bombay: Bharatiya Vidya Bhavan, 1984.

Cousins, James. H. *The Renaissance in India* Madras: Ganesh, 1952.

Dasgupta, R.K. *Swami Vivekananda on Indian Philosophy and Literature*. Calcutta: The Ramakrishna Mission Institute of Culture, 1996.

An Encyclopedia of Religion. Ferm, Vergilliius: The Philosophical Library, 1945.

Gandhi, Kishore. *The Poetry of Sri Aurobindo: A Journey from Ego to Self*. Meerut: Anu Books, 2001.

Ghatak, Nirmalya. *Sri Aurobindo—The Poet and Thinker*. Howrah: Smt. Kuntala Bhattacharya, 1984.

Ghose, Sisir Kumar. *The Poetry of Sri Aurobindo*. Calcutta: Chatuskon, 1969.

_____. "Poet as Seer." *Sri Aurobindo: An Interpretation*. Ed. V.C. Joshi. Delhi: Vikas, 1973. 43-63

_____. "The Poetry of Sri Aurobindo." *Sri Aurobindo Circle*: 20. Bombay: Sri Aurobindo Society, 1964. 86-95.

Gokak, Vinayak Krishna. *Sri Aurobindo: Seer and Poet*. New Delhi: Abhinav, 1973.

Grover, Verinder, ed. *Sri Aurobindo Ghose: A Biography of his Vision and Ideas*. Delhi: Deep and Deep, 1998.

Gupta, Mahendranath.(denoted as M.) *The Gospel of Sri Ramakrishna* Trans. and Introduction Swami Nikhilananda. Madras: Sri Ramakrishna Math, 1996.

Gupta, Nalini Kanto. *Poets and Mystics*. Madras: Sri Aurobindo Library, 1951.

Harshananda, Swami. *A Dictionary of Advaita Vedanta*. Bangalore: Ramakrishna Math, 2000.

Harshananda, Swami. *Hindu Scriptures: A Brief Anthology*. Bangalore: Ramakrishna Math, 2000.

Harshananda, Swami. *The Ten Cardinal Upanishads—A Brief Study*. Bangalore: Ramakrishna Math, 1998.

Hick, J. *Philosophy of Religion*. London: Cambridge University, Prentice Hall, 1963.

Hiriyanna, M. *Outline of Indian Philosophy*. London: Allen and Unwin, 1964.

Iyengar, K.R. Srinivasa. *Indian Writing in English*. (5th ed. 1985) New Delhi: Sterling, 1995.

_____. *Sri Aurobindo—A Biography and a History*. Pondicherry: Sri Aurobindo International Center of Education, 1972.

Jitatmananda, Swami. *Swami Vivekananda Prophet and Pathfinder*. Rajkot: Shri Ramakrishna Ashrama, 1998.

Joshi, Shubhada. "Rgveda and Sri Aurobindo." *Sri Aurobindo and Vedic Interpretations*. Ed. Kala Acharya and Shubhada Joshi. Bombay: Somaiya, 1996. 56-66

Jyothirmayananda, Swami, ed. *Vivekananda (His Gospel of Man-Making with A Garland of Tributes and A Chronicle of His Life and Times with Pictures)*. 2nd ed. Madras: Swami Jyothirmayananda, 1988.

Kallury, Syamala. *Symbolism in the Poetry of Sri Aurobindo*. New Delhi: Abhinav, 1989.

Kattackal, Jacob. *Religion and Ethics in Advaita*. Kottayam, Kerala: CMS Press, 1982.

Keats, John. *Select Poems*. Comp. Raghukul Tilak. Meerut: Rajhans Prakashan Mandir, 1995.

Khatri, C.L. *Vivekananda Speeches and Writing: A Critical Study*. New Delhi: Prestige Books, 2000.

Kumar, Pushpendra. *Sakti and her Episodes: On the Basis of Ancient Indian Tradition and Mythology*. Delhi: Eastern Book Linkers, 1986.

The Life of Swami Vivekananda by his Eastern and Western Disciples. Calcutta: Advaita Ashrama, 1960.

Maheshwari, H. *The Gita's Gospel in Sri Aurobindo's Light: A Movement from Crisis to Liberation*. (based on Sri Aurobindo' s Essays on the *Gita*.) Pondicherry: Sri Aurobindo Ashram, 1999.

Maitra S.K. *The Meeting of the East and the West in Sri Aurobindo's Philosophy*. Varanasi: Banaras Hindu University, 1988.

_____. *An Introduction to the Philosophy of Sri Aurobindo*. Pondicherry: Sri Aurobindo Ashram, 1965.

Mannumel, S.J. Thomas. *The Advaita of Vivekananda: A Philosophical Appraisal*. Madras: T.R., 1991.

Mishra, Kamalakar. "Facets of the Tantric Wisdom." *Sri Aurobindo and Vedic Interpretations*. Ed. Kala Acharya and Shubhada Joshi. Bombay: Somaiya, 1996. 92-110

Mohapatra, A.R. *Philosophy of Religion: An Approach to World Religions*. New Delhi: Sterling, 1990.

Mother India, Monthly review of culture. Pondicherry: Sri Aurobindo Ashram (March, June, 2004).

Mukherjee, Jugal Kishore. *Sri Aurobindo's Poetry and Sanskrit Rhetoric*. Pondicherry: Sri Aurobindo International Centre of Education, 1990.

Mukhyananda, Swami. *Om Gayatri and Sandhya*. Madras: Sri Ramakrishna Math, 1989.

Murti, T.R.V. *The Central Philosophy of Buddhism*. London: George Allen & Unwin, 1960.

Nadkarni, Mangesh. *Savitri: A Brief Introduction* (four talks). Pondicherry: Sri Aurobindo Society, 1990.

Nandakumar, Prema. *Sri Aurobindo: A Critical Introduction*. Delhi: Sterling, 1988.

Naravane, V.S. *Modern Indian Thought*. London: Asia, 1964.

Narasimhaiah, C.D. *The Swan and the Eagle*. Shimla: Indian Institute of Advanced Study: 1987.

Nehru, Jawaharlal. *Sri Ramakrishna and Swami Vivekananda*. Calcutta: Advaita Ashrama, 1963.

Nikhilananda, Swami. *Hinduism: Its Meaning for the Liberation of the Spirit*. Madras: Sri Ramakrishna Math, 1968.

_____. *The Gospel of Sri Ramakrishna*. Calcutta: Sri Ramakrishna Math, 1942.

_____. *Vivekananda, the Yogas and Other Works*. New York: Ramakrishna-Vivekananda Center, 1953.

Panda, N.C. *Maya in Physics*. New Delhi: Motilal Banarsidas, 1991.

Pandit, M.P, comp. *Vedic Symbolism: Sri Aurobindo*. Twin Lakes (USA): Lotus Press, 2001.

———, ed. and comp. *Sri Aurobindo on the Tantra*. Pondicherry: Dipti Publications, Sri Aurobindo Ashram, 1967, rep. 1999.

_____. *Sri Aurobindo* (The Builders of Indian Philosophy Series). New Delhi: Munshiram Manoharlal, 1998.

Pearson, Richard and Kailas Javeri. "Be Like a Flower." *Life Positive Plus*. Special issue entitled, *Sri Aurobindo: an adventure of Consciousness*. (April-June, 2004): 52-54

Prasad, Harimohan and Chakradhar Prasad Singh, ed. *Indian Poetry in English*. New Delhi: Sterling, 1985.

Prasad, S.K. "Sri Aurobindo's Poetry as the Mantra of the Real" *Contemporary Relevance of Sri Aurobindo*. Ed. Kishore Gandhi. New Delhi: Vivek, 1973. 203-23

Prayers and Meditations of the Mother. Pondicherry: Sri Aurobindo Ashram, 1914.

Princeton Encyclopedia of Poetry and Poetics. Macmillan Reference Books. Ed. Alex Preminger. Associate editors: Frank .J. Warnke and O.B. Hardison Jr. London: Princeton U P, 1986.

Purani, A.B. *Life of Sri Aurobindo*. Pondicherry: Sri Aurobindo Ashram, 1958.

Radhakrishnan, S. ed. *History of Philosophy: Eastern and Western*. Vol. I. London: George Allen and Unwin, 1952.

_____. *Indian Philosophy*. 2 Vols. London: George Allen, 1923.

_____. *The Principal Upanishads* London: George Allen & Unwin, (1953). 2nd ed. 1968.

Rai Chaudhuri, Sanat Kumar. *Swami Vivekananda—The Man and His Mission*. Calcutta: Scientific Book Agency, 1966.

Rajendra Prasad, Akhouri. "The Poetical Corpus of Vivekananda." *Indian Writing in English*, ed. Krishna Nandan Sinha. New Delhi: Heritage, 1979. 77-82

Raju, P.T. *Introduction to Comparative Philosophy*. Delhi: Motilal Banarsidas, 1972; rep. 1997.

Ramakrishnan, R. *Swami Vivekananda: Awakener of Modern India*. Madras: Sri Ramakrishna Math, 1972.

Rao, P. Nagaraja. *Contemporary Indian Philosophy*. Gen. Ed. K.M. Munshi and R.R. Diwakar. Bombay: Bharatiya Vidya Bhavan, 1970.

Ray, Parthapratim. "Prophet of Transformation." *Gentleman* (May, 2000): 30-35

Reddy, V. Madhusudhan. "Sri Aurobindo's Philosophy," *Sri Aurobindo: An Interpretation*. Ed. V.C. Joshi. Delhi: Vikas, 1973. 14-42

Reminiscences of Swami Vivekananda by his Eastern and Western Admirers. Calcutta: Advaita Ashrama, 1964.

Rishabhchand. *The Integral Yoga of Sri Aurobindo*. Pondicherry: Sri Aurobindo Ashram, 1953.

Rolland, Romain. *The Life and Gospel of Vivekananda*. Calcutta: Advaita Ashrama, 1970.

Runes, Dagobert D. ed. *A Treasury of Philosophy*. Vol. II New York: The Philosophical Library, 1973.

Sarma, S. Krishna. *Seed of Grandeur: Commentary on Sri Aurobindo's Poems*. Vijaywada: Kamala Publications, 1972.

Satprem. Sri Aurobindo or the Adventures of Consciousness. Trans. Michel Danino, Paris: Instut de Recherches Evolutives, 1996 & 2000.

Sengupta, Santosh Chandra. *Logic of Religious Language*. Calcutta: Ashok Ray Prajna, 1978.

Sethna, K.D. *The Vision and Work of Sri Aurobindo*. Pondicherry: Sri Aurobindo Ashram, 1968.

Shanmukham, N. Jaya. *Sri Aurobindo and the Indian Tradition*. New Delhi: Crown Publications, 1988.

Sharma, Chandradhar. *Indian Philosophy: A Critical Review*. New York: Barnes & Noble. 1962.

Sharma, K.K. ed. *Indo-English Literature—A Collection of Critical Essays*. Ghaziabad: Vimal Prakashan, 1977.

Sharma, Krishna. *Bhakti and the Bhakti Movement: A New Perspective, A Study in the History of Ideas*. New Delhi: Munshiram Manoharlal, 1987.

Sharma, L.N. *Kashmir Saivism*. Varanasi: Bharatiya Vidya Prakashan, 1972.

Singh, Shail Kumari. *Religious and Moral Philosophy of Swami Vivekananda*. New Delhi: Janaki Prakashan, 1983.

Sircar, Aniruddha. "Introducing Sri Aurobindo's Poetry," *Mother India*, Monthly review of culture. Pondicherry: Sri Aurobindo Ashram; (March, 2004): 217-25.

Sivaramakrishna, M. and Sumita Roy. ed. *Reflections on Swami Vivekananda (Hundred years after Chicago)*. New Delhi: Sterling, 1993.

Sri Aurobindo: Views and Reviews. (Reprint from *Arya* a monthly magazine between 1914 and 1920) Pondicherry: Sri Aurobindo Ashram, 5th ed. 1997.

Sri Aurobindo and his Ashram. Pondicherry: Sri Aurobindo Ashram, 1985.

Srimad Bhagavad Gita (with Sadhana Vyakhya). Trans. S. Subba Rao Hyderabad: Sri *Gita* Grandhalaya, 1969.

Srivastava, Rama Shanker. *Sri Aurobindo and the Theories of Evolution*. Varanasi: The Chowkhamba Sanskrit Series Office, 1968.

Sri Vishnu Sahasranam (Commentaries by Shankaracharya and Parasara Bhattar), trans. E. Parthasarathy. Madras: np, 1972.

Subba Rao, M. *Readings in Indo-Anglican Literature—Prospective and Retrospective*. Vol. II New Delhi: Kanishka, 1995.

Sullivan, H.P. "Sri Aurobindo on the Supermind and the Creative Process." *Sri Aurobindo A Garland of Tributes*, ed. Arabinda Basu. Pondicherry: Sri Aurobindo Research Academy, 1972. 205-23

Swahananda, Swami. *Hindu Symbology and Other Essays*. Madras: Sri Ramakrishna Math, 2001.

Talari, Anantha Babu. *God and the Householder*. Hyderabad: Sri Ramakrishna Math, 1994.

Tejasananda, Swami. *A Short Life of Swami Vivekananda*. Kolkata: Advaita Ashrama, 2001.

Tripura Rahasya Ed. Swami Sri Ramananda. Tiruvannamalai: Sri Ramanasramam, 1971.

Vaudeville, Charlotte. *Myths, Saints and Legends in Medieval India.* Comp. and Introduction. Vasudha Dalmia. Delhi: Oxford U P, 1999.

Vijayasree, C. "The Poet as a Seer: A Note on Vivekananda's Poetry." *Perspectives on Ramakrishna, Vivekananda Vedanta Tradition*, ed. M. Sivaramakrishna and Sumita Roy. Hyderabad: Ramakrishna Vivekananda Seva Samiti, 1991. 166-73

Visitor's Guide to Sri Aurobindo Ashram. Pondicherry: Sri Aurobindo Ashram, nd.

Vivekananda: The Man and his Message. By his eastern and western disciples. Kolkata: Advaita Ashrama, 2004.

Wilson, H.H. *The Religious Sects of the Hindus*. Madras: The Christian Literature Society for India, 1904.